The Gods in Their Cities

Also by Richard Leviton

Seven Steps to Better Vision

The Imagination of Pentecost: Rudolf Steiner and Contemporary Spirituality

Brain Builders! A Lifelong Guide to Sharper Thinking, Better Memory, and an Age-Proof Mind

Weddings by Design: A Guide to Non-Traditional Ceremonies

Physician: Medicine and the Unsuspected Battle for Human Freedom

The Healthy Living Space: 70 Practical Ways to Detoxify the Body and Home

What's Beyond That Star: A Chronicle of Geomythic Adventure

The Galaxy on Earth: A Traveler's Guide to the Planet's Visionary Geography

The Emerald Modem: A User's Guide to the Earth's Interactive Energy Body

Signs on the Earth: Deciphering the Message of Virgin Mary Apparitions, UFO Encounters, and Crop Circles

Encyclopedia of Earth Myths. An Insider's A-Z Guide to Mythic People, Places, Objects, and Events Central to the Earth's Visionary Geography

Fraser's Angel

The Gods in Their Cities

♦

Geomantic Locales of the Ray Masters and Great White Brotherhood, and How to Interact with Them

A Primer on Earth's Geomantic Reality, No. 1

Richard Leviton

iUniverse, Inc.
New York Lincoln Shanghai

The Gods in Their Cities
Geomantic Locales of the Ray Masters and Great White Brotherhood, and How to Interact with Them

iUniverse books may be ordered through booksellers or by contacting:

iUniverse
2021 Pine Lake Road, Suite 100
Lincoln, NE 68512
www.iuniverse.com
1-800-Authors (1-800-288-4677)

ISBN-13: 978-0-595-38339-9 (pbk)
ISBN-13: 978-0-595-82712-1 (ebk)
ISBN-10: 0-595-38339-4 (pbk)
ISBN-10: 0-595-82712-8 (ebk)

Printed in the United States of America

To Ray Masters Saint Germain and Portia, thanks for your patience, insight, and expeditions

Contents

Introduction xi

Chapter 1   THE GREAT WHITE
            BROTHERHOOD 1

What the Brotherhood Is 1

What Is Ascension? 4

What the Brotherhood Does 5

The Einherjar's Mythic Guises 8

The 48,000 Rishis and the Seven Rishis 10

Where the Rishis Reside 31

Activities on Earth of the Ray Masters 33

Manifesting the Virgin Mary Apparitions 40

Designated Places for Meeting the Einherjar 43

An Architectural Model of Amaravati 48

Mount Meru—The Larger Context for the Celestial Cities of
the Gods 51

Indra, Leader of the Ascended Host, and His Residence 54

Camalate as Indra's Palace, *Vaijayanta* 60

Chapter 2   VALHALLA 64

Mythic Descriptions of Valhalla 64

The Geomantic Actuality of Valhalla .70

A Valhalla in Full Activation 74

Likely Experiences Inside Valhalla 78

Current Activities Inside Valhalla 84

How to Interact with a Valhalla 89

Chapter 3   RESIDENCES OF THE 14 RISHIS 93

The Glass Mountain and the Crystal City 93

The Rainbow Bridge, Bifrost, and Its Guardian 99

The Importance of the Light City to Silver Eggs 103

How to Interact with the Light City 106

Chapter 4   PHYSICAL RETREATS 111

Inside the Hermetically Sealed Caves 111

What the Retreats Do for the Earth 115

Preparing Human Helpers for Geomantic Events 117

Chapter 5   ETHERIC SANCTUARIES 124

The Golden Etheric City and Other Sanctuaries 124

Where the Etheric Sanctuaries Are Situated 127

Classical Vedic Descriptions of Sanctuaries 131

Etheric Sanctuaries as Divine Abodes 134

What the Sanctuaries Do 138

How to Interact with an Etheric Sanctuary 139

Shambhala as the Premier Etheric Sanctuary 141

How to Get to Shambhala 143

Chapter 6   TEMPLES OF LIGHT 146

Sitting in the Ray Flame 146

Distribution Pattern of the Color Temples Over the
Earth 149

How to Interact with a Color Temple 150

Chapter 7   RAY MASTER SANCTUARIES 152

1,080 Sanctuaries Originally Assigned to the Earth 152

A Visual Description of a Sanctuary .164

Sanctuaries of Ray Master Jesus of the Scarlet Robe 166

The Scarlet Ray's Complement—The Rose-Pink Ray of
Master Nada 175

Portia's Sanctuaries of the Orange Ray 180

Sanctuaries of the Master of the Pale Orange Robe 187

Lao Tzu's Sanctuaries of the Yellow Ray 189

Kuan-Yin's Sanctuaries of the Pale Yellow Ray 194

Djwhal Khul, Tibetan Master of the Green Ray 196

Ray Master Hilarion of the Pale Green Ray 199

The Cobalt Blue Ray of Divine Will and Power 202

Apollo, Master of the Pale Blue Robe 207

Serapis Bey, Egyptian Ray Master of the Indigo Robe 214

Pallas Athena's Magenta Sanctuaries in Greek and Irish
Culture 221

Master of the Violet Robe—Maha Chohan 234

Saint Germain's Lilac Ray of Transmutation 241

How to Interact with the Ray Masters in Their
Sanctuaries 249

The "15th" Ray Master, the Cosmic Joker Called
Merlin 251

Ray Master Dedicated Outposts, and How to Interact with
Them 256

Chapter 8   THE GREAT WHITE
               BROTHERHOOD IN CURRENT
               TIME 258

Reasons to Interact with the Ray Masters 258

Current Activities of the Great White Brotherhood on
Earth 261

Say Goodbye to the Antichrist 265

Reassuring the Nation's Egregor, the Eagle 270

The Plan Calls for Geometry 274

The Global Geomantic Liturgical Calendar 276

Overall Purpose of the Great White Brotherhood Geomantic
Locales 279

All of Earth Lives in the Womb of Amaravati 282

Bifrost Planet—The Earth Is on the Rainbow Bridge 286

The Blue Room Consortium *289*

About the Author *291*

Introduction

Who runs the world? Why do myths from nearly all cultures attest to a time long ago when the gods ran affairs on Earth, usually in a benevolent manner? Why did ancient peoples speak of meeting with their gods in holy places on the surface of Earth, implying that somehow the gods lived in cities amongst them?

Perhaps even more urgently we might ask: where did all this go?

Today we find hardly any serious discussion of these questions in the mainstream media or culture. It's considered axiomatic that such issues are artifacts from a primitive, magical (meaning fantasy-laden) earlier time on the Earth. It's as if today the mark of education is the automatic disbelief in all this, and we are schooled in regarding "gods" as an imprecise, outmoded remnant of a mythical (i.e., undeveloped or unsophisticated) mind, no longer real or relevant.

However, clairvoyant investigation of the planet suggests otherwise. Let's start with the last question: it didn't go anywhere for it is all still here around us. Ancient peoples were not deluded when they spoke of meeting with their "gods" in certain dedicated sanctuaries atop mountains, in caves, or elsewhere on the Earth. Across the planet's surface are numerous apertures or portals into that supposedly only mythic and therefore unreal realm where the "gods" once (yet still do) reside and which may be accessed by humans today should we wish to.

Some of these portals we now term sacred sites, holy places, and pilgrimage destinations. As the Hindu mystics rightly put it, such places are *tirthas*, or sacred fords across the "river" from the material to the spiritual world; or as the ancient Celts said, the land is dotted with hollow hills and *sidhes* (forts or palaces) in which the gods still live, awaiting their next moment in our history.

The larger context is that surrounding the physical planet and its biosphere is another layer of life, though more subtle than the material realm. This is the planet's visionary geography, a landscape that inspires visions into its true nature, a terrain of Light. Others have termed this the planet's Light body or Light grid, a complex, many-layered auric or subtle energy shell. I point to this with the term "Earth's geomantic reality"; it's a layer of implicit revelation the Earth has for us.

That true nature of the Earth's geography comprises a variety of Light temples (structured Light spaces), exactly, it turns out, the kinds of celestial cities, residences of the gods, and opulent habitations originally reported in all the world's myths as being the homeland of the gods on the Earth. I call this series and its view a Primer in Earth's Geomantic Reality. The *Primer* refers to the introductory, summary overview provided, emphasizing practical ways to interact with it. *Geomantic* refers to the process of discovering and explicating this implicit global pattern. *Reality* refers to the new, deeper, purer, original design and truth of our planet.

The Earth's geomantic reality is a hologram of most of the structures and places in the spiritual world, as described in numerous myths and religious traditions, as well as a fair selection of what's in the galaxy. I call this Light template the *galaxy on Earth*, and at latest count, there are 105+ different types of Light temples found in the planet's visionary geography, and all of these have multiple copies, as if the Earth's designers had a marvellous Xerox machine and made then positioned many duplicates of the same features all over the Earth.

The geomantic features profiled in this book are among those 105+ types.

This book describes seven types of Great White Brotherhood geomantic locales—Valhalla; Amaravati, or the Light City; physical cave retreats; etheric sanctuaries; Ray Master Sanctuaries; Color (or Light)

Temples; and Dedicated Outposts. It offers practical suggestions on how to interact with them to benefit yourself and the local landscape. The recommended interactive exercises do not require any psychic ability, simply the ability to hold your attention (and body) steady for a while as you make and interact with a visualization.

As for the "gods," the Spiritualism and Theosophy movements of the mid-to-late 19th century gave Western culture a new context for understanding what the old mythic gods might be. Theosophists spoke of Ascended Masters, Chiefs, and great Adepts, of a hidden though active Brotherhood of Light comprising men and women of considerable spiritual development who came and went as they wished from human form and culture to accomplish arcane deeds on behalf of humanity and the Earth and in accordance with long-range developmental plans.

Suddenly many of the activities attributed to the old mythic gods were more understandable as the feats of adepts not bounded by matter or physical bodies. Ascended Masters who occupied bodies of Light were protean, fluidic, and free, clearly working according to a plan and on humanity's behalf.

Merely our knowing that this esoteric Brotherhood and their interactive locales across the Earth exist as a minimum leavens consciousness and culture. It starts to dissolve ingrained atheism and materialism that discredits any intermediary effect of the spiritual world or, in the extreme, discounts even its existence. Further, it can inspire hope, confidence, even certainty, that reality, and thus our planet, culture, and individual human lives, have meaning and are purposeful. It lends support to the perception that Earth is a *designer planet*, designed intelligently for us.

The practical application of the research reported here is that we may, should it interest us, interact with these "gods" in our present time, by using a variety of geomantic locales across the Earth specially created for this and profiled in these pages. This book will show you how we can do this, and why.

1

THE GREAT WHITE BROTHERHOOD

In brief: This is the assembly of Ascended Masters drawn from evolutionary streams across the galaxy whose headquarters is in Ursa Major, specifically through the seven stars of the Big Dipper, and whose purposes are sponsoring, mentoring, and governing the evolution of consciousness and the Light on all worlds with sentient life.

What the Brotherhood Is

The "White" in this term refers to Light, as in pure white Light, for all members of the Great White Brotherhood have achieved the state known as ascension or the Philosopher's Stone in which they have transformed their physical body into a body of Light. In the Mysteries of the Christ on Earth, ascension was demonstrated when Jesus Christ rose from the grave in his Light body. This was a public demonstration of the majesty of ascension and possibly the first public display of this mystery on the Earth outside secret initiatory circles though it was unacknowledged or passed over in conventional Christianity in favor of the grimmer, and still misunderstood, crucifixion.

The "Brotherhood" in this sense refers to the collegiality and lateral cooperation exhibited by all members. They all have achieved a basic level of spiritual accomplishment, the creation of the Light body through ascension, and they all have pledged to honor and fulfill the goals of the Ascended Host. Within this vast assembly of Ascended Masters, as they are also called, there are different degrees of initiation, development, and responsibility, but the nature of hierarchy within the Brotherhood is far different than any rigid human concepts we might have of this ordering scheme.

The "Great" refers both to the sheer numbers of the Ascended Host and to the august assemblage of so many thousands of Ascended Masters in Light bodies. A Norse "mythic" description of Valhalla, a coded name for the assemblage of Ascended Masters, says there are 432,000 members.

The term Great White Brotherhood (GWB) is usually familiar only to students of metaphysics and the esoteric. But there are references, veiled by myth, to the Brotherhood elsewhere in our cultural memory. One of the most well-defined references is from the Norse mythic canon in which the Ascended Host is referred to as the Einherjar, slain warriors who feast with Odin, the high god (the Norse description of an aspect of the Supreme Being, i.e., God, the Source, Great Spirit).

The word Einherjar is from the Old Norwegian and means "those who fight alone" or simply "Lone-Fighters." It refers to those slain in battle and brought to Valhalla, Odin's Hall of the Slain. Valhalla (see below) is a warrior's paradise in which the Einherjar spend their days redoing battles then, hale and unharmed again in the evenings, feast on meat from the divine boar Saehrimnir and mead from the divine goat Heidrun, as served to them by the Valkyries, Odin's special female assistants.

The essential fact about the Einherjar is that at Ragnarok, the Norse conception of the Twilight of the Gods or the Christian Last Judgement Day, they will go into battle alongside the gods of Asgard against the Fenris-wolf and other ancient enemies. Valhalla has 540 gates through each of which 800 Einherjar can march at once, thus providing Odin with 432,000 warriors for Ragnarok.

The key to understanding the Einherjar is what is meant by "slain." It is not a matter of physical death as we understand it. The Einherjar are those humans touched by a God aspect within themselves to the point of self-realization and awakening and who have dropped or "slain" the now lower personality and physical body in favor of ascension and the Light body.

The Einherjar are formerly embodied humans who excelled as spiritual warriors in the solitary battle against themselves—hence they are the lone fighters, those who fight alone. But the "fight" is a matter of recognizing, assimilating, and integrating all aspects of themselves—past lives, the Shadow, kundalini and the dragon within, and the controlled illumination of all the bodily chakras (the numerous consciousness-energy centers, 81 in all, found throughout the body).

They are "slain" in that they have succeeded in transmuting their ego and body-based identity, fully waking up, remembering and claiming their divinity, embodying it, and definitively passing out of the human incarnational cycle. They have slain themselves to birth the divine within, touched the God aspect in themselves and ascended permanently into Light of which they are now masters, able to wield it to accomplish arcane goals.

They have *mastered* the energy of God and created their own Light body, hence the use of the term Master. These highly evolved beings have mastered matter and Light and can create with perfect freedom using both. They can precipitate any form, subtle or solid, from what is called the Ocean of Milk or Sea of Electronic Substance, a fundamental reservoir of obedient, protean electrons.

The Einherjar are graduates from humanity, from this planet and many others. They are the Ascended Host, the Arisen Ones. They do not merely wait for Ragnarok to aid Odin; to them, every day is Ragnarok, and they work all the time with Odin to preserve consciousness and the Light at all levels against entropy, distortion, or manipulation, and they foster its continuous wholesome unfoldment.

Other names for them include the Great Brotherhood of Light, Brotherhood of the Grail, Grail Guardians, Great Ones, Legion of

Light, Lords of the Flame, Lords of Light, Mahantas, Perfected Beings, Perfected Ones, rishis, siddhas, and Solar Fathers (Pitris). Some members of the Einherjar collectively have been remembered in myth as the Anunnaki of Sumer and the Tuatha de Danann of Ireland. In both cases, the Einherjar in different guises, appropriate to the cultures and landscapes, were involved in the early unfolding of humanity.

The Ascended Host also comprises what is referred to as the occult Hierarchy of the planet; they have been termed a society of organized and illumined minds, and are known as the Elder Brothers of the human race. By one reckoning, the Hierarchy of "highly evolved Entities" was established on Earth 18 million years ago "to form focal points of planetary force for the helping of the great plan for the self-conscious unfoldment of all life."[1]

What Is Ascension?

Here are three ways of approaching it. Each human cell is said to have about 1.7 volts of electrical potential, and the average human body is composed of an estimated one quadrillion cells. The math works out that the total human body, if all its cells' electrical potential could be realized, equals about 1.7 quadrillion volts. If this potential were realized all at once, it would create like a vast explosion the Light body from out of its own physical matter.

Second, most metaphysical traditions say the human is a microcosm of the cosmos. That means, among other aspects, we—our overall constitution, including the body, auric fields, chakras, meridians, and nadis—contain all the stars of the galaxy. In nearly everyone these stars are dormant, sleeping; but what if they start to awaken in us? What if they all awakened at once, as billions of exploding points of light? It would be the Big Bang inside us, creating the Light body, a miniature galaxy, out of us.

---

1.   Alice A. Bailey, *Initiation, Human and Solar* (New York, NY: Lucis Publishing Company, 1951): 28,29.

Third, the ascension state is pointed to in the mystical concept of the Philosopher's Stone. It may seem an abstruse concept to us, but to the Einherjar, it is an experiential reality, the ultimate spiritual accomplishment. The creation of the Philosopher's Stone was considered the *Magister*, or Great Work, of medieval alchemy, the transmuting of lead into gold, that is, the carbon-based body into light.

The essential goal was to find, release, amplify, and exalt the trapped spiritual light within the human body and to redefine, even recreate, the body with it as a Light body. It was known as the Ascension Body, Diamond Body, Diamond Soul, Electronic Body, Elixir of Life, *filius philosophorum*, Miraculous Stone, Glorified Body, Hermetic Stone, Higher Self, *lapis philosophorum*, the Mighty "I AM" Presence, Seamless Robe, Soul of the World, Spirit of Truth, Stone of the Wise Man, White-Fire Body, and the White Stone by the River.

The 1.7 quadrillion volts of electrical potential, the Big Bang of a billion stars within the human constitution, or the Philosopher's Stone—with these descriptions we get a semblance of an idea of the spiritual status of the Einherjar. Through a variety of geomantic apertures and "cities of the gods" across Earth, detailed below, we are privileged to be able to interact with the Ascended Host.

What the Brotherhood Does

The Great White Brotherhood oversees the development, unfolding, and evolution of consciousness and the Light on the Earth and other planets. Although rarely acknowledged as such by humanity, the GWB is in truth the world's spiritual government and the actual

---

2. Light in this context refers to the spectrum of consciousness, reality, and truth existing in the spiritual worlds as a reservoir available for human experience and assimilation; it evokes the experience of en*light*enment, which, mystics say, is the total illumination of the self by God, the Light of infinity. It refers also in part to the elec tromagnetic field spectrum of visible light, but emphasizes the spiritual or higher aspects of the visible light. We may equate Light with the total array or sea of consciousness.

determiner of the direction human culture takes on Earth. They are
not autocrats, however, and work within the parameters established
by the Supreme Being for Earth as a planet of free will.

Thus the GWB can influence, suggest, or set up opportunities for
human growth, but they cannot force any of this and must wait for
human agreement and participation. I hope that the information in
this book will serve as an inspiration for many to begin the process of
co-creating a Light-enriched Earth and a geomantically aware culture
in cooperation with the GWB.

From the human viewpoint, the Ascended Masters are gods as
characterized in all of the world's myths. "They wield tremendous
God-Power at *all* times" because they are unwaveringly in alignment
with God and thus all power is given to them for responsible application throughout the worlds. They have "guided the expansion of
Light in humanity on this planet from the beginning," and they continuously radiate "Love, Light, and Perfection" and "Wisdom and
Power." Their brief has them working "everywhere in the universe
with complete freedom and limitless power," on a planetary and individual level.[3]

On the individual level, they educate, initiate, and assist people in
expanding their consciousness beyond the ordinary human
level—into the ascended state. In brief, the Ascended Masters direct,
protect, and assist the expansion of Light at the individual human,
group-cultural, and planetary levels. But they also work to dispel negative energy and darkness. The Ascended Master, from his own Body
of Light, is "constantly pouring out Rays of his 'Light Essence' upon
the discords" of the planet, dissolving them the way sunlight dissi-
pates fog.[4]

Western cultural awareness of the GWB was renewed in the 1870s
after a long period of oblivion with the advent of the Theosophical

---

3.   Godfre Ray King, *Unveiled Mysteries* (Chicago: Saint Germain Press,
      1939): 134-5.
4.   Godfre Ray King, *Unveiled Mysteries* (Chicago: Saint Germain Press,
      1939): 136.

movement in the U.S., Europe, and India, spearheaded by the Russian psychic Helena Blavatsky and later by the English clairvoyant, C.W. Leadbeater.

In 1925, Leadbeater described the Masters as "Perfected Men," and late 19th century Theosophical lore had been rich with reports of actual sightings of selected Ascended Masters in the "flesh" in India. Earlier, Blavatsky had reported that "the Masters not infrequently materialized themselves so that all could see them," and that when she lived in Nepal she saw "three of our Masters constantly in their physical vehicles," including the ones known as Master Kuthumi, Master Djwhal Khul, and Master El Morya. Leadbeater said he twice had met physically embodied Ascended Masters.[5]

"The world is guided and directed to a large extent by a Brotherhood of Adepts to which our Masters belong…a great Brotherhood…[whose] members are in constant communication with one another" on the higher planes." Some of these Masters of the Wisdom, Leadbeater said, take human pupil-apprentices.[6]

Starting in 1919, the British writer Alice A. Bailey began conscious communication with one Master specifically, Djwhal Khul, usually called just D.K. or The Tibetan. He dictated a series of metaphysical works to her over the next 25 years, first by clairaudience then by telepathy. D.K. told Bailey that "her major duty as a disciple was to familiarise the public with the true nature of the Masters of the Wisdom" and to correct wrong impressions the public had about this subject. Further, Bailey was to help the public understand that the Plan of the Masters of the Hierarchy is "one of evolutionary development and educational progress towards an intelligent spiritual goal."[7] This in itself was a radical insight for Western culture, so entrenched

---

5. C.W. Leadbeater, *The Masters and the Path* (Adyar, India: The Theosophical Publishing House, 1979): 6, 7, 8.

6. C.W. Leadbeater, *The Masters and the Path* (Adyar, India: The Theosophical Publishing House, 1979): 15.

7. Alice A. Bailey, *The Unfinished Autobiography of Alice A. Bailey* (New York, NY: Lucis Publishing Company, 1951): 255, 257.

in the mistaken notion that life was adrift as a serendipitous accident upon a sea of no-meaning or purpose.

In 1939, the American Godfre Ray King (formerly Guy Ballard) published the first of a series of books called *Unveiled Mysteries* reporting his experiences in 1930 with an Ascended Master, both in the flesh and in visionary states, on Mount Shasta, California. The Master was known as Saint Germain, and King recounted his adventures with and teachings from this "Great Beloved 'Bearer of the Light'" in subsequent books.

The Einherjar's Mythic Guises

Other than to esoteric circles, before the public release of information about the GWB in the late 19th century, the Einherjar were remembered in certain cultures in their mythic guise as the early gods, notably the Tuatha de Danann of Ireland and the Anunnaki of Sumer.

The Tuatha de Danann was a GWB group dispatched along with members of the angelic hierarchy to assist in the terraforming of the land of Ireland and the fulfillment of its spiritual agenda as both land and people on behalf of the Earth.

According to earliest Irish lore, the Tuatha de Danann were a magical race of gods who invaded and inhabited the island of Ireland long ago. They ruled over Ireland for about 3,000 years and successfully fought against the monstrous Fomorians (see below) and the doughty Fir Bolg. Eventually, another invading race, called the Milesians, forced the Tuatha to retreat from the surface of the world and enter the numerous *sidhe* or Otherworld palaces across Ireland. Irish myth then confused their identity and likened them to the elusive Fairy Folk.

The name Tuatha de Danann literally means "Followers or People of the Goddess Danu," the Mother goddess from whom they descended or took their inspiration. They were also called the *Fir Dea,* meaning "Men of the Goddess;" the Ever-Living Ones (because they were immortal); the *Aes Sidhe* ("People of the *sidhes*" or Hollow Hills); and the *Fir Tri nDea* ("Men of the Three Gods").

After their retreat from the physical world, the Tuatha took up residence in ten principal Otherworld dwellings or *sidhes*, many of which are still extant today, although more than ten residences and their occupants are remembered. Many of Ireland's sacred sites are the *sidhe*-palaces of the elusive Tuatha, and the 12th century A.D. *Acallam na Senorach* ("Tales of the Elders of Ireland") lists the locations and inhabitants of several dozen of the Tuatha *sidhes* across the country. Even today these sites are human access places for members of the GWB.

Irish myth also recounts how periodically the Tuatha, either singly or in groups, would emerge from their *sidhes* to meet with a few living Irish people or invite them into their Otherworld palaces for a brief look and maybe a gift and to enjoy the lovely music and singing. The Tuatha had the power of *feth fiada,* or invisibility, which enabled them to roam the human world undetected. In more modern parlance, this means they could manifest fleshly or Light bodies at will.

The term Anunnaki, scholars say, refers to a collective of deities in Sumer (later called Mesopotamia, in today's Iraq). The name was written variously as *a-nuna-ke-ne* or *a-nun-na*, and generally is translated as "those of princely or royal blood." It also means those who came to Earth from Heaven—humanity's early gods. Unlike the Irish Tuatha, individual Anunnaki were not named or remembered, at least in the texts available to us today.

The Anunnaki, whose numbers are given variously as 7, 50, 300, 600, or 900 (300 in Heaven and 600 in the Underworld), are all under the direction of An (or Anu, virtually identical to the Irish Danu), the principal sky god based at Uruk (Erech) where his temple was called *E-anna*, "House of An." It was known as the pure sanctuary, the hallowed, alluring place, the house for his descent from Heaven. One cuneiform text speaks of the *anunna eridu ninnubi*, "the Fifty Anunnaki of the city of Eridu," and elsewhere they are called the "fifty great princes."

The Anunnaki were also based in the *E-ninnu* at the temple of Nirgirsu at Lagash, and probably due to their continuous presence there, Sumer (or Shumer) was known as "the Land of the Ones Who Watch," because the gods were always observing, monitoring, and directing humanity, even building their temples and cities.

The Anunnaki were a delegation from the Great White Brotherhood sent to Earth to develop and oversee one of the planet's early Lands of Light. In the early days of human life on the Earth, several areas were highlighted for special attention. They were Lands of Light, places like An (the Greek Heliopolis) in northern Egypt, Mycenae (in the Peloponnesus of Greece), Ireland, and Sumer, where a certain mix of geomantic features, when amplified by the GWB, had the effect of creating illuminated, psychically-charged regions to support higher consciousness states.

The Anunnaki were sent to Sumer on Earth to create, sustain, and oversee the operation of the numerous Light forms (geomantic features) in that landscape that would make higher consciousness states in embodied humans possible. They would remain, for a time, as benevolent Observers, as the Ones Who Watch.

The 48,000 Rishis and the Seven Rishis

In classical Hindu and the earlier Vedic society of India, what the Norse called the Einherjar were understood to be accomplished, sublime spiritual beings called rishis, of whom seven were described in detail. Although today rishis are regarded by Western scholars as mythic heroes of ancient India (and also, generically, as contemporary Indian seers), at one time in India they were recognized as actual beings; they were highly honored and their wisdom sought.

The word rishi comes from *rsi*, itself deriving from the root "R" which means "sound," and sound in this case means mantric sound, sound currents, primordial creative syllables, aspects of the Word. The numerous hymns of the Vedas were originally delivered from on high through clairaudience to the rishis, that is, by sound. Other sources attribute the word *rsi* to the roots *rs* and *drs*, which mean "to see," so that *rsi-krt* would mean "causing to see" or a "singer of sacred songs" (mantras). One ancient text declared there were 48,000 rishis in practice in the world.

The Seven Rishis, as they were called, were specialists among the vast assemblage of masters. They were seven divine beings and seers, mind-generated by Brahma, the Creator god, to recognize, uphold, and teach the immutable divine laws (*rta*) to humans, as revealed in the holy texts, the Vedas. These laws describe the basic energies that create and sustain life, the essential spiritual mechanisms and rhythms by which reality at all levels runs. Other cultures knew these fundamental laws as asha, ma'at, *me's*, Dharma, the Tao, and for the Greeks, personified as Themis, custodian of cosmic order.[8] The rishis perceived these laws and energies and expressed them as transmittable knowledge. Vedic thought says the world's stability is due to the fact that the rishis perform their reality-preserving rituals (reciting the mantras, making their holy sounds) three times daily without ceasing.

Most often the rishis were depicted as august celestial seers who would occasionally take human form as teachers and appear in every new cycle of creation whenever a new revelation of cosmic law and divine order was needed. In each new cycle, the rishis reappeared though under different names, but mostly it is the same Seven Rishis merely renamed in each new cycle of existence. They are archetypal culture heroes who continuously assume new names and forms.

In the 20th century, the Seven Rishis started to gain some popularity in new age and metaphysical circles in the West, though under different names. One psychic source called them the Lords of the Seven

---

8.   *Rta* refers to cosmic law, order, and the truth of reality; it means eternal law, the correct order and course of things, the setting in motion of the truth of reality, being, and consciousness. It connotes the perfect harmony, established at the beginning of Creation, between the essence of being, called *Sat*, and its activity. At the microcosmic level, *rta* is implicit in the design, array, and operation of all features of the Earth's Light body.

Rays; I was introduced to them as the 14 Ray Masters of Ursa Major (consistent with the Vedic statement that the seven male rishis each has a female rishi consort, making 14, all based in the Great Bear). The Rays refer to the basic color spectrum embodied in the rainbow—red, orange, yellow, green, blue, indigo, violet—but with gradations of each such as red-scarlet and rose-pink; rich blue and sky blue; deep yellow and pale yellow; violet and lilac. The major and minor gradations of the seven colors thus comprise the 14 Rays. The rishis are the masters, administrators, and embodiments of these Rays, and rather than seven, there are 14 rishis.

But it's more than color. The Rays refer to fundamental themes and streams in consciousness, and each Ray Master administers a part of that differentiation. Humans at a soul level (consistent through their sequence of incarnations) have an allegiance or affinity to one of the Rays and may be tutored for initiation by the Master of that Ray or by other masters affiliated with it over lifetimes.

Between the 1930s and 1950s, Alice Bailey published a series of channeled books discussing what she called the Masters of the Seven Rays. Bailey said the seven Rays are wielded by the Solar Logos (an organizing, cohering principle for all stars; see below) as channels through which all consciousness flows. Bailey said they are the seven predominant characteristics or modifications of life, but she documented the activities and qualities of only seven Rays, not addressing (or perhaps not told about them by her mentor, Djwhal Khul) the other seven.

The formal titles for Bailey's Rays, in her language, are the Ray of Will-Power; Love-Wisdom; Active Creative Intelligence; Harmony Through Conflict; Concrete Knowledge and Science; Idealism or Devotion; and Ceremonial Magic, Order, and Ritual. Each Ray is also associated with a profound initiation which, Bailey says, it might take a given soul many lifetimes to prepare to undergo and master.

Each Ray has a Lord, and each human, through one's soul, is affiliated with a single Ray. This Ray colors the mind, determines the temperament, controls energy distribution, predisposes one to certain strengths and weaknesses, and generally flavors the mode of spiritual development and types of experiences one has. Each Ray is a name for a particular type of force or energy and its exhibited quality, and, for Bailey, the Ray is essentially equivalent to its Ray Lord.

Each Ray represents a theme of consciousness and filter for soul evolution, but going beyond Bailey now, all 14 represent the spectrum of consciousness, mythically represented by the Egyptian Osiris. His body of Light was "cut" (diffracted) into 14 parts: these are the 14 Rays. Each Ray represents a basic quality of energy and consciousness, and its Lord administers the relationship of that Ray with humans in affinity with it and its themes.

The Rays are seven channels which flow through all levels of being in a solar system, "the seven predominant characteristics or modifications of life…[each is] a particular force or type of energy."[9] The Rays are radiant qualities, great cosmic lives who impart their essence to all the forms in all the kingdoms and throughout the seven planes of existence. Their nature is consciousness, their "expression is sentiency," they work together, blending, and intermingling, and they "produce cyclically the manifested world."[10] They can best be pictured as "a band of seven colors circling and continuously shifting and moving through the [seven] planes [of existence] back to their originating source."[11]

In the view of the Ofanim[12], an angelic order commissioned to interface with humans on matters of the Earth's energy and Light body, the 14 Rays are the standard qualifications of light, the major subdivisions and manifestations of light. For ease of understanding and reference, I arrange the 14 Ray Masters and their Rays (and

---

9.   Djwhal Khul, *Ponder On This. From the Writings of the Tibetan Teacher (Djwhal Khul)*, (Lynnwood, Pretoria, South Africa: Trulit Publishers: [no date]): 331.

10. Alice A. Bailey, *Esoteric Psychology. Vol. 1, A Treatise on the Seven Rays* (New York, NY: Lucis Publishing Company, 1962): 141.

11. Alice A. Bailey, *Letters on Occult Meditation* (New York, NY: Lucis Publishing Company, 1950): 211.

themes and qualities) in accordance with the electromagnetic spectrum of visible light (see Table 1). This gives us two Ray Masters per each of the seven major visible colors, one for the primary or full tone color, one for the minor, paler but higher frequency gradation of this same color.

---

12. The Ofanim are an angelic order that has provided me the basic outline of the Earth's visionary geography, facilitated my experiences within it, and inspired many people to engage their own spirituality with that of the planet's. In my writings, I have referred to them variously as Blazing Star, the Nimitta, or more avuncularly, Blaise. They are implicit in every human being, as a tiny, expandable pinprick of light just above the navel and a little inside. As an angelic order of about 40.3 million potential manifestations, they have dipped into human culture here and there and left a lasting impression, encoded in myth, in the form of Ganesh, Garuda, Hanuman, Behemoth, Simurgh, Thunderbird, the Eagle (famous in Toltec shamanism), the Ziz, Vocub Caquix (Mayan), and others. Their name comes from the Hebrew, *ofan,* which means "wheel" for they are the wheels of the Merkabah, the Supreme Being's Chariot and Throne. In conventional angelologies, they are the Thrones. The Ofanim are fun, irreverent, deeply knowledgable, protean in their expressions, and with Archangel Michael, Sanat Kumara (the Cosmic Logos), and the Ray Masters, a primary factor in the rejuvenation of the Earth's visionary geography and the project of bringing a sufficient number of humans up to speed on the interaction protocols. The Ofanim are also implicit in the renewal and purification of the Christ Mysteries, being the guides (as in "the Star of Bethlehem") for humans to an authentic, dogma-free experience of the cosmic Christ.

Table 1
The 14 Rays According to the Electromagnetic Spectrum of Visible Light

Red	Orange	Yellow	Green	Blue	Indigo	Violet
Rays 1, 2	Rays 3, 4	Rays 5, 6	Rays 7, 8	Rays 9, 10	Rays 11,12	Rays 13,14
Primary: Jesus	Primary: Portia	Primary: Lao Tzu	Primary: Djwhal Khul	Primary: Paul the	Primary: Serapis Bey	Primary: Maha Chohan
Minor: Nada	Minor: Kuthumi	Minor: Kuan-Yin	Minor: Hilarion	Venetian	Minor: Pallas Athena	Minor: St. Germain
Bailey: Devotion and Idealism	Bailey: Concrete Knowledge and Science	Bailey: Harmony Through Conflict	Bailey: Active, Creative Intelligence	Minor: Apollo Bailey: Power and Will	Bailey: Love and Wisdom	Bailey: Ceremonial Magic, Order, and Ritual

Note: *Primary*=the color's major full tone; *minor*=paler, a higher frequency gradation; *Bailey*=the name and quality of the Ray in Alice Bailey's system

The numbering of Rays and Ray Masters in this book will follow this simple allocation per color (and thus depart from Bailey's scheme) since the color is arguably the most important and fundamental distinction among the Rays and the electromagnetic field spectrum is a commonly accepted model of light.

We must be careful not to be rigid or dogmatic about the exact colors attributed to each Ray Master nor even to this classification scheme as an absolute. It is an approximation, made from the human viewpoint, and may be inherently inaccurate or at least imprecise to some degree. It is based on my recent clairvoyant dialogue with each of the 14 Ray Masters plus cumulative interactive visionary experiences with them and their locales for 22 years. That is the *empirical* basis of the information in this book—my direct experience through clairvoyance of the Ray Masters, their Rays, qualities, lives, locales, and activities. Since this is a corroborable psychic reality, readers may verify or amend these observations based on their own experiences; to help with this, I have provided practical exercises to put one in contact with the Rays.

The Ofanim note that Ray Masters can blend their own color with that of other Masters not of their Ray. Pallas Athena, for example, is of the Indigo Ray yet she is presently blending a little with Jesus of the Scarlet Ray producing a magenta or reddish indigo hue. In present time, Apollo, whose Ray is inherently a pale sky blue, is blending a little with the neighboring green to produce a sky blue-turquoise Ray color. Kuan-Yin's pale yellow is so ethereal, silken, and evanescent as to carry suggestions of a background of scintillating silver.

The Seven Rishis—the 14 Ray Masters—are also known, nonspecifically, as Ascended Masters, Brothers of Wisdom, Cosmic Master Beings, Elders, Lords of Progeny, Lords of the Seven Rays, the Seven *Abdals*, Seven *Apkallu*, Seven Chohans, Seven Ray Lords, and Seven Sages, among other titles. A more functional designation is to say Master of the Golden Robe, Master of the Blue Robe, and Master of the Violet Robe, the "Robe" being the garment of light in which the Ray Master appears and the totality and color essence of their Ray.

Mesopotamian myth recognized an equivalent group of celestial adepts known as the Seven *Apkallu* or Sages. Their task was to teach humanity wisdom and to ensure the correct functioning of the plan of Heaven and Earth. In pre-Islamic Iranian mysticism, the rishis were known as the Seven *Abdals* of the Great Bear constellation, but also as the Seven Poles or *Aqtab*, the seven masters of initiation. They are intercessors invisibly apportioned to the human world, seven apertures through which God shows Himself in the world—God's Eyes, as it were. They are the invisible spiritual hierarchy necessary for the continuation of all life, and they each oversee specific zodiacal energies in the forms of the 12 constellations of the zodiac (and the personal horoscope). See Table 2 for the correlations of the Ray Masters with the constellations in the Western zodiac.

Table 2
Correlations of the Ray, Ray Master, and Astrological Constellations

Deep yellow	Lao Tzu	Aries
Olive emerald green	Djwhal Khul	Taurus
Pale sky blue turquoise	Apollo	Gemini
Gold-dark orange	Portia	Cancer
Indigo-midnight blue	Serapis Bey	Leo
Violet-purple	Maha Chohan	Virgo
Reddish indigo-blue violet	Pallas Athena	Libra
Cobalt blue	Paul the Venetian	Scorpio
Ethereal pale yellow	Kuan-Yin	Sagittarius
Spring green-jade	Hilarion	Capricorn
Pale red, rose-pink	Nada	Aquarius
Scarlet	Jesus	Aquarius
Electric pale orange-gold	Kuthumi	Pisces
Pale violet, lilac	Saint Germain	Pisces

Note: With 14 Ray Masters and 12 zodiacal signs, there are two overlaps in assignments.

In classical Vedic lore, the seven male rishis were named as follows: Marici ("Light"), Atri ("Devourer"), Angiras ("Fiery"), Pulaha ("Bridger of Space"), Kratu ("Inspiration"), Pulastya ("Smooth Hair"), and Vasistha ("Owner of Wealth"). Their female consorts were: Sambhuti ("Fitness"), Anasuya ("Without Spite"), Lajja ("Modesty"), Ksama ("Forgiveness"), Sannati ("Humility"), Priti ("Love"), and Arundhati ("Faithfulness"). Later, we will discover some possibly more formal and possibly familiar Western names for these 14 Ray Masters.

By way of previewing this, let's note that in terms of Western myth and culture, the Ray Masters have occasionally manifested for humans or sometimes in human form, such as in the guise of gods, but other times as mysterious, only seeming humans. Among their god-forms, Ray Master No. 10 (pale sky blue) was Apollo; No. 1 (scarlet) was Hephaistos, the smith and craftsman of Olympus; No. 12 (blue violet-magenta), Pallas Athena, Homer's "grey-eyed Athena" and steadfast Olympian mentor to Odysseus; No. 3, Portia, was the Bodhisattva Avalokitesvara, famous among Buddhists in India, Tibet, China, and Japan.

In the human realm, Ray Master No. 14 (lilac) has manifested as the Comte de Saint Germain, William Shakespeare[13], and Francis Bacon; Ray Master No. 5 (deep yellow) as Lao Tzu and St. Patrick; Ray Master No. 3 (orange-gold) as Benjamin Franklin; Ray Master No. 2 (pink) as Mary Magdalene, Joan of Arc, and St. Bridget. Four of the Ray Masters in their female valency periodically manifest, singly or as a group, as the Virgin Mary and her other cultural counter-

---

13. The metaphysical view seems to be that Saint Germain, as Francis Bacon, wrote all of the plays attributed to Shakespeare and that this latter figure was either an actual actor who agreed to take the credit for the works, to be the "front man" for Bacon who wished to remain in the background, or a made-up name and figure (the name evokes the image of a spear-holder and shaker) that served the same, as it turned out, historical purpose. See: Peter Dawkins, *The Shakespeare Enigma* (London: Polair Publishing, 2004).

parts (the Buddhist-Tibetan Tara; the Chinese Kuan-Yin; and the Aztec Coatlaxopueh).

Often the cosmic pairing of Ray Masters within the same Ray is exemplified in their manifestations in human culture. Master Jesus (Ray Master No. 1, scarlet) was paired in biblical times (and again in current times) with his archetypal consort, Mary Magdalene (Ray Master 2, pink—Aphrodite and Hathor, the Greek and Egyptian love-goddess). In the Puranic tradition of India, this Master was Rama, and Mary Magdalene was his consort, Sita; in earlier Vedic literature, he was Krishna, she was Radha, again, his consort. They could not help but be "consorts" to each other, as they co-administered the same color frequency, the Scarlet Ray.

In H.P. Blavatsky's 19th century Theosophy and its adulation of the secret Himalayan Chiefs and arcane masters, we see a few of the Ray Masters making a cultural appearance such as Kuthumi (Ray Master No. 4), El Morya (No. 10), Serapis Bey (No. 11), and Alice Bailey's celestial mentor for all her books, Djwhal Khul, the "Tibetan Master," Ray Master of the Emerald Ray (No. 7).

The Ray Master Saint Germain (from the Latin, *Sanctus Germanus*, "Holy Brother") has probably been the most popular of the Lords of the Seven Rays recently. For a complete listing and details of the 14 Ray Masters, see Table 3.

Table 3
Ray Masters: Their Ray Numbers, Colors, Qualities, Guises, and Aliases

1 SCARLET	2 PALE RED, ROSE-PINK	3 GOLD-DARK ORANGE
Christ Carrier, the Christ-Smith, Solar Logos Shaper, Fire-Master, Superintends the Sun Centers, Casts Self-Aware Substance into Forms, Initiator, Forger of Divine Weapons, Soul Shaper, Sacrificial Surrender, Scarlet Flame of Surrender, Softener of Metals (Chakras), Creating Vessels for the Father, Fullness of the Father's Love, Creating Embodiments for the Logos •Ray Master Jesus (carrier of the Christ-Logos) •Constellation: Aquarius •Santanda •Subhuti (Buddha's first disciple) •*Feng-hwang*, The Vermilion Bird, the Substance of Flame	*Love, Eros, Beauty, Seduction, Sound, Music, Consort to Jesus Christ, Master of the Palace of Beauty, Administers Candlemass (February 2), Ocean of Sound Currents, Sea of Mantras, Sea-Born, Surrender to the Great Mother, the Softener, the Compassionate Goddess* •Ray Master Lady Nada ("Sound") •Constellation: Aquarius •Mary Magdalene •Aphrodite •Hathor, Ishtar, Astarte •Narada (*rishi*-musician, who taught Gandharvas) •Freya •Irish St. Bridget •Irish Bride (Brid): Keeper of the Flame, White Swan, Bride of the Golden Hair, Bride of the White Hills	*Justice, Wisdom, Mercy, Compassion, Discrimination, Discernment in Transmutation, Righteous Alignment with Truth (Dharma, 'rta, maat, me's), Transcendental Insight into the Emptiness of Form, the Mysticism of Name and Form (Rupa), Burns Away Obstructions to Prajna (Sublime Emptiness), the Discerning View of the Process, Counsels Earth's 72 National Egregors, Administers Heaven on Earth Day, Superintends the Summer Country temple at Glastonbury, Oversees Archetype of Heart Chakra (Venus, Netzach)* •Ray Master Lady Portia

Table 3
Ray Masters: Their Ray Numbers, Colors, Qualities, Guises, and Aliases (Continued)

•Rama	•Irish Tuatha de Danann Goddess Brigit	•Constellation: Cancer
•Krishna		•Tribe: Berbers, Bahrain
•Hephaistos	•Joan of Arc	
•Vulcan (Mulciber, "Smelter of Metals")	•Radha, Krishna's consort	•Benjamin Franklin
•Llassar Llaes Gyfnewid	•Sita, Rama's consort	•Murasaki Shikibu (author, *The Tale of Genji*, 11ᵗʰ cent. A.D., Japan)
•Goibniu, Goban Saor	•Mahavidya Tripurasundari (Sodasi, Lalita)	
•Ilmarinen (Finnish)	•Virgin Mary	•Songsten Gampo, Tibet
•Lochan, Culann		•Buddhist Bodhisattva Avalokitesvara-Chenrezi
•Govannon		
•Wayland (or Weland): Wayland's Smithy		•The 14 Dalai Lamas of Tibet (partial incarnation)
•Apollonius of Tyana		•Avallach, King of the Summer Country
•Desiderius Erasmus		•Evelake the Unknown
•Leonardo da Vinci		•Mahakala ("Great Dark One"), a Dharmapala (Protector of the Dharma as a Wrathful Deity)

Table 3
Ray Masters: Their Ray Numbers, Colors, Qualities, Guises, and Aliases (Continued)

4	5	6
ELECTRIC PALE ORANGE, PALE GOLD	DEEP YELLOW	ETHEREAL PALE, SILKEN YELLOW
Higher Mind, Acquires Transcendent Knowledge and the Self, Dharma-Christ Protector, Prepares the Grail Vessel, Truth Revealer, Lord of Knowledge of God, Revelation of God's Plans, Desert Scorcher, Guardian of the Door into God's Mind, Great Connector and Intermediary, Gate-Keeper of the Dharmakaya	*Taoism, Inner Alchemy, Joy of Movement in Nature, Non-movement in Movement, the Mind That Is Not Moving, Stillness in Transformation and Process, Supervises Og-Min Cave Heavens, Working with Earth Energies and Harmonizing Landscape Protector Spirits, Oversees Samhain, Secret Landscapes of Spirit, Maintains Secret Cultural Reserves and Arks for the Future*	*Compassionate Mother, Emissary of the Mother. Lady of the Peaks, Savior, Goddess of Mercy, the Mountain Born, Taking the High View, the View behind and through the Opposites, View Provider, Vision, Spiritual Perception, Tutor for 8th Chakra (The Mountain), Guardian of Threshold to Sea of Consciousness*
•Master Kuthumi, Koot Humi Lal Singh •Constellation: Pisces •Durga ("Inaccessible") •Perseus, Slayer of Gorgon-Medusa •Teacher of Ascended Master Artemis-Diana •Virgin Mary	•Ray Master Lao Tzu (Old Master, Old Sage, Old Child) •Constellation: Aries •Tribe: Buryat-Mongolians, midway between Ulaan-Bataar and Amarbayasgalant, Mongolia	•Ray Master Kuan-Yin (Chinese: "Who Contemplates the Supplicating Sound of the World") •Constellation: Sagittarius •Tribe: Ainu-Jomon of Japan

Table 3
Ray Masters: Their Ray Numbers, Colors, Qualities, Guises, and Aliases (Continued)

•Sekhmet, Egyptian Lion-Goddess, "The Powerful One"
•Vairochana ("He Who Is Like the Sun": a transcendent Buddha)
•Samantabhadra, a transcendent Bodhisattva
•Maitreya Buddha (the Buddha to Come)
•John the Baptist
•Emperor Shah Jahan, builder of Taj Mahal
•Pythagoras
•St. Francis of Asissi (Francesco di Pietro Bernardone)
•Sir Thomas More and Isaac Newton (partial incarnations)

•Tonpa Shenrab Miwo, "The Lord of Man, the Conqueror," founder of Tibet's Bön
•St. Patrick
•Lord Lanto
•Chinggis (Genghis) Khan, "Oceanic Ruler," or "Emperor of all Emperors", Mongolia

•Gauri ("The Yellow")
•Parvati, daughter of Himalaya-Himavat, consort to Shiva
•Green, White, Red, Yellow Tara
•Dolma (Tibetan)
•Virgin Mary
•Tonantzin, Coatlicue, Coatlaxopueh (Aztec)
•Miao-shan ("the Wondrously Kind One")
•Saint Theresa of Avila (Teresa Sanchez Cepeda Davila y Ahumada)

Table 3
Ray Masters: Their Ray Numbers, Colors, Qualities, Guises, and Aliases (Continued)

7 SPARKLING OLIVE-EMERALD GREEN	8 SPRING GREEN-JADE	9 COBALT BLUE
Messenger of the Masters, Teacher of Cosmic Law, Mentor in Occult Philosophy, Guide to Buddha Lands, Certainty in Spiritual Perception, Universal Analzyer, the Model of Universal Operations, Guide to the Infrastructure of the Buddha Mind, Geographer of the Higher Mind, Guide to the Dharmakaya Realm of the Earth's Landscape, Oversees Wesak Festival, Developer of New World Religion, the Universal Systematiser, the Seeker's-Scholar's Ray Master, Preparation for Buddhahood	Developing Intuition, Growth and Vitality, Nurturing and Stimulating Growth and Activity, Especially in Culture, Quickening of New Buds in Consciousness and Nature, the Eucharist-Asvamedha, Preparing the Space-Container for the Christ-Logos Experience, Nurtures Seeds of Christ Consciousness, Spiritual Mentoring, Associated with Sun Temples	Poised Stillness of God's Force, Focussed Application of Divine Will, Devouring Selfhood, Dismemberment of Illusory Selfness, Stripping Away Falsehoods in Being, Divestment of Self, Guide to the Bardo and Duat-Underworld, Funerary-Initiation Rites, Necropolis Psychopomp, Master of the Cinvat Bridge. Supervises Scorpio Illumination Day (Oct. 22)
•Ray Master Djwhal Khul, Alice Bailey's "Tibetan Master"; source of H.P. Blavatsky's *The Secret Doctrine*" (1888)	•The Cretan Ray Master, Hilarion •Constellation: Capricorn •Tribe: an obscure folk group in Albania •Centaurus, Father-Leader of the Centaurs •The Asvins, Nasatya and Dasra ("Possessed of Horses") •Cheiron, the Centaur •The Sage Cyavana ("Activity")	•Paul, the Venetian Ray Master (Paolo Caliari Veronese) •Constellation: Scorpio •Kali the Black One •Virgin Mary •Supervisor of the Persephone-Kore-Daena initiation at Eleusis, Greece •Persephone as Queen of the Dead-Underworld

Table 3
Ray Masters: Their Ray Numbers, Colors, Qualities, Guises, and Aliases (Continued)

•Constellation: Taurus •Tribe: the Basque, northeastern Spain •Infiltrated Henry Cornelius Agrippa	•Saul-Paul of Tarsus, the Apostle Paul	•Minos, King of Crete, Judge of the Dead •Sokar, Egyptian funerary god

Table 3
Ray Masters: Their Ray Numbers, Colors, Qualities, Guises, and Aliases (Continued)

10	11	12
PALE SKY BLUE-TURQUOISE	INDIGO-MIDNIGHT BLUE	REDDISH INDIGO-BLUE VIOLET, MAGENTA
The Power and Will of God, Opener of the Golden Door, Power of God to Heal (Father of Asclepios), Express (Mousagetes: Leader of the 9 Muses), and Excel (Pythian Games), Lord of the Silver Bow, The Archer, Far-Shooter, The Healer, Purification and Pollution, Prophecy, Oracles, Divination of God's Will, Psycho-pomp-Guardian of Magical City of Findias, Oversees Beltaine (May 1), Supervises Arcs of Developing Consciousness, Hyper-borea Emissary	*Voyage and Process of the Discovery of Truth, Concentration in Objec-tivity, Release of Sub-jectivity, Love and Wisdom, Supervises the Sphinxes and Mystery Pyramids, the Ray of Revelation, Facilitator of the Mystery Revelation, Supervises the Celestial City of the Nagas, Psy-chopomp for Summer Solstice Mystery Initia-tion, Mystery of the Blue Door*	*The Star Initiator, Psy-chopomp to Psychic Reality of Stars, Defense of Clear Per-ception, Voyages to the Mind of God (Zeus), Hero-Helper, Move-ments Towards Truth (Odysseys), Truth-Holder, Lived-Wisdom, Psychopomp to Mysti-cal Sanctuaries (Beyuls), Chaperone of Landscape Zodiac Experiences, Mentor to Astrology, Vajra-Wielder, Mystic Initia-tion, Mentor to the 144,000, Supervises the Sword in the Stone (Scabbard) Ritual, Guardian of Vajra Spots, Supervises Gor-gon Medusa Initiation-Mystery*

Table 3
Ray Masters: Their Ray Numbers, Colors, Qualities, Guises, and Aliases (Continued)

•Ray Master Apollo •Phoebus Apollo, "The Shining One" •Constellation: Gemini •Tribe: Aborigines of Arnhem Land, Australia •Djanggawul (Arnhem Land culture hero-god) •Nuadu (Nudd) of the Silver Hand (Irish) •Arjuna •Ascended Master El Morya (Theosophy) •Oenghus mac Oc •Bel, Belinus, Baal •Solomon •The Apostle Peter	•Ray Master Serapis Bey •White Flame •Constellation: Leo •The Egyptian Master, Osorapis (Sarapis): Assumes Apis Bull or Sphinx form at Serapeum •White Buffalo Maiden (Lakota) •Socrates •Nagarjuna ("The Great Naga, Great Adept")	•Ray Master Pallas Athena •Constellation: Libra •Vajravarahi (Dorje Phagmo), the Dakini Diamond Sow Goddess •The Morrigan (Irish) •Morgan le Faye •Brynhildr, the Valkyrie •Major inspiration behind Homer, Ferdinand Magellan

Table 3
Ray Masters: Their Ray Numbers, Colors, Qualities, Guises, and Aliases (Continued)

13 VIOLET	14 PALE VIOLET, LILAC
Applied Energized Knowledge, Magic-Qabala, Protean Applications in Ritual, Ceremony, Protocols, Esoteric Curricula and Formulae, Guardian-Master of the Spear, Psychopomp to Magical City of Gorias, Magic Used to Create Forms, The Magician-Magus, Oversees Lughnasadh (August 1) •Ray Master Maha Chohan, *Great Teacher* (Literally: "Lord of the Dharma") •Constellation: Virgo •Tribe: Inuits of Alaska •Thoth-Djehuty, Hermes Trismegistus •Issac Luria (1534-1572), "The Sacred Lion," Holy Ari (influential Qabalist)	*Transmutation, Alchemy, Freedom, Ceremony, Hierarch for America and Aquarian Age, Transmutative Energy of the Christ, Purification, Light Grid Activation, Dragon Network "Plumber," Lilac Containment Fields for Lucifer, Anti-Christ Dissolution, Awakening America as the Cup of Light Prominent in Wild Hunt (Winter Solstice, Yuletide), Ghost Dance-Cup of Light Realization for America, Blending Science and Spirit, Innovation and Deepening of Science, Great Instauration* •Ray Master Saint Germain, from *Sanctus Germanus*, "Holy Brother"

Table 3
Ray Masters: Their Ray Numbers, Colors, Qualities, Guises, and Aliases (Continued)

•Lugh Lamfada, the Long-Armed (Irish hero), *Samildanach* ("Possessing many arts, trades, crafts"), "The Shining One": possessor Spear of Lugh •Lleu Llaw Gyffes (Welsh Lugh) •Crom Dubh ("Black Crescent"), legendary pre-Christian Irish chief	•Constellation: Pisces •Eolia •Bellerophon (Greek) •Le Comte de St. Germain •St. George (British dragon-slayer: d. 303 A.D.) •Francis Bacon •Roger Bacon •William Shakespeare •Christian Rosenkranz •Haroun al Raschid, 9th century caliph of Baghdad •Christopher Columbus •Herakhan Baba •Prince Rakoczy •Khorlo Demchog (Wrathful Deity) •Chakrasamavara, Heruka consort to Dorje Phagmo

Where the Rishis Reside

The rishis reside in the seven stars of the tail of the constellation Ursa Major (the Great Bear), commonly known in the West as the Big Dipper and in other cultures as Arthur's Wain, the Plough, the Great Chariot, Seven Bears, Himmel Wagen, Car of Osiris, the Government, among many others. The Seven Rishis were each assigned one of these stars as a residence, according to the Vedas, and each has a consort at that star, making fourteen Big Dipper-based Ray Masters. Two Rays emanate from each of the seven stars in the Big Dipper, or the Great Bear (functionally, the Dipper is the Bear), and thus two Ray Masters occupy and work from each star where their Ray is grounded.

Of course, this begs the question of how rishis can "live" in a sun. It is helpful to conceive of the stars in our galaxy as the outer physical expressions of great spiritual beings, what the Chaldeans anciently called the great Star-Angels. Some metaphysical traditions, including Anthroposophy and the insights of its founder, Rudolf Steiner, testify to the experience that the stars as we see them and think we understand them all have great conscious beings within them and that the apparent fiery, gaseous composition of the stars is a physical façade for spiritual depths. We have to free ourselves of the materialist conceit that what we see is what (and all) there is in our galaxy. The stars, clairvoyants and mystics tell us, are but the facades of great beings.

In the *Mahabharata*, India's fabulous mythic saga, Arjuna witnesses thousands of "shining beings of great beauty" flying around in chariots; they were so bright the region around them glowed. "You have seen their shining abodes from the Earth as stars in the firmament," he is told. Arjuna was on his way to Amaravati, the Celestial City of Indra, chief of the gods.[14] Amaravati is one of the seven geomantic locales of the GWB to be discussed below.

---

14. Krishna Dharma, *Mahabharata* (Los Angeles: Torchlight Publishing, 1999): 258.

In support of this view, the clairvoyant (Rudolf Steiner) commented: "If we have acquired the faculty of Intuitive Knowledge, the stars are the revealers of Cosmic Beings, spiritual Beings. And with Intuition we behold in the spiritual Universe, instead of the physical stars, colonies of spiritual beings at the places where we conceive the physical stars to be situated."[15]

So we might think of the seven stars of the Big Dipper, in a subtler dimension, as a colony of spiritual beings known as the rishis or Ascended Masters. Or perhaps more truly, we might conceive of the Great Bear stars as portals or points of focus through which these august spiritual beings of the galaxy move in and out of various realms of manifestation and activity. It's not so much that they "reside" in or at the seven Great Bear stars, but that these are laserlike foci for their Rays to be disseminated throughout the Milky Way galaxy and the Earth.

Vedic lore says the rishis soar effortlessly through space to the mysterious initiate's realm called Svetadvipa, a pure, mystical, paradaisal land (or island) on the northern side of the Ocean of Milk. This is said to be 32,000 miles above Mount Meru (the cosmic mountain or *axis mundi* of both Earth and the cosmos; see below). There all the residents are rich in *Jnana* (knowledge) and exude a perpetual fragrance indicative of the purified, exalted state of their being.

The rishis also glide out across the galaxy from the Great Bear. As an animal, the bear is large, powerful, and physically daunting to behold. Similarly, the Great Bear as a conclave of stars is a formidable galactic presence, a *mass of consciousness* just as the physical bear is a mass of flesh and bones. The Great Bear continuously sends out "agents" in the form of rishis to supervise the development of solar systems, planets, and the varieties of sentient life resident there. Of course, this is a materialist way of putting it; probably the case is more that the Rays with the Ray Masters implicit in them are continuously streaming out, almost automatically, from the Great Bear.

---

15. Rudolf Steiner, *Karmic Relationships, Esoteric Studies. Vol. V,* Translated by D.S. Osmond (London: Rudolf Steiner Press, 1966): 73.

It could be said the rishis supervise the incubation of new solar systems and their planets and encase them in a placenta of "colored ribbons" or rays of light. For solar systems, such as ours, with arguably more advanced sentient life forms than is represented by a fetus of the galaxy, the Great Bear's agents oversee initiations, dispense esoteric knowledge, act as a spiritual governing body, and stimulate our further conscious evolution. Two of Earth's prime geomantic features for interfaces with the Great White Brotherhood, Valhalla and the Celestial City of Amaravati, are based in Ursa Major. The Earth has numerous holograms of both (360 and 108, respectively), which serve as visionary portals to the original "place," accessed through actual physical sites.

The *fact* of their existence on Earth is part of our planet's design rationality. Implicit in the model of visionary interactive geography is the fact that Earth is a *designer planet*, rationally, intelligently, purposefully designed. It was designed to execute a purpose: to facilitate the expansion of consciousness within material forms on a physical (or densified) planet. The means by which this would happen is the Earth's Light grid or Light body, also called its visionary geography—the array of more than 100 different subtle energy features or Light temples, all in multiple copies, across the planet's surface, all primed for our interaction and known to us outwardly, if sketchily today, as sacred sites.

For us to be able to *use* portals within the planet's Light grid to consciously interact with representatives of the true "government"—those who truly "run" or guide the world—was, and remains, a central design feature of this plan.[16]

Activities on Earth of the Ray Masters

One of the prime functions of the GWB in general and of the Ray Masters specifically is to supervise the expansion of Light (consciousness) within humanity, that is, the ability to have embodied higher consciousness states. We have already seen how delegations from the

GWB, remembered in myth as the Tuatha de Danann of Ireland and the Anunnaki of Sumer, worked to activate those Lands of Light. The 14 Ray Masters and their GWB adepts also have had particular geomantic assignments.

In the Earth's earliest days, when its array of visionary geography features was being installed and "turned on," a prime responsibility of the Ray Masters was the grounding and progressive activation of the Earth's 1,067 dragons. These dragons are authentic astral beings commissioned by the Supreme Being to fulfill certain geomantic tasks on the Earth working through its visionary geography; though they have been trivialized or fancified over time by myth and disbelief and even recent Hollywoodization, their presence on Earth is crucial to the progressive release of the Light into planetary and human matter.

Perhaps it is helpful to picture a dragon as the embodiment of the complete electromagnetic field (EMF) spectrum of light, including those frequencies (the bulk of them) not currently seeable by humans. The Australian Aborigines' name for the dragon, Rainbow Serpent, points in this direction, the name suggesting the color spectrum; so does the Vedic myth of Indra slaying Vrtra, the cosmic demon-drought dragon, forcing it to release the waters (of Light and higher consciousness states). Vrtra and the Rainbow Serpent both contain the cosmic "waters" which the Earth needs, which means they contain

---

16.   This is not meant to invalidate the fairly widespread sense of there being a single, inimical, and secret shadow government behind the apparent national ones. This government behind the government is an expression of the antithesis to the Earth's Light body called the dark grid. It is a manifestation of the Antichrist. However, the GWB has a deeper magic than the Antichrist, as C. S. Lewis would say, and their level of planetary, solar, and galactic government is both more benign and more far-seeing than the machinations of the supposed secret manipulators of world events. The GWB lets them run their power and world control games for a while in accordance with their larger plans in which the self-styled world controllers are but the unconscious, unwitting agents of the larger benevolent plan for the Earth.

the full EMF spectrum of light and its subtle consciousness states. We might say the dragon holds both light and the Light.

The Ray Masters ground their own energies and the spectral array from Ursa Major through the Earth's 1,067 dragons. These exist at three levels: the Midgard Serpent is the Earth's primary Mother dragon who encircles the planet; then there are 13 major dragons, each capable of generating up to 81 progeny (1,053 minor dragons, the third tier of dragons). It is also correct to say the 13 primary or master dragons among these 1,067 seed the energies (the seven primary Rays and their seven subtleties) of the Ray Masters, enabling them to affect the Earth in positive ways to support growth.

Then, in mimicry of Indra's cosmogonic act, the Ray Masters also "slay" the dragons, meaning they serially activate them, one by one, allowing the planet to register the energy impact of these awakenings and energy releases. Perhaps the image of a spigot on a water tank is more apt: the Ray Masters, as appropriate for the state of world and human evolution, crank open the dragon spigots a little.

Here is another way to picture this: The Ray Masters slice up the Rainbow Serpent into 14 pieces, each a different color. More precisely, for our solar system, they slice up the visible light portion of the full spectrum, that is, the fourth of seven frequency domains according to conventional science, with a wavelength spectrum of 4,000 to 7,000 angstroms.[17] Ray Master Jesus, for example, takes the scarlet wedge; his consort, Ray Master Nada, the rose-pink. Each Ray Master is responsible for grounding this Ray (its energy and consciousness) on the Earth and in humanity and for managing its expression and evolution in a planetary context. The totality of the seven (or 14) colors in the visible light spectrum is white; as said above, one mythic name for this totality is the Egyptian high god, Osiris, who was sliced up into 14 pieces.

More recently, beginning around 1988, the Ray Masters have been "wiring" the 14 Rays of Ursa Major to an increasing number of the Earth's domes. A dome is a geomantic term I use to denote an etheric energy canopy, a half-sphere averaging 5-15 miles in diameter and half that in height, set over a mountain, plain, or town. Each dome transmits the energy and holographic presence of a single high magnitude star.

In December 1988, I participated in a "dome wiring" as part of my initial introduction to the 14 Ray Masters. The site was a small village in Lincolnshire, England, called Tetford; it is canopied by a dome representing Sadalmelik, or alpha Aquarius. The event was conducted by the Ofanim, as mentioned, an angelic order intimately involved in all energy aspects of the Earth and its Light grid. One by one, they introduced each of the Ray Masters to me; each Master allowed an image of himself to form (as well as a hint of his or her color or Ray) for my psychic perception. As I made contact with each, the Ofanim attached that Ray into the top of the dome.

At the finish of the introductions, the dome appeared to have 14 brightly colored ribbons of light attached to its top; these ribbons streamed out into the night sky, terminating, I later understood, in the seven stars of the Big Dipper. Since I had, as an embodied human,

---

17. The spectrum of electromagnetic radiation has seven divisions, including radio waves, microwaves, and infrared (the slowest frequencies), and then visible light, followed by ultraviolet, X-rays, and gamma rays (the fastest frequency vibrations). Whether this model has reality and complete descriptive accuracy beyond the Earth, solar system or galaxy is uncertain. One wonders. What about the other six domains—do they have colors? Why can't we see them? One possible answer, speculatively applied here, comes from Djwhal Khul, Ray Master No.7: He says there are seven great rays in the cosmos, but in our solar system, only one of these rays is in operation; that ray is divided into seven portions, and these are the Seven Rays, each with their Lords (as in Ray Lord or Ray Master). My speculation is that perhaps the other six great cosmic rays represent the (to us) nonvisible portions of the electromagnetic spectrum; elsewhere in creation, perhaps in other solar systems or galaxies, those six portions are visible because the six other cosmic rays are operational there. Djwhal Khul, *Ponder On This. From the Writings of the Tibetan Teacher (Djwhal Khul)*, (Lynnwood, Pretoria, South Africa: Trulit Publishers: [no date]): 331.

been similarly "wired" with these Rays, on future occasions, the Ofanim and/or Ray Masters used that precondition to wire up more domes in whose vicinity I happened to be. I observed this in 1990 at Mount Palomar, near San Diego, California. While I was conducting an outdoor workshop there on geomantic topics, the Ray Masters wired Palomar's dome (which represents Alnitak in Orion, the middle belt star) to Ursa Major.

By June 1990, they had wired 42 more of the planet's 1,746 domes, and since then, presumably many more, although definitely not the full complement as that would be ill-advised. The Ofanim explained why: "A dome is an energy matrix imprint from the 4th dimension. The light of the Rays facilitates the activity of this energy matrix. The more Rays that are connected to domes, the more the planet's energy matrix becomes effective. We would never activate them all as this would have a negative effect"—something like over-eating rich desserts, they suggested.

Implicit in this explanation is the illustration of a macrocosmic fact. Ursa Major is energetically connected—"wired"—to the other stars in our galaxy. As a mass of galactic consciousness, it is perpetually feeding the galaxy's stars with the spectral array of Light, the 14 Rays. This pattern is copied on Earth through the star-domes, although obviously Earth has vastly fewer stars (as domes) than the galaxy. But Ursa Major, through its agents, the Ray Masters, secures the energy connections between the Mother Bear and the stars (analogically, the "children") present on Earth as domes by "wiring" some of them (as noted, only a portion of the 1,746 total) with the 14 Rays.

Individual Ray Masters also have affiliations with specific constellations within the Sun's ecliptic, that is, the annual apparent path of our Sun through the zodiac. For example, Ray Master Portia (Orange Ray) is affiliated with Cancer; Lao Tzu (Yellow Ray) with Aries. We might usefully think of Cancer, for example, as a highly advanced adept within the Orange Ray and whose evolution as the Logos (the central, master cohering principle) of a vast star system (the Cancer constellation and its many stars) is supervised by Ray Master Portia.

Similarly, Lao Tzu monitors the evolution and spiritual mastery of the galactic intelligence whose outer star-body is called Aries. Refer again to Table 3 for more details on these correlations.

This arrangement of Ray Masters and zodiacal constellations has application on the Earth level too, on at least three accounts. First, each of the twelve seats at King Arthur's Round Table is supervised by a Ray Master (two Ray Masters are for this purpose implicit within another Ray). The Round Table has many nuances, but the one germane here is that it represents twelve stages in the maturation of the human into the Christed Self. Each zodiacal station, such as Cancer and Aries, represents a portion of that totality of the Self that must be assimilated. A Ray Master supervises that assimilation within those humans wishing to do this.

The second aspect pertains to a geomantic feature called landscape zodiacs. These are holograms of a selection of the galactic stars templated in various sizes upon generally flat areas of the landscape for human interaction. Each zodiac (the diameter range is ½ mile to 100+ miles) is topped and contained by an even larger etheric energy canopy called a zodiac dome. Each of these large domes is under the influence of one zodiacal energy, such as Aries or Cancer.

In the case of a landscape zodiac influenced by the constellation Aries, you will probably find Ray Master Lao Tzu, Master of the Yellow Robe, supervising it. In other words, he will administer all fractalized geomantic expressions of his primary charge, the galactic star field of Aries. Sometimes Ray Masters will position one of their special features called a Ray Master Sanctuary (see below) in proximity to a zodiac under their care so that human interactions with this holographic energy feature can be locally guided and inspired.

A third aspect to the correspondence of Ray Masters to zodiacal constellations is more arcane and generally secret. It pertains to what are exoterically known as the Twelve Tribes of Israel; however, the truth of this term has nothing originally to do with Judaism but with a geomantic fact. One aspect of the Earth's Light body, when perceived geometrically, has twelve pentagonal faces or windows, each of equal size and adjacent to one another. Each of these bears a zodiacal influence, usually for 2,100 years, then it receives a new one. Over a 25,000-year period, each "window" and its fractalized contents below on Earth has experienced all twelve zodiacal influences.

Within the scope and influence of one of these vast pentagonal "windows" is a group of indigenous people who have lived there seemingly from humanity's beginnings. Very long ago, these peoples were given a task by the spiritual world: to maintain a specific vibration, to keep valuable archival records of the history of Earth, and each to preserve an identical jewel (an Emerald from a crown with 13 emeralds belonging to a high archangelic being called the Lord of Light or Light Bringer) until such time as it would be asked for again, in the far future (our present time).[18]

Each Tribe got a copy of the same Emerald; they were to keep it safe, interact with it on behalf of a region of the Earth and its inhabitants, and one day, present it back to the Light Bringer in a complete, whole condition. Largely, the identity of these groups has been kept secret, though it is most likely that the Hopi of the American Southwest and the Aborigines of Australia are two of the twelve original, geomantically-comissioned Tribes.

Each group or Tribe is supervised by a Ray Master, and each has a central, and, again, secret, physical location for their activities. Ray Master Portia of the Orange Ray, for example, supervises the Berbers, probably in Bahrain. Yellow Ray Master Lao Tzu mentors the Tribe in north-central Mongolia; Violet Ray Master Maha Chohan oversees the Inuits of Alaska; and Emerald-Green Ray Master Djwhal Khul looks after the Basque of Spain, probably at their holy site, Guernica.[19]

---

18. There was a 13th Tribe known as the Hyperboreans but it was not associated with any specific pentagonal window of the Earth. The 13th was a free-roaming Tribe and did not belong to the Earth in the same way as the members of the 12 Tribes. The Hyperboreans originally came from the Pleiades.

These Ray Masters periodically will visit their Tribes appearing sometimes as a majestic angelic bird or as a golden apparitional human. Think of each of these Tribes as a people acting like a specialized tuning fork set to a specific vibration; this vibration is congruent with the general geomantic disposition of the pentagonal "window," its astrological influences, and the variety of its geomantic contents. See Table 3 again for some of the tribal affiliations of the Ray Masters.

Manifesting the Virgin Mary Apparitions

In terms of the Earth's timeline, a fairly recent project of four of the Ray Masters has been to serially stage the Virgin Mary apparitions. Virgin Mary apparitions, whose incidence has accelerated since the start of the 20th century, began fairly soon after the presumed histori-

---

19.   With Guernica, Spain, we witness a disturbing political aspect, seemingly based on esoteric geomantic knowledge. The Euskadi is the Basque name for the provinces in northeastern Spain that comprise their ancestral homeland; Guernica is the epicenter of their holy land, and following a special 16th century dispensation from the Spanish monarchs Ferdinand of Aragon and Isabella of Castile, the Basques were permitted their own legislative assembly, the Juntas Generales, that met under a sanctified oak tree in Guernica. Euskadi was not only the holy capital of the Basque but a source of mineral, manufacturing, and shipbuilding wealth. Evidence now documents that General Francisco Franco, leader of the Spanish rebellion, organized the bombing and destruction of Guernica on April 26, 1937, to break the back of the Basque spirit and to mobilize support for his rebellion. Insidiously, Franco then blamed the bombing on the Communists. Franco apparently hated the Basque's fierce independence and self-confident nationalism, and vowed to annihilate both. Geomantically, it is uncanny that the holy site of the Basque and, one presumes, the site of their Tribal archives and the Emerald in safekeeping, was selected for this political act. See: Russell Martin, *Picasso's War. The Destruction of Guernica, and the Masterpiece That Changed the World* (New York: Dutton/Penguin Putnam, 2002): 10-17.

cal time period of Jesus' mother, Mary, the Christ, and the Apostles. It has been underway for almost 2,000 years, building great momentum through the 19th and 20th centuries.

Four different Ray Masters (Rays 2, 4, 6, and 9), each assuming a feminine guise for the occasion, jointly create the apparitions, creating a fourfold feminine presence that exemplifies the virgin, mother, crone, and wild woman aspects of the Great Mother for whom the Virgin Mary is but the Catholicism-filtered emissary. These four include nuances not familiar to the modern Western psyche, or if so, they carry a disturbing or unclear valence: the fierce warrior-goddess Durga and the death and destruction goddess, Kali the Black, both from Indian lore. These and the virgin-mother aspects are part of the Great Mother, whose emissaries are these four Ray Masters manifesting in their differing feminine guises.

While the reports of the Christian visionaries always emphasize the traditional Virgin Mary valence (the young virginal mother, often a 16-year-old girl), in many cases what could be seen at the apparitional sites by fuller clairvoyance are four feminine deities standing in quadrants on a slowly rotating pedestal, each revealing an aspect of the Great Mother as that portion of the pedestal rotates into our view.

The Marian apparitions are not occurring to propagate Catholic dogma. After all, in the majority of cases, the Catholic Church refuses to validate or even acknowledge the apparitions and it actively discredits or discounts them, apparently because their contents and the sheer fact of their existence departs uncomfortably from dogma. Yet the appearances of the spiritual form of the Virgin Mary are deeply purposeful. First, they inundate prepared geomantic locales[20] with a pure spiritual input, a blessing of the Earth by the Divine Mother through her Ray Master agents; second, they create what I call a global Net of the Mothers of Christ, a kind of distributed planetary staging ground for individual initiations into the Christ reality.

---

20.   There is no single geomantic feature used for the apparitions, but rather a variety of them, such as Ray Master Sanctuaries (e.g., Lourdes, Fatima) and about 15 other features.

Metaphysical tradition calls this the second birth, the birth of the Christ Child, or the incarnation of the Higher Self within the embodied human. It involves a reformulation of the parameters of identity to include the cosmic Christ as the epitome (and foundation) of complete, wakeful, spiritual cognition. Here an important aspect of Christ cognition is the ability to extend our awareness into the next dimension, to emulate, as much as possible, the meaning of Vishnu's name (Vishnu is the Hindu perception of the Christ) which means to pervade and permeate space with wakeful awareness. It is similar to the function of the Western Logos (also another name for the Christ): to connect and link all space, like the threads of a lace doily. To connect all points in space is to link all the states of consciousness within it too—the lives and states of being of the great Star-Angels of the galaxy, and beyond. Hindu myth gives us a wonderful image for this: Vishnu lies on the Ocean of Milk and out of his skin pores millions of universes flow in and out of existence with his breathing.

The Marian apparitions elevate our perceptual norm to the threshold of the spiritual worlds, to what is often called the fourth dimension, or 4D reality. This is like raising our heads above the clouds of normal materialistic consensus reality and terrestrial parochialism to suddenly behold the vast array of 4D star-beings embedded in a new, different, strange, and only vaguely rumored layer of reality in which awareness is distributed throughout a vast star net.

We might conceive of the Marian apparitional project as a slow-motion upgrade of human conscious awareness through numerous repeated Marian inputs making it eventually possible and inevitable that we each will birth the Christ within.[21] This is not the same as becoming a Christian or a "born-again" Christian. Rather, this is the nondogmatic attunement with the Christ as a cosmic fact and initiation experience and as the model for an equivalent birth within each of us in the sense of a metanoia, a profound change of mind or turn-

---

21.   See: Richard Leviton, *Signs on the Earth. Deciphering the Message of Virgin Mary Apparitions, UFO Encounters, and Crop Circles* (Charlottesville, VA: Hampton Roads, 2005).

ing about in the deepest seat of consciousness. The Christ upgrade becomes the new basis for human identity and consciousness. With each new Marian apparition, the invitation to us to voluntarily participate in this globally offered initiation sequence is re-extended through a freshly energized geomantic location.

Designated Places for Meeting the Einherjar

The Marian apparitions alert us to the specificity of landscape locales for meetings with the GWB. Behind the physical façade of an apparitional site is a geomantic feature, a particular type of Light temple. The Irish mythic memory of the Tuatha de Dannan in their fabulous, otherworldly *sidhes* gives us a clue about a geomantic secret, and an opportunity. There are places—"homes of the masters in the heaven-world"—set aside within the Earth's visionary geography for humans to meet with the GWB.[22] The Ascended Masters maintain a variety of retreats and sanctuaries of either physical or etheric substance across the Earth, as well as holograms of their celestial residences and even larger GWB galactic assemblages, such as great Cities of Light, Sun Centers, and the Golden Etheric City of Light.

We will examine seven different types of residences or geomantic facilities of the GWB "gods" present in the Earth's geomantic network. These include Valhalla, Amaravati (one of eight Celestial Cities), physical cave retreats, etheric sanctuaries and retreats, Ray Master Sanctuaries, specialized Color or Light Temples, and Ray Master Dedicated Outposts. Each of these seven are intended for human experience and may be visited and interacted with in a visionary-clairvoyant mode.

Let's sample the mythic descriptions of these meeting places. The classic Irish mythic text, *Acallam na Senorach* ("Tales of the Elders of

---

22. Mark L. Prophet and Elizabeth Clare Prophet, *The Masters and Their Retreats*, Edited by Annice Booth (Corwin Springs, MT: Summit University Press, 2003): 397.

Ireland") gives a virtual Baedeker's of the ancient, Tuatha de Danann-occupied Irish *sidhe.*

In the *Tales,* Cailte and his nine companions on tour of Ireland were brought inside a *sidhe* and placed in chairs of bright crystal on a central platform; they observed a bird with an iron beak and tail of fire perching on a golden windowsill. In the evenings it shook so violently all the spears, shields, and swords rained down on the people inside.

One day a woman in a purple-fringed cloak with a gold pin announced to Fionn mac Cumhaill, the Irish hero, that she was from the *sidhe* of Aed at the Hill of Howth (near Dublin), and he was invited to visit. Fionn brought two thousand of his Fianna (equivalent to the Celtic Knights of the Round Table) inside the *sidhe* where they sat on the music platform in the royal house and were amply fed and attended to by a yellow-haired woman named Etain Fholtfhinn. She was the favorite of the Tuatha, and she continuously dipped a white silver cup into a vat of mead to serve the beverage to her guests.

Another time, 400 warriors and 400 boys entered the great shining *sidhe* at Slievenamon (the "*sidhe* of the Fair Women") and received a glorious song of welcome, fresh foods and wines, and were toasted and feasted for three full days. Often, human mortals describe their visits to the Tuatha's *sidhes* in similar terms: they were great bright places, occupied by exceedingly handsome men and women, that sported wonderful crystal chairs, inexhaustible supplies of mead or ale and food, and an abundance of horns, chalices, and goblets of crystal and white gold.

Typically, human mortals would be greeted by the Tuatha in the daytime out in the green fields of Ireland, but there would be something otherworldly and divine about these wanderers; it was like encountering a celestial apparition only haltingly visible and formed. For example, St. Patrick and Cailte were greeted by a warrior in a fair green cloak, yellow silk shirt, and fine golden-yellow hair. He was from the *sidhe* at the Hill of Ardmoll (Rathlin). Later, they met a woman in a green cloak, a yellow silk tunic, and glistening gold-yellow hair; she came from the Cave of Rathcroghan, another numinous Tuatha *sidhe*. You can sense the liminal quality here, as otherworldly higher beings "magically" appear in our world. In the 20th century, Godfre Ray King had the equivalent experience when he was met by a seemingly fleshed-out form of the Ray Master Saint Germain on the slopes of Mount Shasta.

Residents of the *sidhe* often were accomplished musicians. Cailte and St. Patrick in their journey across Ireland met Cas Corach, a master dulcimer player. His music was so melodious and beguiling it brought sleep upon its listeners. The *sidhe*-folk were also master healers. Cailte declares this tribute to his hosts: "A blessing on the people of the *sidhe*, their king and queen. I have had all their service and been made completely whole."[23]

Where exactly were the *sidhes* of the Tuatha de Danann? On the top of the Mount of Women (Slievenamon), also called Mount of Aige, Cailte said of the place upon which they stood: "It is the mountain of a *sidhe*, and it contains a *sidhe*-palace, though it has never been discovered by any one except once by Finn with six of his warriors."[24] The Irish understood the *sidhe*-palaces to be accessed *through* special mountains, such as Slievenamon, or hills, hillocks, cairns, caves, barrows, mounds, hill-forts, grave-mounds, and fairy-hills. Always, the *sidhe*-palace was far larger on the inside than the outside physical shape suggested. The physical feature somehow *contained* the numinous one or was the access point, the magic doorway into it; this suggests the physical and numinous features occupied the same space but at a different vibrational frequency. Starting at the mound, hill, or mountain, you sensitized yourself, rendered your awareness more subtle and fluid, and passed into the *sidhe*.[25]

It was the same understanding that certain landscape sites are otherworldly portals that informed the British folktales of Hollow Hills

---

23. *Tales of the Elders of Ireland*, Translated by Ann Dooley and Harry Roe (New York, NY: Oxford University Press, 1999): 203.

24. *Tales of the Elders of Ireland*, Translated by Ann Dooley and Harry Roe (New York, NY: Oxford University Press, 1999): 139.

that housed sleeping warriors or in Ireland, the departed Tuatha de Danann, the People of the Hills. You pass through a physical portal, marked by a hill or stone structure, into the Light-filled domain existing parallel to the outer visible one.[26]

To Slievenamon three times each year came the lords and chieftains of the Tuatha De Dannan from their *sidhes* all over Ireland (18 are specifically named). Irish myth says they came to battle the 28 Tuatha brothers still resident there (originally they had numbered 28,000) and to ravage their land. More likely, the "battle" was not a fight at all, but a triannual working assembly of Ascended Masters (the Tuatha) to discuss or plan events in Ireland.

These various retreats, memorialized as the *sidhes*, have many practical geomantic functions. They enable the GWB to anchor certain energies in the Earth and they serve as a platform to broadcast them around the planet or to selected areas. The retreats maintain physical archival records of past, and to us, forgotten or unsuspected civilizations, and through the retreats the GWB offer instruction, study, learning, and initiation to interested and qualified humans. Typically, such people will journey there in their astral bodies at night, although

---

25. You find a similar perception of the subtle landscape in Tibetan accounts of their sacred geography. Jamgon Kongtrul Lodro Taye, a 19th century Tibetan Buddhist teacher and writer, traveled to numerous pilgrimage spots in eastern Tibet and based on his clairvoyant viewing characterized the types of spiritual beings present. At one place, ideal for meditation, he observed that "spiritual heroes and *dakinis* gather here and countless accomplished masters of the past have visited this place." Every feature of the local landscape there contained celestial palaces in which resided spiritual masters of the present and past, "assemblies of deities, spiritual heroes and *dakinis*, groups of protectors and guardians of the spiritual teachings." He described many other sacred sites in similar terms, as the habitats of sublime, enlightened spiritual beings. The similarity between this and the Irish description of the *sidhe* inhabitants should be clear and suggestive. Ngawang Zanpo, *Sacred Ground. Jamgon Kongtrul on "Pilgrimage and Sacred Geography,"* (Ithaca, NY: Snow Lion Publications, 2001): 183.

some may access the sites and interact with the GWB during their waking hours through embodied clairvoyance.

In this light, it is exciting to contemplate the *Tales of the Elders of Ireland* as the clairvoyant account of numerous visionary visits to the GWB's centers. I have found that the core story line or description in myths all over the world is reliable descriptive shorthand left by earlier clairvoyants of the geomantic landscape. Myths are psychic maps of the visionary geography and the protocols of successful interaction left to us by our psychic ancestors in the form of a picture language. It's just a matter of figuring out how to decode them, eliminate the "barnacles" and detritus, and isolate the key elements; then you verify the story through current-time clairvoyance.

You can see this starkly in modern accounts that do not rely on mythic language. In the 1970s, American trance-medium Elizabeth Clare Prophet experienced both the physical and subtle aspects of some GWB retreats. While in an airplane in 1974 flying over Cuba (she already knew the island had an etheric retreat "over" it), she marveled at the sensation of "passing through the exact area where the retreat is anchored in the etheric plane above the island." Prophet described the Retreat as "a focus, a flame of freedom" and noted that physically being near it gave her (and would give anyone, she said)

---

26. Hindu sacred geography speaks in terms of *tirthas*, or sacred fords that span our material world to the next, the spiritual domain. The Australian Aborigines use the term Dreamtime to refer to the original morphic field out of which all physical creation was precipitated. The Dreamtime is equivalent to the Earth's Light body as the master subtle environment overshadowing its visionary geography. The Tuatha live in the Dreamtime; their *sidhe*-palaces exist there; similarly, the Hollow Hills of Celtic lore are portals into the Dreamtime. We could picture the *sidhe*-palaces or Hollow Hills as existing in the Dreamtime or Earth's Light body and the various hills, cairns, hill-forts, and other physical structures as being place-markers, showing us where in the landscape to cross the bridge (*tirtha* or ford) into that subtler realm of Light, much like passing from 3D to 4D reality or moving across levels of reality.

"access to expand greater energies."[27] Prophet was describing her encounter with a *sidhe*-palace but free of the old mythic language.

On another occasion, she had a visionary experience of what she called the Ascension Temple and Retreat of Serapis Bey at Luxor, Egypt. Serapis Bey was a Lord of the Flame in Prophet's language, the same as what I call a Ray Master. His Light temple is superimposed over the ruins of the Luxor temple. In the square Flame Room are 12 white pillars that surround a central dais on which the ascension flame burns, Prophet reported; this flame is "an intense fiery white with a crystal glow." All the Retreats she visited are based on fundamental geometric patterns and emphasize a central flame upon an altar as the signature of that Retreat's focus.[28]

The presence of the flame in the Retreat is one reason why the GWB members are called Lords of the *Flame*, Solar Fathers, or Lords of Wisdom. That is because they help humanity develop the *Manas* (mind principle) and discernment in consciousness, which is appropriately represented by the image of fire or a flame.

An Architectural Model of Amaravati

These Irish mythic snapshots give us a general sense of the meeting places for the GWB, and the specific geomantic features they reference could well be any of the seven types I will profile. The Hindu myths seem to give us the bigger picture, a workable architectural model of the entire GWB as a meeting place.

The largest or most-encompassing classification is a place the Hindus called Amaravati, a Celestial City of Light—in fact, one of eight such Light Cities. Amaravati is the home of Indra, chief of the Hindu

27. Mark L. Prophet and Elizabeth Clare Prophet, *The Masters and Their Retreats*, Edited by Annice Booth (Corwin Springs, MT: Summit University Press, 2003): 407-9.

28. Mark L. Prophet and Elizabeth Clare Prophet, *The Masters and Their Retreats*, Edited by Annice Booth (Corwin Springs, MT: Summit University Press, 2003): 405, 422, 423.

gods (i.e., the GWB); his opulent palace is called *Vaijayanta* ("Palace of Victory"). The Earth has 108 copies of this Celestial City, which means we can access it from many different locales. It's important to know that the Hindu Indra is the same celestial being as the Celtic King Arthur, for Arthur is the leader of the host of the Great White Brotherhood. This equivalence in identity is explained in more detail below.

Amaravati ("Immortal City" or "Full of Ambrosia") has 100 palaces in addition to Indra's *Vaijayanta* and a delightful flower and pleasure park called *Nandana*, "Abode of Delight." Another name for this celestial city is *Devapura*, "City of the Gods," situated within *Devaloka*, the world, realm, or dimension (*loka*) of the gods (i.e., "the gods' realm"), but this is also known as *Svarloka*. Eight gods each guard a direction (the four cardinal plus their half-way points) or a *loka*, and are known as *Lokapalas*, or World Guardians; Indra is the *Lokapala* of the East.

As to what Amaravati looks like, we can put a picture together based on present-time clairvoyant viewing and ancient mystic accounts of the residence. It will yield an approximate picture of the architecture of Amaravati. It probably does not, ultimately, resemble this description too closely, but at least we will have a functional if sketchy idea of how it is laid out. The practical reason for this is that it makes it easier for us to interact with Amaravati through any of its 108 copies throughout the Earth's visionary geography if we know roughly what it looks like.

Basically, Amaravati contains six functional divisions, arrayed in concentric circles around a center. Indra's central palace is surrounded on all sides by the huge assembly of the Great White Brotherhood in a structure I call Valhalla, from the Norse descriptions. It resembles a vast circular sports stadium. This is surrounded by the residences of the 14 Rishis or Ray Masters; each of these has a 1/14th wedge of the entire circle of the "sports stadium" of Amaravati, although in the Earth's copy of this all 14 wedges are within a single circular temple. We might say Indra's palace sits in the playing field of the sports stadium while Valhalla is the seating area within the stadium; the 14 "wedges" are equal divisions according to Ray color among the rows of seats. Each of the wedges carries or is imbued with a single Ray color, and the GWB members within that wedge are adepts and Ascended Masters in that Ray.

Hindu descriptions of Amaravati say 100 palaces surround Indra's palace; we might equate these in principle (as the numbers do not correspond) with the 195 GWB etheric retreats around the Earth, their 212 physical though veiled cave retreats, and their 49 Temples of Light (Color Temples) that focus individual Rays (all described below). Or perhaps these palaces represent residences or teaching stations for the Ray adepts. The 14 Ray Masters each have dedicated Ray Master Sanctuaries (1,080 in all), which, if not literally, then at least functionally, occupy almost the farthest inner perimeter of the great Celestial City. Again, using the sports stadium and seating image, these Sanctuaries would be specialized clusters of seats within the Ray wedges. In the highest tiers of seats and furthest from the playing field are Dedicated Outposts with a single Ray flame burning, unattended by a Ray Master.[29]

Within the Earth's visionary geography, these different components of the unified Amaravati are expressed individually and in multiple holographic copies. One could have the impression they are all separate features, but celestially they are all part of the one Amaravati, itself one of eight Celestial Cities. For ease of explanation, I have sep-

---

29. Norse mythology gives us a description of this same place in their perception and call it Asgard, but they provide less architectural detail. Asgard means "Home or Enclosure of the Aesir [singular: *As*: "god"]." Asgard includes Valhalla (Hall of the Slain Warriors), *Hlidskjalf* (Odin's throne room from which he surveys the world), and *Idavollr* (an idyllic, self-rejuvenating Avalonish plain and the locale of the new world after Ragnarok). Originally, the Aesir contracted with the Frost Giants of Niflheim to construct a fortified castle for them, a city of the gods, or, in other accounts, just the massive wall surrounding the city. Asgard is connected to Mitgard (Middle-earth) by Bifrost, the quivering rainbow bridge of fire.

arated out all the parts of Amaravati and discussed them as discrete geomantic locales. There is justification for this in that across the planet Amaravati is templated according to its parts; but keep in mind that at the celestial level, the seven parts are all facets of the one Amaravati, the seat of the Great White Brotherhood in Ursa Major.

So as I review each of these components separately below, remember that in terms of the feature's original celestial expression, it is all one big place. And throughout our visits to the copies of the seven aspects of Amaravati, it's important (and invigorating) to continually remember its primary reality is in Ursa Major.

Mount Meru—The Larger Context for the Celestial Cities of the Gods

Amaravati is one of eight divine abodes described in Vedic literature as Celestial Cities arrayed around Mount Meru. This is the cosmic mountain at the center of the universe and the heart of creation. Each of the eight *Lokapalas*, the World Guardians and Regents of the Directions, has a Celestial City, and these are considered each to be a zone of the one central City of *Brahmapuri* in *Brahmaloka*. In Hindu myth, Brahma is the prime creator god, and among the oldest too; the Vedic model of time is reckoned in Days and Years of Brahma, whose cosmic life totals 311 trillion years. That's just his age for one vast cycle of creation and destruction; these cycles are continuous, so Brahma's ultimate age is far older, probably infinite.

Vedic lore describes Mount Meru as the ultimate axial mountain and abode of all the gods. A golden peak, it rises at the center of the universe, directly under the cosmic North Pole, and it stands 84,000 *yojanas* high (about 350,000 miles) and penetrates the Earth to a depth of 16,000 *yojanas* (128,000 miles); its summit is 32,000 *yojanas* across (256,000 miles), and its base, 16,000 *yojanas* (128,000 miles), making it twice as broad at the top as at the base and thus cone-shaped.

Brahma, the creator god, occupies *Brahmapuri*, a square golden city, in the topmost center of the mountain; the eight *Lokapalas* have their Celestial Cities in the eight cardinal directions around Meru's slopes (e.g., southeast, northwest, west). According to the Vedas, Indra's City is 15 miles high by 450 miles wide and 300 miles long. Thus, Indra's City occupies 135,000 square miles on the side of Mount Meru[30]; the seven differentiated assembly places of the GWB, mentioned above, lie within this area, and they are probably referenced by Indra's 100 palaces.

Each of the zones of *Brahmaloka* is copied, in differing quantities, as Light temples on Earth. The eight Celestial Cities have collectively 3,546 copies in Earth's visionary geography, including 108 of Amaravati. I will discuss only three of these Cities below as they pertain directly to the Great White Brotherhood and its administration; the other five Cities are more focussed on facilitating deep spiritual experiences and processes within the sentient beings who visit them.

Just as the eight Celestial Cities are templated across the Earth within its visionary geography, so too is Mount Meru present on

---

30. Should we automatically dismiss these measurements as wild, exaggerated figments of the Vedic imagination and at best see them as purely metaphorical for the extent and puissance of the place mentioned? Maybe not. Richard Thompson in his explication of Vedic astronomy and mysticism presents evidence that some of the key measurements in the Vedic and Puranic texts may be psychically obtained and fairly accurate descriptions of things on a galactic scale, such as the width of the solar system or the Sun's ecliptic. Fabulous numbers, such as a dowry of 90,000,000 horses presented for a king's daughter, might refer to activities taking place in a higher dimensional reality, Thompson suggests, and thus be accurate at that level of reality. Our physical Earth, the old texts imply, is "part of a region called Bharata-varsa in a larger, higher-dimensional structure called Bhu-mandala." Bhu-mandala, a higher dimensional reality, is described in the Puranas as "a vast disc that extends for millions of miles into space but is not perceivable by our present senses." Richard L. Thompson, *Vedic Cosmography and Astronomy* (Los Angeles: The Bhaktivedanta Book Trust, 1989): 62, 65,66.

Earth, though singularly. A virtual Mount Meru is situated somewhat to the east of the South Island of New Zealand. It is physically present on the Earth yet phase-shifted (or protected by a force field) out of accord with our physically perceivable reality. You could sail right past it in a boat and never notice it because the force field surrounding it would simply push you away. You can postulate its existence, but just never get to it physically.[31]

It is possible for people to visit Mount Meru psychically but only by invitation and/or angelic escort, and understandably what portion of the vast city you might see is variable.

If you visit Amaravati through any of its 108 "local" portals or copies, it is metaphysically exciting to remember its true or ontological location is on the slopes of Mount Meru, both "on" the Earth (as a hologram) and "in" the cosmos (as the original). Its relative, galactic location is in Ursa Major, and its virtual, planetary location is at the 108 sites or place-markers on Earth.

This is also true for the other seven Celestial Cities: when we contact one of their copies (holograms), we are interacting with the holographic "original" and singular expression of the City on the slopes of Mount Meru as templated in the Earth's Light body and at the actual original location in the cosmos. Visiting Amaravati, you are in a sense stepping off the planet into the galaxy, yet you are also engaging the Earth at its subtler, soul level, as it were, stepping into a node in one of its delicate auric sheaths. We must keep in mind the essential paradox, from a human standpoint, of location: these Cities, ultimately,

---

31. This is how French metaphysical writer Rene Daumal conceived of it. He called Mount Meru "the ultimate symbolic mountain," or Mount Analogue, and noted its "inaccessibility to ordinary human approaches." Daumal proposed that this mountain was encased "in a 'shell' of curved space" or "a closed ring of curvature, spacious and impenetrable, which surrounds the country at a fixed distance with an invisible intangible rampart." Rene Daumal, *Mount Analogue. A Novel of Symbolically Authentic Non-Euclidean Adventures in Mountain Climbing*, Translated by Roger Shattuck (New York: Penguin Books, 1974): 42, 66.

are located not so much at a specific place or space, mapped by geo-detic coordinates, as at a level or realm of consciousness.

Indra, Leader of the Ascended Host, and His Residence

The *Mahabharata* recounts how Arjuna, a highly accomplished spiritual adept, spent five years in Indra's magnificent Celestial City. The city was astonishing, Arjuna said: opulent beyond belief, a luxurious, effulgent place of celestial music, saints, rishis, flowers, dancers, perfumes, sensual and aesthetic delights, and more.

The saga reports that Indra, the thousand-eyed god seated beneath his regal white umbrella with a gold handle, was in fact Arjuna's father. Airavata, the regal white elephant of ancient lineage with four tusks, was Indra's royal mount and guards Amaravati. (Airavata is a disguise for the angelic order of the Ofanim, and indicates their close working relationship with the GWB and its chief.) While there, Arjuna learned the correct use of numerous celestial weapons (potent spiritual powers), such as Indra's thunderbolt, the *vajra*, conch, and fierce lightning flashes.

Indra's heaven, Arjuna learned, is also known as *Svarga* (from *svar*, meaning the light of Heaven, i.e., the Sun), and Indra is also *Svarga-pati*, Lord of Heaven as well as *Divapati*, Lord of the Gods; *Jisnu*, Leader of the Celestial Host; *Bajri*, He Who Wields the Thunderbolt; *Meghavahana*, He Who Rides on the Clouds; and *Vrtraha*, Destroyer of the Drought-Demon, Vrtra. Only the "sinless" may perceive *Svarga*, and only the "good" (the spiritually accomplished) may dwell there.

Indra is the Vedic perception of King Arthur at the celestial level. This is a complicated equation, but a reliable one. Indra as *Jisnu* is Leader of the Celestial Host, and the Host are the "gods," the Great White Brotherhood. He's the leader because he is the Logos of the stars, a position called the Solar Logos. That is the central, cohering principle that holds the vast star-weave of stars together and energizes it. Indra is the Vedic and King Arthur the Celtic name for the one Solar Logos. The stars in this equation include the great Star-Angels and the membership of the GWB.

King Arthur (Indra) has reality at both the celestial and human levels. At the level of the galaxy, he is the Solar Logos, the Logos or Word (the Christ) of all the suns (stars). In terms of human culture, King Arthur represents the Christ expressed in the warrior class and tradition. His name means "Sun-Star," but as Solar Logos, his name, in terms of its function, is Qabalistically derived and means growth and change.

On the Earth, however, he is more than a myth, metaphor, or symbol. At the human level, King Arthur has overshadowed 15 human Arthur exemplifiers, so far, in different cultures, including Celtic, Irish, Persian, Mongolian, and Teutonic. That means periodically the actual celestial King Arthur (Indra) infiltrates an embodied human for a lifetime so that this human may exemplify some of Arthur's qualities. He will gather around him other humans exemplifying other vital aspects of the Arthurian mythos. All of this will be overshadowed, supported, and mentored by the GWB so that for a time terrestrial and galactic events and initiatives synchronistically reflect each other.

If we picture the Ascended Masters as arrayed about a vast Round Table, like the one attributed to the Celtic King Arthur (a big wooden round table with a hollow space in the center), then this central open part is where King Arthur sits. Except he doesn't really sit, so much as shine, like a brilliant sun illuminating the table from its center. The Solar Logos fills this spot also in the form of a golden rotating spindle, enlivening, quickening, energizing, and completing the array of the Ascended Host and the different qualities of consciousness they embody and transmit to the galaxy. Arthur-Indra is the Sun and Light of Heaven that illuminates *Svarga*.

The Solar Logos, as King Arthur or the spinning golden bore, itself occupies a position (one of twelve: the heart chakra seat) in a more august Round Table, that of the Cosmic Logos known, among other names, as Sanat Kumara (the Eternal Youth). The Cosmic Logos is the rational, cohering principle at the level of galaxies; this Logos sits at the center of the cosmos and rationalizes the multiple galaxies just as Arthur sits at the core of the galaxy and coheres the multiplicity of stars. This same pattern of Solar Logos to Cosmic Logos is repeated across the Earth as a generic energy template underlying all landscape temples, that is, geomantic nodes and their features. Under each sacred site, there is a hierarchical template including both.

The Cosmic Logos, or Sanat Kumara (actually six beings or "brothers" of nearly the same name, according to Hindu myth) is also based in Ursa Major. According to the Ofanim, originally the star Sirius (and its celestial beings) focused the energy from what was called the Great White Lodge.[32] Although the Lodge's energy originated in Ursa Major, it was first focused and developed within Sirius in Canis Major (the Greater Dog). Then after the focus and the beings managing it had become sufficiently developed, the focus and its attendants were relocated to Gaia, planet Earth (through a Celestial City called Shambhala; see below), and the Lodge was renamed (or reformulated as) the Great White Brotherhood.[33]

Despite the fact that King Arthur or Indra enters the assembly of the Ascended Masters from a higher level (the Round Table of the Cosmic Logos), he has a point of reference or grounding within Ursa Major in the star Megrez (*delta Ursae Majoris*). That is the star at the place where the handle joins the dipper. The name comes from the Arabic *Al Maghrez* and means "Root of the Tail." Fittingly, an old Hindu text says Megrez rules the other stars of the Great Bear, and the Chinese astronomers called it *Tien Kuen*, "Heavenly Authority." This is Arthur's seat. Appropriately, it has a specific Earth correlate, a place called Tintagel, on the far western tip of Cornwall; Tintagel is famous in England as King Arthur's birthplace. What secures the connection is that the star-dome for Megrez is situated there.

---

32. The Ofanim note that beyond the Great White Brotherhood is an even more arcane assembly, to which the Ofanim belong, called the Great School. This has no fixed location and has no limits of any description.

The important observation here is that already we encounter two famous figures from myth, the Celtic and Vedic, occupying the same key GWB role. What we had thought was a myth, turns out to be a façade for an occult truth. Known as King Arthur or Indra, this is a real celestial being, not so much a "god" any more which means made-up, metaphorical, vanished, or an inaccessible reality, but a highly evolved spirit in charge of thousands of Ascended Masters and all the stars in the galaxy.

It is possible for aspiring Grail Knights (apprentices on the path towards Ascension) to have an encounter with the actual celestial King Arthur as part of the Grail Quest (the training in interacting with the Earth's visionary geography). Here's an example: Once while meditating on a hill called Ivy Thorn outside Glastonbury, England, I

---

33. Consistent with this description is the fact attested to in Vedic myth that Sanat Kumara is the son of and possibly the avatar (incarnation or descent) of Shiva, whom the Vedas associate with Sirius. As the progeny of Shiva-Sirius, Kumara was called Skanda ("Spurt of Semen"). Thus as Cosmic Logos, Sanat Kumara developed mastery over the Lodge's focus just as that energy was being grounded through Sirius as a whole. His name means Everlasting (Sanat) Adolescent (Kumara), and sometimes Chaste Adolescent, since he remains perpetually young, single, and never had a mother. The myths say he was reared by six Pleaides (called Krttikas) and was thus called Karttikeya ("Son of the Pleaides"); Kumara developed six faces to be able to drink their milk (Light). His strength is immense; he was regarded as the lord of war, the secret chief of the gods' army; he rode a magnificent peacock called Paravani ("The Year"). Other of the 31 names for him include the Secret One, Lord of Armies, the Great Captain, Captain of the Realized, Six-Faced. He is captain of the armies and lord of war because as Cosmic Logos he withstands all assaults on the Light at the cosmic level. He guards the cosmos against entropy. In the Arthurian mythos, he is called the Emperor Lucius who at one point commands King Arthur's obedience. Lucius, whose name embodies Light (*Luc*), portrays an aspect of the Cosmic Logos. According to the Ofanim, Sanat Kumara was conceived at the Great White Brotherhood (Hindu myth says he was a Mind-born son of Brahma, the creator god) and never took bodily form, nor was intended to.

had the visionary experience of travelling to Megrez, 65 light years from Earth. There I was met by a man. He was regal, kingly, with a gold crown, sparkling blue eyes, white hair, and a short white beard. His famous sword, Excalibur, was long and gleaming, his shield bore the Pendragon image (a rearing dragon encased in lilac flames) and the image of the Mother of Christ with the holy infant. In his heart I saw the Holy Grail, an effulgent golden Grail chalice, and inside that, the Christ in human form.

Without a further *Hello!* King Arthur shoved Excalibur into my heart.

I was fairly certain he had good intentions at the time. Technically, this was to quicken something, to spark it to life (I figured this out later), although it surprised me. As part of my training I was incubating a white seed inside a visualized Grail chalice inside an emerald inside my heart chakra. With the touch of Excalibur, the seed caught fire, blazed into a white stone on fire, and sprouted roots and leaves.

Arthur, as Indra, was known by the Hindus as the Kindler, the stimulating force that kindles thoughts, deeds, rain, agriculture, fertility, life—awareness. Kindling that white seed in my heart chakra is part of what he does within the human realm. In some respects Excalibur is equivalent to the *vajra* (Indra's thunderbolt): it embodies and transmits the pervasive electrical force of the universe, like a modulated thunderbolt or lightning strike. His power is generative and virile, causing crops to quicken, livestock to reproduce, rain to fall, Grail Knights to awaken. Indra-King Arthur *sparks* fertility and *causes* growth, movement, change. He kindles awareness, ignites awakening, fertilizes consciousness, waters the self. These are some of the qualities of the Solar Logos, the great light of the galaxy.

This one celestial being, in his guises as Indra and King Arthur, fulfills a very important function in the galaxy as the Solar Logos, and his qualities and activities are indicated by the numerous Vedic epithets for Indra. Simplified, we could say the Solar Logos is the spiritual intelligence behind or within the Sun.

The Solar Logos is the Word made manifest in the flesh, that is, in material things. It is the energy of the Sun (not our solar system's sun, but the Great Central Sun, sometimes called the Sun within the Sun, at the heart of the cosmos) expressed through communication (occult sounds, like mantras or sound currents) for the benefit of the human, plant, mineral, and animal kingdoms. It is the solar energy stimulating growth and change, in matter and consciousness; the surprising fact is that its correct pronunciation, delivered as a forceful shout, is actually its activation: *Ar-Thur-humg!* If intoned correctly, it is in part the sound of Arthur as the rotating golden spindle.

Ar comes from the Hebrew *AWR* (also written *OR*) which means Light and its spirallic unfolding and represents the Sun (or solar part) and change[34]; *Thur* represents the Word or Logos aspect which is growth; and *Humg!* is the way the declared name and its energy and insight are grounded like a sword shoved into the Earth. Arthur's name, when spoken, (or better, shouted in a mantric way) is the attunement to the Solar Logos, which is the manifestation of the Word (Christ) in the flesh. In some respects, Arthur's invocation is Indra's *vajra*, or thunderbolt.

In recent phases of geomantic node stimulation, King Arthur as Solar Logos has been brought to a particular locale to energize it in the form of a massive rotating golden spindle and inserted into a key place within an overall Light temple to catalyze movement, growth, and change in that system. The Solar Logos is grounded at only one place on the planet at a time, but copies of it may be made and transferred temporarily to locales requiring this energy infusion. In mythic imagery, it is just like Indra brandishing his *vajra* at or Arthur inserting his sword into a particular place.

---

34. *AWR* in Hebrew (the Hebrew letters are also numbers; decoding this is called gematria) spells 16200, embedded in which is the rounded-off value (162) for phi, the Golden Mean, of 1.1618...., the irrational, infinite number repesenting the uneven division of a line, thus generating the asymmetry that drives the spiral and thus unfoldment and change,

Camalate as Indra's Palace, Vaijayanta

Indra's palace has a Western equivalent known as King Arthur's Camalate. In the Celtic Arthurian mythos, Camalate is understood to have been the headquarters of the Round Table and Grail Knights, and their efforts to have been military primarily, with a slow segue into the mystical quest for the Holy Grail. Historians reluctantly attribute the historical Arthur (circa 6th century A.D.) to a place in Somerset called South Cadbury Castle, today a ringed grassy hilltop. That may be where Arthur flourished, but he was born elsewhere, at Tintagel to the west.

King Arthur may be accessed through many geomantic venues on the Earth, but one place that especially facilitates that access is Tintagel in Cornwall, England. In Arthurian lore, this is where Arthur was conceived and born; in esoteric reality, this is the sole location for the star-fall (called a dome; see below) of Megrez in Ursa Major on Earth. Tintagel actually means "tints of angels"—the variously hued Ascended Masters arrayed about Arthur's Round Table in anticipation of their completion, namely, that the Solar Logos may be born in their midst as King Arthur. This has to do with the dialectic between individuation (represented by the Ray Masters) and the unitive consciousness of the Self; Arthur as Solar Logos is the connecting link.

Tintagel is the once and future birthplace for Arthur because as the Solar Logos, already present in the etheric and astral sphere of Gaia, Arthur is always available there to be birthed as a fresh initiatory experience in men and women. Lest this be confusing, contact with Arthur is always available there as a human experience, yet in his function as Solar Logos, Arthur now is grounded in northern New Mexico.

In the earlier Irish version of the Arthurian saga, King Arthur's Palace was at the *sidhe* of Almu, now known as the Hill of Allen in Leinster, Ireland. This was the royal seat and *sidhe* of Fionn mac Cumhaill, the Irish expression of King Arthur as the Solar Logos. Almu ("All-White") was crystal bright, pure white, as if all Ireland's lime had been used for it; originally it was the *brugh* or spectral home of and built by Nuada of the Silver Hand, chief Druid, King of Ireland, and a Tuatha de Dannan. Its ramparts enclosed many white-walled dwellings and a great towering hall.

Almu was named after an eponymous Irish goddess honored in Leinster Province, and her hill was once the sacred capital of this province and the seat of its kings. Both the goddess and the *sidhe* were known as All-White, and folklore said an invisible entrance to the Otherworld was accessed here. Significantly (as with Tintagel), Almu was Fionn mac Cumhaill's birthplace. Thus the Solar Logos, personified by Fionn, was once "born" and grounded here too, and it can still be experienced here by the sensitive, as at Tintagel, as a living spiritual force.

We could say then that wherever Arthur was "born" on Earth, that is, where his energy was grounded in a cultural landscape, that is the same as Indra's *Vaijayanta* palace. But it is also any place where the Solar Logos is grounded amidst an array of the GWB, such as at a Valhalla (see below) or a dedicated application of this, called Camalate, the mythic name for King Arthur's headquarters for Grail Knights.

The manifestation of King Arthur through human culture was not a unique or only twice-accomplished affair. There have been, so far, 15 King Arthurs. Each time, the celestial figure overshadows a human who embodies some or a lot of his archetype. During the 15 occasions in which the celestial King Arthur has overshadowed a human exemplifier of that energy, the terrestrial headquarters has been known secretly as Camalate (also spelled Camelot). Many of these manifestations were not in Celtic or English-speaking lands, but as an esoteric center it has always been Camalate. Camalate, though seemingly an English word, is derived from Qabala and carries levels of phonetic, gematrial, and spiritual nuances, much like a charged mantra.

At the risk of confusing matters, it is important to note there have been 26 Camalates in the history of the Earth but only 15 Arthur exemplifiers at a Camalate[35]. That means 11 Camalates were incomplete, without the quickening presence of the Solar Logos. At the 15 Camalates that were complete, the Solar Logos was resident, such as at Arthur's South Cadbury Castle or Fionn MacCumhaill's Hill of Allen. It may sound whimsical, but the terrestrial Camalate was a place to which *came a lot* of people for initiation in the protocols of Earth's visionary geography and GWB interaction.

Whether or not all of the physical features of an active and complete Camalate were present at the specific site is not important; residential and teaching facilities may have been distributed throughout a region under the palpable influence of the Camalate. But the energetic and geomantic structures would definitely be present and functioning at a complete Camalate, and to an extent, these energies may still be sampled today by visiting a former Camalate.

To summarize, Tintagel and Almu were places where previously the Solar Logos was established on the Earth for a time, planted, as it were, into the prepared geomantic matrix at both sites. In a sense, Arthur was more fully born at Tintagel because of the Megrez star connection through its dome; this is the only place on the planet where Megrez in Ursa Major is grounded in this definitive manner. Camalate was the actual working headquarters and outreach platform for Arthurian Knights. The Camalate locations were not birthing places of Arthur for the planet, yet they facilitated the birth of the Arthurian initiation within Grail Knight candidates; that means, men and women, if they wished, could receive training in Arthurhood. It's helpful to think of "Arthur" and "Arthurhood" here in terms of a generic station of development, like chief magus.

---

35. Two of the other Arthurian incarnations or overshadowings were Rustam, who was king of the Sistan region of southeastern Persia (today's Iran), and Gesar of Ling, based either in the Ling or Kham provinces of Tibet or somewhere in Mongolia, where he was known as Bukhe Beligte. To the extent these seemingly mythic though historically actual figures (but not provable by conventional means) had a geographic and namable base, then there we will find the residues of a former active Camalate.

Now that we have a generalized picture of Amaravati and its parts and how they have been known in different myths, we can start focusing on its components, starting with the one called Valhalla.

2

VALHALLA

In brief: This is an assemblage place much like a packed sports stadium for the Great White Brotherhood and a place for human interaction with this group or selected members, accessed through physical sites; 360 copies of this feature are present on the Earth.

Mythic Descriptions of Valhalla

Both Irish and Norse myths offer descriptions of this feature though they present this locale in physical terms as if it were visitable in an ordinary human material sense. It is not. To the Irish, it was a *bruiden* or *brugh* (plural: *bruidne*); to the Norse, it was Valhalla, the Hall of the Slain (warriors slain on the battlefield). Each description offers a vivid picture of a specialized Light temple with geomantic expression on the Earth.

Irish legend speaks of five *bruidne* distributed across the landscape of Ireland (called Eriu) long ago in the time of King Ailill and Queen Maeve. A *bruiden* was an inn, hostel, or spacious banquet hall, noted for the sumptuous and constant feasting and drinking of its guests and its tendency to cater to warrior prodigies. Each *bruiden* had a magic cauldron that cooked precisely what each individual guest desired and yet also offered a seemingly inexhaustible supply of freshly cooked pork. When you study the details, it's clear the *bruidne* have an otherworldly ambiance and clientele. There just aren't such magical places in the physical world, certainly not the one we know.

The five *bruidne* were named: Bruiden Da Derga; Bruiden Fhorgaill Manaich; Bruiden Meic Da Reo; Bruiden Da Choca; and Bruiden Meic Da Tho. Only approximate locations were given for these five, and their physical dimensions seem to far exceed architectural plausibility. Of course there was a sixth, the famous *Brugh na Boinne*, the Hostel on the River Boyne, now known as Newgrange, near Dublin and on the Boyne River, but this inn had a different function than the above-named *bruidne*. Two of these *bruidne* were described in some detail in Irish myth.[1]

In "The Story of Macc Da Tho's Pig," Macc Da Tho is described as the king of Lagin (Leinster County), and he plays host to other kings and queens of the land at that time, including Ailill, Maeve (Medb), and Cet, all of Conachta (Connaught County); and Conchobor, Fergus, Loegure, and Conall Cernach, all of Ulaid (Ulster County). Thus representatives from three of Ireland's five classical counties are named as guests at Macc Da Tho's hostel. The bulk of this brief story deals with the carving up of the pig, the serving of the champions' portions, garrulous, boastful feasting, and a bit of fighting among the rowdier, more competitive guests.

---

1. *Brugh* (also spelled *bruig, bru*) is Irish for farmhouse, abode, region, district, even cultivated land, but the general nuance pertains to the spirit and fairy-folk world, specifically to the interior of a fairy mound. *Bruiden* (also *bruidhean* or *bruighean*) is also an Irish word denoting a hotel, large banqueting hall, mansion, house, and sometimes, royal residence; general usage of the word has shifted the emphasis to the otherworldly quality. Early Irish literature identified six *bruidne*, but later with the term *sidhe*, the number of otherworldly dwellings identified and accessed through the physical landscape, considerably increased. The Irish term *sidhe* denotes a fairy mound and generally the realm beyond the five senses. The *sidhe* is accessed through (or copresent at) a barrow, tumulus, round, flat-topped hill, or hillock, anciently used to bury royal figures; Irish lore said the *sidhes* mark the places where the Tuatha de Danann long ago fled the physical world of Ireland for the Otherworld.

The tale gives the hostel's dimensions, and this valuable clue gives it away that the hostel is not of this world: it has seven entrances with 50 paces between each, and inside, seven hearths and seven cauldrons. Each cauldron offers cooked beef and salted pork, and Macc Da Tho's pig is so large that 40 oxen easily may lay across it. This pig had been nourished by 40 milk cows for seven years and was delivered to Macc Da Tho with the 40 oxen already placed upon its immense girth.

"The Destruction of Da Derga's Hostel" is a much longer tale and a standard fixture in Irish legend. Da Derga, whose name means "The Red One," is a king in Leinster who owns ten great vats containing a nut-brown ale; the vats were a present from Conaire Mor, King of Ireland at the Hill of Tara, who plans to visit. Da Derga is red-haired and sports a green cloak, and his cauldron has never been taken from the fire since he built and opened his inn; he has been constantly cooking food for the men of Eriu ever since. Hence he is called Eriu's Chief and Royal Hospitaller.

His hostel has seven doorways with seven rooms built between every two doorways: that's 49 rooms, and the description suggests the hostel is circular and set on the main road through Lagin (Leinster); in fact, the great road of Cualu goes right through it though, confusingly, the hostel is said also to sit on the banks of the River Dodder. In fact, the *bruiden* was placed on the road so that no one might pass by it shelterless. Traveling this road, presumably, you would have to deliberately depart the road to avoid passing through the magnificent hostel: it's *that* accessible to travelers.

Seventeen of Conaire's chariots were parked at each of these seven doors and yet from a distance you could see through their wheels into the house and its fires. That's 119 chariots parked adjacently on the perimeter of the *bruiden*. As for the fire, it is huge and called a *torc caille*, a "boar of the forest"; it has seven outlets and the flame of each is the size of a burning chapel. The inn is always open and is likened to a man's mouth open to yawn; it is called a *bruiden* because "it resembled the lips of a man blowing hard upon the coals of a fire to awaken it."[2]

Let's consider the dimensions of this hostel: with 17 chariots parked, presumably side by side between each of the seven doors, if a chariot's width is set at ten feet, plus the same for the seven doors, that gives the hostel an approximate perimeter of 1,260 feet, a diameter of 630 feet, and a radius from central "boar of the forest" to outer walls of 315 feet. Within this space, yet some safe distance from the massive hearth, are 49 rooms filled with guests, all of them exceptional.

Da Derga's hostel and its guests are described from the viewpoint of a band of hidden raiders who plan to destroy the place, but that action occupies only a small, concluding, and incidental (if not irrelevant) portion of the tale whose purpose seems more to provide a set-piece description of this otherworldly inn and its formidable, even unbelievable, guests. The point of the story is not the narration of the destruction of the inn, for that is almost an after-thought; the point is the description of the guests and the implicit understanding this all is a psychic reality perceived.

Here are just a few of them: Nine immortal pipers from *Sidhe Bregia* (an otherworldly fortress); Mac Cecht, Conaire's champion, whose sword stands thirty feet high and whose eyes are like two large lakes next to a mountain (his nose); the Fomorians, ancient giants with three heads and three hundred teeth apiece; Tulchinne the Juggler, who carries nine swords in his hand, nine silver shields, and nine golden apples; the three chief champions, each of whose limbs is as thick as a man's waist and whose lances each will kill nine men at one throw; Conall Cernach, whose curly golden hair was the size of a reaping basket and reaches his hips; Sencha, Dubthach, and Goibnenn, the three chief champions whose limbs are each the thickness of a man's waist.

---

2.   Randy Lee Eickhoff, *The Destruction of the Inn* (New York: Forge/Tom Doherty Associates, 2001): 101.

The poet of the tale specifies the color and quality of the cloaks worn by the guests, and these details are significant: green mantles, black capes, mantles of different colors, silken mantles, cloaks of speckled red, tufted purple cloaks, a cloak like a summer mist, a speckled mantle of various colors, crimson capes, purple plaid linen tunics, mixed plaids, gray floating mantles, blue mantles, gray-speckled mantles, and mantles of silver mist. We'll come back to the meaning of these in a moment.

The Norse description of Valhalla, the Hall of the Slain, is less detailed about the individual feasters but equally precise about its architecture. The Hall belongs to Odin, chief of the Asgard, the Norse gods, and is a paradaisal banquet facility for the noble, slain warriors brought here, even pre-selected, from the battlefield by the nine Valkyries (Odin's "Wish-Girls") led by Brunnhilde (Old Norwegian [ON]: Brynhildr, "Bright Battle").

These warriors are the Einherjar, and they spend their days practicing their feats of war and physical prowess, often simulating death. At night, they are all restored and resume feasting on the boar and drinking mead that flows from the udders of Heidrun, Odin's celestial goat (who feeds on leaves from the Tree of Life, Yggdrasill, converting them to mead). The cooked pork comes from Saehrimnir, the massive boar whose flesh is inexhaustible. No matter how much meat is sliced off his flanks during the evening banquet, the next morning he is whole, ready to be cooked and carved all over again.

Valhalla (ON: *Valholl*, "Hall of the Slain;" *valr*, "those slain on the battlefield" [the Einherjar], and *holl*, "hall") has 540 gates through which 800 Einherjar can (and will) march at once in defense of Asgard in the future at Ragnarok, the end of the world and final judgement of the gods. That's 432,000 Einherjar assembled in Odin's sumptuous, capacious hall. This gold-bright great hall, also called Carrion Hall, is thatched with spears and shields, and the Einherjar's armor (possibly equivalent in essence to the Irish mantles and cloaks) is displayed on benches. A central gate called Valgrind offers one access to the Einherjar from the outside—interesting: one door in, 540 doors out.

Valhalla is much larger than Da Derga's Hostel. With 540 doors and the expectation of 800 Einherjar storming through each, this presumes the Einherjar are all inside Valhalla. A space capable of housing 432,000 people would be about five times larger than the largest outdoor sports stadium we presently have.[3]

The Icelandic poet Snorri Sturluson, who codified much of Norse myth in the 12th century A.D., places Valhalla in Gladsheimr, a division of Asgard ("the Enclosure of the Aesir"), thus clearly part of the spiritual world. Sturluson says Gladsheimr ("Happy Home" or "Gleaming Home") is a temple with 12 seats, "the best and greatest building made on earth; outside and inside it is like a single piece of gold."[4] Valhalla, Sturluson implies, appears to be a room among many at Gladsheimr.

From these examples we realize the myths are actually psychic descriptions of perceived spiritual environments, story and picture notes from clairvoyant visions. The physically implausible measurements indicate the locale's spirit potency and quality, and the warrior guests and feasting Einherjar similarly suggest beings of awesome spiritual advancement. We already have made the connection of Einherjar as Lone-Fighters to mean those touched by a God-aspect (Odin) in their quest for self-transcendence. So when the Norse poet seems to exaggerate the champions' and warriors' macho prowess, the reference really is to their spiritual "size" and puissance.

Our model of Earth's visionary geography adds the surprising element that these spiritual locales are actually present and psychically

---

3. One of the world's largest sports stadiums is Maracana Stadium in Ipanema, Brazil; a capacity crowd is 90,000 (which means Valhalla is 4.8 times larger), but once in 1969, the stadium held 183,341 people.

4. Snorri Sturluson, quoted in John Lindow, *Norse Mythology. A Guide to the Gods, Heroes, Rituals, and Beliefs* (New York: Oxford University Press, 2001): 145.

visitable through landscape portals positioned across the planet, at specific geomantic nodes I call Valhallas.

The Geomantic Actuality of Valhalla

We needn't hold the Irish and Norse psychics to any standards of literal, Earthly accuracy in their descriptions of the hostels or Valhalla. The architectural details and size estimations are physical frames of reference for nonphysical places in the spiritual world.

Here are the essential elements: the places are huge and accommodate many prodigious warriors; there is a central massive fire; a boar whose flesh is inexhaustible is continuously roasting, being carved up, and restored to wholeness; heavenly-derived mead is served; fighting takes place during the day, followed by feasting and revelry at night; there is an owner and inn-keeper, Da Derga in one case, Odin in the other, although technically Odin is not the pork-roaster: that is Audhrimnir.

One difference between the Irish and Norse accounts is site specificity. The Irish tell us the location of that country's *five* hostels; since the hostels are clearly otherworldly in character, the physical sites are portals into their realm. The Norse explicitly state Valhalla as a *singular* after-death destination is in the spiritual world but do not provide landscape site locations that would be gateways for the living into Valhalla—except in one case, easy to miss because it is disguised with a different name.

Known formally in Old Norwegian as *Urdar brunnr*, which means Urd's Well or Well of Fate, Urd's Well was one of the three springs under the roots of Yggdrasill, the World Tree or Tree of Life in Norse myth. Every day the gods of Asgard ride across Bifrost, the magical rainbow-hued bridge, and assemble for council at Urd's Well; here they decide the fate of humanity and the Earth, possibly in conjunction with the three Norns, the Norse version of what the Greeks called the Fates.

Remarkably, these supposedly mythic—"only mythic," skeptics would say—references have actual landscape correlations, including Yggdrasill. The planet's sole, original, and massive Tree of Life is rooted at a tiny hamlet in central Norway called Rondablikk in the Rondane Mountains. This tree exists in the Light realm, but its physical measurements are considerable: it stands 150 miles high, its roots extend 15 miles into the Earth, and its trunk spans 4.5 miles. If you want to stand in the core of its trunk, visit Rondablikk. It even has a hotel inside our planet's sole Tree of Life.

The geomantic expression of Urd's Well is located in a nearby deep valley called Rondvassbu, reached by an easy four-mile walk along open country. The Well at which the Aesir assemble everyday to discuss affairs of the world is actually a meeting place for the Great White Brotherhood and is the same place as what I refer to as Valhalla. Let's be clear: there is, ultimately, one Valhalla in the spiritual world; the Norse called it Urd's Well. But Valhalla has 360 virtual copies or holograms across the planet; one of the Norse Valhallas is here at Rondvassbu, and in the long ago visionary perception of the Norse, this Valhalla at Ronvassbu was also called Urd's Well. Here we encounter the assembly of the Ascended Masters.

In essence, each of the 360 Valhallas is identical though it may be clothed in or filtered through different cultural and mythic attributions and earlier psychic perceptions. Paradoxically, each of the 360 copies is both a portal to the one Valhalla (in the galaxy) and an experiencable, nuanced Valhalla itself, as in Irish-flavored, Norse-flavored, even American-flavored, for there are Valhallas in the U.S. too. Think of the specific cultural picturings of this locale as a filtering, silk-screened membrane; you just see through the printed imagery on the screen to the reality.

The Valhalla at Rondvassbu resembles a vast sports stadium or massive colosseum, whose seats are occupied by what initially seem to be crystalline facets with a splash of color. On closer examination these are revealed to be an assortment of angels and members of the Great White Brotherhood, each emitting a different and specialized frequency (color) congruent to their nature. Here we appreciate the specificity about the cloaks and mantles of the guests at Da Derga's Hostel or of the shields of the Einherjar: they indicate the figure's spiritual frequency (Ray alignment), initiatory status within the GWB, and to a degree their function and assignments.

Another important nuance to this color-frequency spectrum is the fact that Valhalla with its assembled angelic and hierarchical host is a vivid fleshing out of what Hinduism calls the jewelled altar of the inner heart chakra (the *Ananda-kanda*, "Place of Bliss"). This altar stands before the *Kalpataru* (Kalpa Tree or Wish-Fulfilling Tree: it's the Norse Yggdrassill or Tree of Life) within the inner heart center. The jewelled altar is the GWB spectrum array of ascended beings and angels, like many-hued crystals, and all of this is an *outer*, geomantically grounded presentation of the spiritual reality of the *inner* human heart chakra. The Urd's Well Light temple is a projection of the generic structure of the inner heart chakra out into the visionary geography of Earth to enable us to interact with it through a psychic focus.

On the galactic level, correspondingly, Ursa Major, seat of the Great White Brotherhood, is the *Ananda-kanda* (inner heart chakra) of the galactic body.

Thus when you are physically situated at a geomantic node that embodies a Valhalla as a numinous feature you are also sitting within your own inner heart chakra, extrapolated outside you and expanded to be an interactive Light temple environment and remembered millennia later through "mythic" imagery. Hindu iconography of the chakras shows that beneath the central heart chakra, the twelve-petalled *Anahata*, hangs the red lotus of eight petals (the *Ananda-kanda*), its head upturned. "It is in this (red) lotus that there are the Kalpa Tree [Yggdrasill], the jewelled altar [Valhalla] surmounted by an awning and decorated by flags and the like, which is the place of mental worship."[5]

---

5. Arthur Avalon, *The Serpent Power* (New York: Dover Publications, 1974): 383.

Mental worship means making a direct connection to God, supervised, as the Irish myths suggest, by the Red One, Da Derga, its chief host. But the host is also Odin, the Norse perception for the Supreme Being in His executive function. So Da Derga and Odin, the chief hospitallers and boar-servers are aspects of the Supreme Being. Valhalla or the inner heart chakra is where you may easily make the contact.

It gets even better, for Yggdrasill literally means Odin's Steed. His steed (*drasill*) is the magical eight-legged horse called Sleipnir; while *Ygg*, which means the "frightening, awe-inspiring one," is a familiar Norse reference to Odin. In simple terms, the horse is the tree, and both are Odin. In actuality, Odin does not ride his horse at all; rather, it is we, when visiting the Valhalla (the outer expression of the eight-petalled inner heart chakra) who ride this chakra "to" Odin as the Supreme Being under the tutelage of the jeweled GWB assembly, only to discover Odin was there all along inside and as the Tree of Life in the inner heart.

Here is another classical description of this spiritual-geomantic place: The *Ananda-kanda* is the seat of the "'Ista-devata under a beautiful awning (Candratapa), surrounded by trees laden with flowers and fruits and sweet-voiced birds.'"[6] Sweet-voiced birds correspond to the singing angelic host and the mellifluous members of the GWB as well as to the musical *sidhe*-dwellers. The Ista-devata is an aid, guide, or principal deity within a temple who helps worshippers attain the ultimate goal of meditation, union with Brahman (i.e., Odin, Da Derga, the Supreme Being). Mythically, we can construe this deity as akin to Da Derga, Macc Do Tho, and the other royal hospitallers of Eriu as well as the valiant boar-carver of Valhalla.

---

6.   Arthur Avalon, *The Serpent Power* (New York: Dover Publications, 1974): 378.

A Valhalla in Full Activation

Let's come back to King Arthur's Camalate in Somerset for here we may see a Valhalla in action on the Earth plane. The Valhalla accessed through South Cadbury Castle, a traditional ringed hillfort (or henge) in Somerset, England, is not remembered as being a Valhalla, but it was once known as King Arthur's Palace. In the 1960s, archeologists tentatively established that King Arthur or a King Arthur-like Celtic king occupied the hillfort in roughly the 6th century A.D.

They further proposed that the legendary "Camallate" (Camelot), King Arthur's fraternal headquarters for the Grail Knights, was also situated at Cadbury Castle.[7] This is based on the now famous statement by British antiquarian John Leland in 1542: "At the very south ende of the chirch of South-Cadbyri standith Camallate, sumtyme a famose toun or castelle, apon a very torre or hille....The people can telle nothing ther but that they have hard say that Arture much resorted to Camalat."[8] Local legend attests to the belief that King Arthur and his Knights even today sleep inside the hill in a secret cavern (it's a Hollow Hill, according to Celtic myth: a *sidhe* or *brugh*), awaiting their call to return to life and worldly action.

The Knights who are sleeping within the Hollow Hill of Cadbury Castle are not the former human-embodied Grail Knights but the immortal Einherjar of the Great White Brotherhood, and the "sleeping" refers to the dormancy of this Valhalla and a period of nonactivity in terms of its egress into human culture and awareness. If anyone is sleeping, it's us: the Einherjar there are fully awake and very busy.

Outwardly, Cadbury Castle was the site of King Arthur's Camalate[9], an initiation and training center for Grail Knights inter-

---

7. In England, you have the curious situation where many ancient sites are called Castles even though there is no evidence of there having been a building on it. It turns out the Castle is the Light temple present there.

8. John Leland, quoted in Leslie Alcock, *'By South Cadbury, is that Camelot...' The Excavation of Cadbury Castle 1966-1970* (London: Thames and Hudson, 1972): 11.

facing with the Earth's visionary geography to develop themselves spiritually. Inwardly, these activities were centered at the geomantic overlap with a Valhalla, thus providing the Knights access to the entire assemblage of the Great White Brotherhood. You had the archetypal assembly of the GWB Knights and their temporal reflection, the human Grail Knights at the same place, an excellent *congruence* of intention and activity, one based on expert knowledge of the local geomantic terrain and its optimal uses by people.

On the human level, the various male and female Knights embodied the qualities of the different characters of the Arthurian myth. One person expressed the essentials of Arthur, another of Gawain, others of Lancelot, Bors, Galahad, and the rest. In this expression they were also overshadowed, influenced, even infiltrated by Ascended Masters who inspired and modeled these "parts." Into this gathering of Grail Knights at Cadbury Castle would come the actual, galactic King Arthur, leader of the Ascended Host of the Great Bear, in the form of a rotating golden spindle and perhaps sometimes in his celestial-human guise as a regal king with all the trimmings.

A golden shaft of light would come down into the center of Cadbury Castle, into the center of all its physical, geomantic, and visionary features, including the Round Table (present as both an actual table and a geomantic energy construct). The spindle would rotate rapidly like a contained and focussed tornado, sending off sparks of solar light (almost like lateral lightning strikes) to all assembled, to the hill, and the surrounding landscape with all its physical and geomantic features. This sparking, golden spindle is a dynamic way in which the Solar Logos may appear to us.

---

9. I prefer the eight-letter spelling of Camalate for its congruence with the eight-petalled reality of the inner heart chakra. This chakra is said to have eight Sanskrit syllables inscribed on its petals; occultly, it is more accurate to say this chakra has an eightfold vibratory field that generates eight petal shapes as a continuous cymatic pattern. Cymatic refers to the demonstration of sound shaping matter, as illustrated by the effect of vibrational frequencies on sand or lycopodium powder on a glass plate.

King Arthur, at this level of expression, is the Solar Logos, which as mentioned above is the Logos or Word (thus an aspect of the Christ) at the level of all the stars of the galaxy, transmitting the energies of growth and change, for Nature, consciousness, culture, and the planet. Arthur is the leader of all the stars and thus "king" of them as well as of the Great White Brotherood; Arthur's *Palace* or Cadbury *Castle* was where the Solar Logos resided for a time on the Earth, the terrestrial equivalent of Indra's heavenly Palace of Victory, *Vaijayanta*. Cadbury Castle was the local access point, the landscape's placemarker, for the Einherjar (GWB) of Valhalla and their chief, and the terrestrial Camalate was the achieved human recognition and conscious use of this specialized feature.

With the Solar Logos resident there for a time (the epoch of the Celtic King Arthur, one of 15 such expressions over time), the connection between our physical, human world and the higher spirit world of the Great White Brotherhood remained open and fluid. Camalate was the grounded manifestation of the archetypal celestial pattern of Arthur-Indra present at his Palace, Castle, or *Vaijayanta* surrounded by the jeweled altar of the GWB (Indra's 100 palaces). In other words, the elements of the pattern through the Earth's geomantic locale matched and lined up in perfect congruence with the celestial originals during that period of time. That's probably why the Arthur myth still reverberates in Western culture. That was such a grand demonstration of it.

We may think of Camalate (Arthur's Palace) as the *activated* terrestrial version of Indra's *Vaijayanta* situated at the heart of the Celestial City of Amaravati; it is activated or illuminated when the Solar Logos becomes resident in the template. The human experience here would be of interpenetrating realms: the celestial template of Camalate overlaid on the physical manifestation of it, so that both realms, Heaven and Earth, were united and co-present at a landscape site. This actually is one of the goals and purposes of the Earth's visionary geography, to achieve this level of wakeful congruence and coincidence of the above and below, or archetype and copy.

At such times, there was a match-up of inner and outer expressions. Inwardly, the Great White Brotherhood, enlivened and focussed through King Arthur as the Solar Logos, would transmit their jewelled presence through the Valhalla at Cadbury Castle out into Somerset. Outwardly, the Grail Knights, trained in accordance with the Great White Brotherhood protocols, were physically arrayed across the landscape. It was a powerful and focussed *overlap* of spiritual and physical presences. With King Arthur as Solar Logos energizing the GWB, their presence streamed right out of the spiritual world and Ursa Major into the British landscape to infiltrate it with Light.

The perfect overlap and simultaneous activation of the inner and outer aspects of this Valhalla, as just described, does not happen often on Earth. Certainly, various of the 360 Valhallas may be "open for business," but the grounding of the Solar Logos through one is a rare event on Earth, and happens at only one Valhalla on Earth in a given epoch. There have been only 15 coincidences of the King Arthur-Solar Logos residence at a GWB-filled Valhalla (outwardly expressing itself as a Camalate) in the history of humanity on Earth, and not all in Britain either. King Arthur coincidences have occurred in Mongolia, Persia, and Ireland, too.[10]

Thus out of 26 attempts to create and ground Camalate on Earth, 15 were completed and moved on to the Arthur-Solar Logos residency and activation. Here the match-up was apparently exact, and the Solar Logos irradiated both the celestial and terrestrial expressions of the same GWB Celestial City template. Perhaps this helps us understand, even feel into, the famous expression and its implicit yearning regarding King Arthur: *rex quondam, rexque futurus*: Arthur, the once and future king.

---

10. The Irish equivalent to Arthur's Palace at South Cadbury Castle (and another Valhalla portal) was Almu, the Hill of Allen (as described above), a hillfort in Leinster County, the home and seat of kingship for the Irish King Arthur, Fionn MacCumhail. His Fianna were the equivalent to the British Knights of the Round Table.

Likely Experiences Inside Valhalla

Usually, a Valhalla node serves as a meeting place for humans, alone or in groups, with the Ascended Masters of the GWB, as the next examples show. As for Valhallas in current times, at the Rondvassbu Valhalla I led a small group in an initiatory sequence called the Christed Initiation in the Buddha Body. At the start of this five-day geomantic experience, it was necessary, by angelic invitation, to have a human conscious interface with the hierarchy of the angelic realms and the Great White Brotherhood to facilitate further initiatory experience in the Rondane landscape temples and others the group would encounter elsewhere and later on Earth.

On this occasion, the Archangel Michael appeared in the central open area of the "sports stadium," his sword upraised, his shield held out before him. All of the assembled angelic host and Einherjar copied this gesture, upraising their swords, facing in towards Michael. Then they lowered their swords, but kept them pointing towards the central open area where in a visionary state our small group was assembled. This seemed to be a kind of *adoubement*, the lowering of the king's sword to the kneeling knight apprentice's shoulders. The GWB host turned around to face outwards to the world, their swords again raised upwards.

Later, observing this physical site from a distance (a small lake surrounded by bare land, large boulders, and ringed by snow-capped mountains), I saw a lilac flame-shaped lotus perhaps five feet tall and wide holding a large pearl in the place where our group had sat. It was a replica of what the Christ called the Pearl of Great Price, created through the interface here of our group and the Einherjar.

The Pearl was a seed that would grow within this Light temple and be a touchstone for future aspirants visiting this site to experience the grounded reality of the Christ. It would also help people contact the Michaelic stream of consciousness, crucial in these times since the Archangel Michael is in charge of planet-wide Aquarian-era efforts to rekindle Earth's link to its own Light body.

As for all the swords, these indicate another initiatory aspect to this interface with the Einherjar at a Valhalla. The Celtic tales of King Arthur spoke of the Sword in the Stone: a young Arthur proved his worthiness to be king of all England by being the only one who could withdraw a sword stuck into a stone.

The sword refers to the psychic ability to penetrate in vision into the spiritual world; in effect, you insert the sword of your clairvoyance into the stone of the spiritual world, the stones or colored crystals of the jewelled altar. It's a stone because to non-clairvoyant vision, the spiritual world is dense and seems to offer great resistance to our seeing through it: it's hard to penetrate, *stonelike*. The sword is like the corn of the unicorn, the extended sixth chakra of psychic insight. At the same time, the assembled host insert their swords into your subtle bodies, probing for merit and catalyzing further spiritual unfoldment. The Sword in the Stone ceremony takes place in the inner heart chakra *and* its outer expression as a geomantic Valhalla.

We can see the Irish King Conaire and his retinue visiting Da Derga's hostel in a similar light: the hospitality they sought was the interface with the Einherjar. King Conaire was well known to the Einherjar, and possibly one of them walking about in embodied human form for he wore over his mist-like, iridescent cloak a wheel of gold that reached from his chin to his navel, a regal sign of initiation and merit. His hair was as fair as well-beaten gold, his sword was gold-hilted and seemed to sing, and the light reflected from his scabbard was so bright it would illuminate the darkness outdoors. "Of all the forms I saw [said one of the pirates planning to destroy the hostel], his was the most beautiful."[11]

Conaire, interpreted as an embodied Irish monarch, fulfils his role as king by being a spiritual leader as well, leading the human-Einherjar interface on behalf of the well-being of land, Nature, and humanity. "Thus the Celtic kings' mission is to *regere*, that is to say, to cast the brilliance of his regard about him as far as he can, to play the role

---

11. Randy Lee Eickhoff, *The Destruction of the Inn* (New York: Forge/Tom Doherty Associates, 2001): 131.

of the sun that gives prosperity and richness to the world."[12] Conaire may well have been a GWB member walking about in human guise, for the wheel of gold is a mark of high spiritual accomplishment. He may even have been a *Chakravartin*. In ancient India, the golden wheel was the *Sudarsana*, Vishnu's Discus (or Chakra), and the *Chakravartin* was the world-master who wielded it to create optimal conditions in a landscape for human spiritual development.

We can now appreciate the other formidable guests at Da Derga's hostel as either still embodied humans of exceptional spiritual development or as ascended Einherjar. The Fomorians are representations of the angelic order called Elohim, for whose early but formative work on the Earth they were usually remembered as giants (because they assumed giant human form), and often as Cyclops (one-eyed giants, such as Ireland's Balor of the Evil Eye or the bible's Goliath). The single round eye stood for unitive vision, their attention and essence never departing from the blissful state of unitive consciousness and their eye from God and God's vision for the world. In the qualities of the spears, swords, and shields of Da Derga's guests we may also discern indications of their clairvoyant prowess, psychic abilities, and auric field brilliance.

The massive "boar of the forest" portrays the powerful illumination an activated Valhalla (one with regular human-Einherjar interfacing) sends into our world, for ultimately one of the prime purposes of the Valhalla installations around the planet is to provide apertures for spiritual Light to flow out like a river of fire and burn up our world of consensus reality, ignorance, and obliviousness. "The doors were open [to Da Derga's hostel], and Mac Cecht's fire shone out like the red heart of a mountain when the Faery People are feasting within it."[13] We want—today we desperately need—this spiritual presence as

---

12. Jean Markale, *The Epics of Celtic Ireland. Ancient Tales of Mystery and Magic* (Rochester, VT: Inner Traditions, 2000): 164.
13. "Conary Mor," in *Celtic Wonder-Tales*, Retold by Ella Young (New York: Dover Publications: 1995): 188.

an antidote to the entrenched atheism, materialism, and cultural entropy enveloping all cultures on the planet.

The Einherjar of Valhalla or the guests at Da Derga's hostel feast perpetually on the inexhaustible boar's flesh. What is this boar? It is a vivid image for Christ Consciousness, for the Christ Himself as a cosmic, ever-renewed Eucharist, self-sacrificing of his "flesh" and "blood" to feed the soul. More subtly, we could say the Einherjar do not actually "eat" the boar or consume the Christ at all; as ascended beings, their bodies of Light already consist of Christ Consciousness, or the universal Light. They are made of the Light of Christ. The boar's flesh is ever renewed for the Light is endless as the Logos permeates and coheres all cosmic space. They perpetually enjoy the boar's flesh, as it is their permanent psychic reality, an unbroken, continuous, pure, all-pervading state of cosmic consciousness. This is their ascended Light-body state, and the eating of the flesh is a formality, even an anachronistic one: truly, they all are Christed boars of the forest.

As for the mead from Heidrun, this is the Norse name for the Vedic *soma* (or *amrita*), the Greek ambrosia, and the Persian *haoma*, the much-desired, highly prized beverage that bestows (or maintains) immortality. Since the gods, or Einherjar, are immortal by definition, the mead bestows an immortality of consciousness, that is, an unbroken *continuity* of the awareness of unitive consciousness that exists before (and after) anything—beings, consciousness, subtle matter—was ever differentiated. The mead signifies perpetual deep wakefulness, of never sleeping, spiritually, that is, forgetting one's Source. Like the boar's flesh and the Christ Light, they already have the mead: it is their life "blood." Soma, says Hindu myth scholar Roberto Calasso, is "'among the gods, he who is awake'…a god who is also an edible substance." Soma is "perfect wakefulness…the nearest to the elusive flow of consciousness."[14]

Embodied humans, such as our group at Rondvassbu, visit a Valhalla to get a taste of the perfected Christ, boar's flesh straight from

---

14. Roberto Calasso, *Ka. Stories of the Mind and Gods of India* (New York: Vintage Books, 1999): 255.

the cooking spit, a mouthful of the heavenly mead, and an experience of the community of Ascended Masters who embody this reality. This taste and experience is a powerful spiritual nutrient for the individual and, by extension, for the culture and landscape, both parched for a taste. The geomantic Valhalla, when operational, provides the *conduit* for this nutrient to flow from the spiritual world into the physical body of planet and humanity.

On another occasion in my experience, a Valhalla served as a meeting place for spiritual aspirants around the Earth, again under the auspices of the Archangel Michael. This Valhalla was accessed through Ivy Thorn Hill, just outside Glastonbury, England, at the time of the autumnal equinox, which on that day in 1985 was 1.30 a.m. I went to this hill in my physical body, while my colleagues and housemates were transported in their dream-bodies by the angelic host to Valhalla. Again, it was like a massive sports stadium, and this time in addition to the Einherjar, there were thousands of Grail Knights (men and women on a path of geomantic initiation) on the playing field.

I had been instructed by my angelic mentors to intone certain phrases many times in preparation for this event, namely, *O Michael uplift us now*, and during the assembly to say this out loud: "O Knights of the Grail. O Knights of the Grail. Be with me now. The time is right for a blessing to come on. I write a book. Help me to sharpen my sword that I may speak the truth from this, the Ivy Thorn." Both of these focussed utterances can be used in interactions with a Valhalla; merely substitute what it is you do (e.g., I paint a picture, I teach children) for "I write a book."

I was surrounded by thousands of brothers and sisters of the Sangreal (the fellowship of the Grail Quest), and though I had met none in the flesh, they all seemed familiar, like colleagues. We raised our Grail swords in honor of King Arthur, the once and future king of the GWB, who stood toweringly before us in the open central area of the sports stadium. All hail Arthur! All hail Indra! All hail Michael! We brandished our swords as an explosion of rainbow light enveloped us and the blades. Somehow as we hammered our swords against

Michael's one great celestial blade as if it were an adamant anvil. all our individual swords became part of it.

Michael swept through the assemblage of Grail Knights and dubbed each on the shoulder as if lighting 100,000 straw torches from his single flame. During this, all our swords were taken from us momentarily, sharpened, then returned *bright*. A celestial personage next arrived: robed in emerald, she was a woman of unspeakable beauty and grace but whose face was veiled (maybe I just couldn't see it). She anointed all the Grail Knight swords with an emerald wand, and all the tips blazed bright green.

Later, comparing notes, my housemates and me discovered we had each been presented with an aspect of the mystery of the Sword in the Stone. The Grail Knight convocation at Valhalla was a training and demonstration of this, an introduction—and a testing—of the protocols for piercing the spiritual Stone (that is, using clairvoyance to see into this realm and to stay awake while seeing)[15] so as to arrive wakeful in vision within the Hall of the Einherjar, mentors for all Grail Knights.

We can appreciate then that one of the human benefits to the existence of 360 Valhallas around the Earth is to facilitate, in fact, to propel, the development of clairvoyance (acquisition and training in the use of the sword) sufficient to penetrate the stone of the spiritual world to reach the place where the angelic and hierarchical host assemble. Then the next benefit is to be penetrated by their con-

---

15. Staying awake while seeing means you are able to keep the thread of bodily awareness, self-identity, and the basic continuity of spacetime on Earth going while you have your vision of something outside spacetime. Often, people feel they reach a point where they blank out or seemingly fall asleep; it is not sleep exactly, but more like an inability to run the psychic perception as a parallel, consciously-maintained track alongside bodily-physical world perception. The former subsumes the latter, and often afterwards you can't remember what happened. The Sword in the Stone is about staying awake at both ends of the sword insertion experience.

sciousness and to be able to assimilate it. It is, after all, a powerful energy for the body to accommodate.

This infusion of higher celestial energy acts as a catalyst for your further development. As part of this, your sword (clairvoyance) is activated, blessed, and focussed by the GWB; then the Ray Masters form the precious scabbard of fourteen jewels around your sword and aura, so you may carry this imprint with you wherever you go. All of this starts to infiltrate your world and self-identity.

Current Activities Inside Valhalla

Not all of the 360 Valhallas are on-line or in active status or their apertures into our world in full operation. They would be if we had the interest. In the Earth context, they may wax and wane in terms of their operation and human interface possibility, somewhat as if they were all originally preset for intermittent on/off status like clockwork. One in particular recently came back on-line in coincidence with an important political event in the United States. On February 15, 2003, I was present at the reactivation of the Valhalla accessed through the backyard of Thomas Jefferson's estate called Monticello in Charlottesville, Virginia.

At the time, an estimated six million people in 600 cities were protesting the United States' recently initiated (second) war on Iraq. Monticello, Jefferson's former residence, is a geomantic site with many features; one is that it is the *Ananda-kanda* landscape chakra within a large regional system that includes Washington D.C. as its solar plexus chakra. Energetically, the Monticello chakra is higher up the consciousness hierarchy than Washington, D.C., more subtle even than the outer heart chakra, and a suitable place from which to focus benevolent attention on the power center of the U.S.[16]

Seemingly in support of the six million antiwar protestors active around the globe that day, the GWB opened the doors to this Valhalla, swung open Valgrind, the one main gate in for outsiders, and revealed their jewelled presence to me in the midst of a fierce blizzard.

Usually, it is necessary when geomantic activations happen from the inside—from the spiritual world trying to work out into ours—that at least one embodied person (more are preferred) be present to observe the event and to help ground the activation in Earth reality, human consciousness, and bodily experience.

I entered the newly opened Valhalla, performed some meditative protocols that put me in congruence with the Ofanim (long-time mentors of mine and central to all activations in the planet's Light body), and generally allowed my body, chakras, and auric field to be a conduit for grounding the reality of this Valhalla activation. In simple terms, the GWB needs people present to greet and say *Hello!* to a newly awakened geomantic aperture. It's all bridge-work: the real activation is of the bridges, the portals into the holographic copy. The bridges are what get awakened anew in each epoch. The Valhalla opened its doors and revealed itself, a huge jewel of many facets—more like 432,000 jewels—many-hued and as large as the hill.

The opening of the front gate to this Valhalla, due to its crucial geomantic positioning with respect to Washington, D.C., supported the global antiwar protest in that it allowed an inrush of higher consciousness and truth to enter a geomantically defined system enabling

---

16. This may seem confusing at first glance. The Valhalla geomantic feature is equivalent to what Hindu texts call the jewelled altar, located within the inner heart chakra. However, not all of the Earth's 360 Valhallas pertain to the inner heart chakra as such in terms of landscape correlates. The assembly of the Great White Brotherhood, or Valhalla, condensed as the jewelled altar, represents one aspect of the inner heart chakra. In other situations, specific landscape temples fulfill the function of the inner heart chakra for a local, regional, or even global "body." The Rondane Mountain area, focussed around Rondablikk, is the planet's singular inner heart center; the composite Light temple (with 24+ geomantic features) at Charlottesville, Virginia, is the inner heart chakra for a regional geomythic "body," encompassing 1/12th of the planet's surface. The Charlottesville landscape temple has a Valhalla portal (at Monticello) as well as being the inner heart center for 1/12th of the Earth, the two features overlapping.

people to be clearer in their perceptions and freer in their choosing, to be less fettered by unwholesome psychic conditioning. The addition of Light to the world grid system enabled people to *choose* more *freely*; it was not a matter of forcing a political position through the Light grid, but of illuminating lies and darkness through the sheer, irresistible potency of the Light flowing through the node and letting people choose.

Washington, D.C. was buried under more than two feet of snow that day, more than any other area. It's amusing because from the spiritual world's viewpoint, snow, rain, and other forms of water-based precipitation are infusions of consciousness (to them water equals Light and consciousness) and also a kind of printer's watermark on the paper, a signature from On High of a good event.

Once you become familiar with the energetics of a Valhalla, it is not always necessary to be physically present at one of its holograms in the Earth's visionary geography to enter it. In late 2004, I was invited to visit via clairvoyance a session of the Great White Brotherhood at their Valhalla in Ursa Major; it was the original or primary one, at least for this galaxy, but perhaps itself a hologram of a greater reality higher up the hierarchical system. This meeting took place immediately after the 9.0 South Asian tsunami-earthquake of December 26, 2004.

Particularly interesting was that while the meeting appeared to be taking place, to be ontologically grounded in Ursa Major, it was being broadcast like a CSPAN live television coverage through the 360 Valhallas on Earth. One could, theoretically, have witnessed the Great White Brotherhood meeting through these individual Valhallas, though this probably would have required either an invitation (equivalent to a premium cable channel subscription) or the ability to perform the Sword in the Stone demonstration as one's *bona fides*.

Here's what it looked like: The Valhalla is a vast assembly, like a political convention center during a presidential election year, or, as mentioned, like a huge, people-packed sports stadium. The many thousands of Einherjar are situated according to their Ray affinity: the seating areas are apportioned into 14 wedges, each vibrating visibly at the specific color of that Ray. Saint Germain's lilac wedge, for example, is filled with his Ray colleagues, adepts, apprentices, students, and visitors. Into the center of the stadium comes a column of blazing white light, the "parent" of the 14 Rays. This is the Supreme Being (in mythic terms, Zeus, Odin, Da Derga, Osiris) saying *Hello!*

It is also an invocation and blessing on the assembly from On High. The Supreme Being envelops the Valhalla in a brilliant, adamant gold sphere offering protection and blessing; outside the sphere numerous spirit beings are posted as sentries against discordant energies seeking entrance. Also on the outside you can see streamers of the 14 Rays like colored ribbons moving out across the galaxy as if threading the interior of an inflated balloon, hunting for resonance and receptivity among sentient life forms throughout the star fields.

Intermingling with these streamers are energy-color emissions like solar jets shooting off in all directions as if from the Sun's corona. So intense is the concentrated spiritual energy present in Valhalla that beneficial discharges and emissions spark off continuously like this throughout the meeting.

As each Ray Master has areas of responsibility and influence throughout the galaxy and across the Earth through various geomantic features, these areas now flush that color. Saint Germain's dedicated Sanctuaries throughout the many planets flush lilac; those dedicated to Lao Tzu are inundated with the rich yellow of his attention.

On this occasion, Saint Germain addresses the assembly, though presumably at other times, different Ray Masters have their turn. His podium is in the open central portion of the stadium (where the playing field would be), and he seems to have some ultra-technological devices to aid his presentation: gauges, consoles, screens, projectable holographic displays. No doubt these are visual metaphors for my benefit. Through one set of gauges, Saint Germain monitors the energy effects of the earthquake. From their viewpoint, the tsunami-earthquake combination was a "controlled burn," planned in advance (in conjunction with Gaia, the primary Earth spirit, and all the human souls who would die), all of it calibrated and carefully executed, its after-effects, both geological and political-cultural, now being monitored.

Saint Germain shows us a view of the Earth from space. A big slit or fissure runs north-south in the area of the tsunami-earthquake, and it has dark gold flames spitting out of it like a fire fountain. The fire-fountain fissue appears perpendicular to the equator and the presumed flow of the pressure wave of the tsunami. Inside the flames, I see a "gas-burner" close up with 100 holes in it, as you would see on a lit gas stove. Of course this is a visual metaphor, yet an instructive one. Saint Germain shows how the GWB "lit" one of the gas-burner outflow holes in the planet and allowed the "gas" to ignite (presumably the earthquake's epicenter), and then allowed the one burning hole to ignite three more nearby, but no more.

The site of the earthquake was carefully chosen so that this sudden flaring up of Earth energy could burn through a series of dark grid lines that crossed that area. The dark grid pertains to the Antichrist and is the antithesis to the Light grid. It encases the planet like a cancerous growth of dark tendrils and cords and weakens the benevolent effect of the Light grid. The earthquake was designed with the same precision building demolition experts set their charges to bring down a structure without collateral damage; here the intent in part was to burn off dark grid cords.

We also saw how Gaia, the Mother spirit of the planet, was looking after the physical Earth. She was in angelic guise perhaps 20 times the size of the planet, holding it in her arms and encasing it in her diaphanous wings, preventing the Earth from being destroyed or irreparably traumatized by this event. She had two aspects: the compassionate Madonna and Kali the Black Destroyer, for while She is perpetually committed to this planet, she has a limit for how much abuse she will tolerate.

Many people afterwards said this event was a planetary wake-up call. We saw that in the spiritual world. Kali is said to be the consort to Shiva, one of Hinduism's trinity, the god of death, dissolution, and transcendence of all form—like the Greek Hades times one thousand. Saint Germain showed us Shiva with a big hammer striking hot metal on an anvil, sending out a fierce shower of sparks in all directions. The hot metal is humanity's attention, its dense, materialistic focus, riveted by this massive event and its implications and no doubt the fear that more catastrophes like it will follow.

Each spark contained the force of Shiva's wake-up call, the shattering of illusions. The sparks were circulating around the planet like volcanic ash; where they landed on people, they started to dissolve illusion and delusory states of mind. It might seem like the world was suddenly full of death and destruction, but that is just the outer husk of the message Shiva was delivering en masse to the Earth. Wake up! See reality! Drop your callous indifference to who you are, to what the planet is! Awake! From another perspective, Shiva was supporting the GWB's intent to loosen the stranglehold of the dark grid on Earth and its continuous support for delusory states.

St. Germain activates what resembles a flat screen television monitor though one hundred times larger. On it are projected numerous Light grids for different planets, engineering schematics for a geometry of Light as a framework for consciousness. Saint Germain and his colleagues discuss the different parameters set by these Light grids for the evolution and amplification of consciousness on respective planets. Presumably, the meeting moved on to other topics, but as I was a visitor, this was the point where my presence there began to fade and I returned to "normal" life.

How to Interact with a Valhalla

Here are two ways to make contact with and enter a Valhalla. Ideally, you need to be physically situated at a geomantic copy of a Valhalla; see Table 4 for a selected list of locations. Once you have physically visited a Valhalla site, you need not be there again bodily to enter it for your subtle energy bodies have an imprint of the locale. Bring to mind the physical qualities of the landscape site and pretend (actively visualize) you are there in your body. A portion of your awareness actually will be.

Table 4
Selected Locations of Valhallas or Urd's Well
Planetary Total: 360

1. Da Derga's Hostel, Bohernabreena-Cuala, County Dublin, Ireland

2. Rondvassbu, near Kvam, Rondane Mountains, Norway

3. Ivy Thorn Hill, near Glastonbury, Somerset, England

4. St. Paul's Cathedral, Ludgate Hill, London, England

5. Arthur's Palace, Cadbury Castle, South Cadbury, Somerset, England

6. *Brugh Da Choca,* Breenmore Hill, Athlone, County Westmeath, Ireland

7. Holyfell Hill, Iceland

8. Forgall Manach's Hostel, Breifne, Ireland

9. Macc Da Reo's Hostel, Breifne, Ireland

10. Monticello, Charlottesville, Virginia

11. Macc Da Tho's Hostel, Leinster County, Ireland

12. Blue Lake, Mount Wheeler, near Taos, New Mexico

13. *Doo-ko-oslid,* San Francisco Peaks, near Flagstaff, Arizona

14. Almu, Hill of Allen, Leinster County, Ireland

First: at the physical site or from a distance having visualized the site, picture an immense domed sports stadium, its thousands of seats occupied by jewlled figures of Light; that is, the Light emitted by the various beings (Ascended Masters and their adepts) is like an array of glittering jewels. See yourself standing on the open playing field. Choose one of the 14 Ray colors (refer to Table 1), whichever one appeals to you. Surround yourself in a towering flame of that one specific color. Visualize a golden rose with a short stem; on the rose petals, write the word *Hello!* on it and toss the rose out into the stadium. Wait for a response: it may have the quality of an image, word, sensation or even an interactive lucid dream, now or later; it may take time for it to percolate into your daytime awareness.

Second: again picture the immense sports stadium. Stand outside it at the front gate. Surround yourself in a towering lilac flame, rising up from the Earth, surrounding you on all sides and rising high above you. Ask your Higher Self (or what Ray Master Saint Germain, Master of the Lilac Ray, calls the "Mighty I AM Presence") to conduct you into the audience of the Ascended Masters of Valhalla. In effect, your Higher Self (we all have one; you do not have to "see" it to interact: just trust you have made contact) acts as your sponsor and guide. You may be assigned a "Visitor's" seat on the outskirts of the stadium.

While the Irish and Norse myths portray activities at Valhalla largely in terms of unending sumptuous feasting and drinking, it is prudent to remember this is a metaphor for the spiritual warriors' thorough, total, uninterrupted immersion in Christ Consciousness. They do not have to eat the divine boar's flesh, because their Light bodies already are compounded of this endless, pure Christ Light—a perfect example of the dictum, "You are what you eat." In fact, Saint Germain emphasizes that "the very atmosphere of the place is permeated with this Christ Light." If anyone actually feasts on this "flesh," it is we, the parched and hungry mortals seeking a "taste" of the pure Christ Light.

3

RESIDENCES OF THE 14 RISHIS

In brief: This is a portion of Amaravati, perceived as the Light City or Crystal City of the 14 Ray Masters, each Ray Master having a 1/14th wedge of its interior space; the feature is topped by a Glass Mountain, a tetrahedral crystalline pyramid of Light sometimes appearing green; 108 apertures to the Light City (or virtual copies of it) exist on Earth.

The Glass Mountain and the Crystal City

In a functional sense, Valhalla is defined, by way of boundary and administration, by the residences of the Ray Masters. At the galactic level, this is the heart of Amaravati, but within the Earth's visionary geography, the Ray Master residence aspect is templated separately with 108 copies. In simple structural terms, picture the circle of the GWB inside Valhalla as divided into 14 equal portions, each like a wedge; each wedge is dominated by a single Ray color and contains all the GWB members in affiliation with that Ray. The 14 Ray Masters administer all activities and supervise GWB members to do with their Ray.

I call the Ray Masters' residences the Light City, and though all of Amaravati (with its seven enumerated parts) is the Celestial City, in functional and locational terms, I designate the Ray Masters' part as the Celestial City. Here is how their Light City first appeared to me and colleagues. We were sitting at the Ofanim's invitation on Hamdon Hill, a flat-topped prominence about ten miles from Glastonbury in England. A large dome topped the hill; within the dome and seemingly set on and somewhat in the hill was a huge, sparkling green pyramid. It emitted a steady green radiance, and its surface was geometrical, as if comprised of innumerable cut-glass squares, like the Great Pyramid of Giza with an emerald plate-glass siding.

Beneath the pyramid and apparently within the hill (though not in the physical dimension at that spot) was a futuristic crystalline city. For a while, in fact, we called it the Crystal City because all its buildings seemed made of quartz crystal and glittered with a tremendous light. It had roads and buildings, but they were all crystalline (i.e., made of solidified or "frozen" light): everything seemed to be vibrating, giving off a blue electric aura. The green pyramid sat above the Crystal City like a lid or a sheer mountain of glass such as you read about in myths.

Perhaps this is why the motif of a Glass Mountain located at the edge of the known world is popular in Celtic, Polish, Russian, and Scandinavian myth. That tells us earlier psychics may have seen this sparkling green pyramid. The Glass Mountain is described as an otherworldly locale exceedingly steep, high, and slippery as ice whose sides of sheer glass make it impossible for valiant knights or heroes to climb up or penetrate them. Glastonbury was once called in Welsh *Ynys Witrin*, the Glass Island, but the reference seems to refer specifically to the Tor, an anomalous hill in that town. For good reason: Glastonbury Tor has a Glass Mountain over it.

What's inside the Glass Mountain? The Russians said a fierce dragon; the Celts said it was a land of the dead, a realm of nine maidens, or a magical place of safety. A Scandinavian myth said a young princess with a golden crown and a golden apple sat on its apex; whoever scaled the mountain could marry her. A young knight never manages to penetrate the Glass Mountain, but on a splendid steed and himself equipped with golden armor, he was able to ride at full speed up to the summit to claim the apple (and thus the maiden) before he slid off.

A Ukrainian myth of the Glass Mountain said it was the home of a ferocious dragon who the longer it lived there the bigger the mountain grew. First it was a hillock, then, as the dragon fed on people, the hillock became a huge glass mountain that dominated the kingdom. It kept growing so that by the time Ivan, the dragon-slayer, arrived, the Glass Mountain of the Ukraine physically occupied three-quarters of the kingdom. Yet somehow by inserting a blade of wheat under the base of the Glass Mountain, Ivan melted the glass and drained off the liquid that constituted the glass and the mountain dissolved. Ironically, this great sudden wall of rushing water drowned the dragon.

In geomantic terms, the Glass Mountain is the outer husk and boundary of the Crystal City. Initially, to enter this domain and pass through the apparently impenetrable glass walls, you must activate a point of light located just above the navel and a few inches inside (known as the Blazing Star, an aspect of the Ofanim) and then enter the Emerald, the Heart within the heart chakra (a third aspect of the heart center, located to the right of the sternum in the upper chest; it's in between the outer and inner heart centers). These are your *bona-fides*—the fruits of initiation, it would seem—to prove your worthiness (or mastery of the ability) to enter the Ray Master's Crystal City. In your subsequent visits, the green pyramid tends not to be as visible or relevant as at your first encounter with this feature. It seems you need scale and penetrate the Glass Mountain only once to enter the Crystal City regularly.

As the myths cited above suggest, learning how to negotiate the Glass Mountain is a test of one's merit, but it's important to emphasize that physical might or swiftness or even guile will not do the trick. Sophistication of clairvoyant insight and perhaps an angelic handicap will get you through the glass.

To some extent, the Glass Mountain is a force field, a merit-testing membrane of seemingly solidified light, most likely the brilliant emanation of the Light City. It is also possible, based on some of my early perceptions of this realm, that your first access is through the apex, where the princess with the golden crown sat. In that myth, the Glass Mountain was first seen by the valiant knight from his perch atop a fir tree, itself on a mountain summit. There he saw, at some distance, a spacious palace glittering in the sunlight. That "some distance" could just as well have been *beneath* him, as possibly he sat on the apex of the Glass Mountain, looking down.

Paradoxically, not only does the Crystal City not exist in our present planetary physical space, it's not in our current time period either. It is an aspect of Shambhala (another GWB outpost, only larger, discussed later in the book) that ontologically exists around 3,000 A.D. That means by approximately this time a sufficient portion of humanity will have advanced cognitively to be able to perceive and interact with the Crystal Cities already in their midst. Yes, it is visitable through clairvoyant and visionary means today by some, but in doing so, we are actually time-traveling into our planet's future. The Crystal City represents a level of consciousness that humanity collectively will grow into in the next thousand years; it also facilitates the movement of consciousness across dimensions (us getting through the Glass Mountain and back again) and time.

In support of the sublimity of this destination, Sumerian lore offers us a Glass Mountain inference, saying that Enlil, the high god (equivalent to Zeus and known as "Great Mountain") resided in *E-Kur*, which means "Mountain House." In Judaic myth, the prophet Enoch in a visionary trip saw a Crystal Palace in Arabot, the highest of the Seven Heavens; he described it as a heavenly palace made of crystals with tongues of fire burning between them, rivers of living fire (i.e., Light currents) encircling it, and innumerable angels and archangels coming and going, and sometimes even the Ancient of Days (the Supreme Being) was seen entering it.

From the Native American perspective, we get another view. The Sioux visionary Black Elk visited the Light City when he was all of nine in 1872. It was, in his words, the Flaming Rainbow Teepee of the Six Grandfathers. He accessed it on Harney Peak, a sacred mountain in the Black Hills of South Dakota. The Teepee, he said, was "built and roofed with cloud and sewed with thongs of lightning;" above it was a flaming rainbow (a sign of the Ray Masters and of Bifrost) and underneath it Black Elk saw "the wings of the air"—in other words, it was *above* Harney Peak. The Six Grandfathers sat in a row and welcomed him, while behind them in the cloud were "faces thronging without number, of the people yet to be."[1] It is possible the Six Grandfathers were some of the Ray Masters, or at least GWB members.

Here is another view from the psychically opulent canon of India. The great rishi Narada describes his visit to Indra's hall, Puskaramalini. It is marked by a "resplendence of fire," he says, and it measures 100 leagues wide by 150 leagues long and five leagues high; it is aerial and freely moving. Within, Narada beheld numerous celestial trees, Indra's superb throne, innumerable divine seers, ascetics, and siddhas in their "divine forms and beautiful ornaments" who wait upon Indra the Mighty, "immaculate, sinless, and radiant like fire." The Apsaras (celestial dancing girls) and Gandharvas (celestial musicians) provide dances, music, songs, and entertainments, and all the heavenly seers ride celestial chariots of various types that "blaze like fire, garlanded and adorned" or are "beautiful looking like the moon on their moon-like chariots" as they come and go from the delightful Puskaramalini.[2]

On one occasion, at the D.A.R. State Forest in Goshen, Massachusetts, as if observing it from above, I saw the Light City as a crystalline disc with many hexagonal facets, like a fly's composite eye when seen magnified. The crystalline disc seemed like a flower about to open, the petals folded over the center just starting to unfurl to allow the light from within the Crystal City to radiate out.

---

1.   Nicholas Black Elk, *Black Elk Speaks*, Edited by John G. Neihardt (Lincoln, NE: University of Nebraska Press, 2000: 33-37.

2.   *The Mahabharata. 2. The Book of the Assembly Hall. 3. The Book of the Forest*, Translated and Edited by J.A.B. van Buitenen (Chicago: The University of Chicago Press, 1975): 46, 47.

At Hambledon Wood near Oakham in Rutland, England, I saw the Light City below me as if I were sitting on its massive crystalline roof. It seemed like a giant, domed, glass greenhouse with sparklingly clear glass panes. Inside the "greenhouse," I saw numerous spikes of solidified light, or maybe they were crystalline towers, giving me the impression of a multichambered City of Light or a many-spoked crystalline wheel; each chamber or spoke seemed to emit a different color.

What does the Light City look like closer up? This of course will vary according to your picture-making style (the way the sixth chakra decodes energy into images). The more times you see it, the more of it and the better you see it. Here is one way: Picture a large circular City of Light, seemingly made of pristine white marble. It looks like a broad, thick typewriter-ribbon spool laid on its side, and its central portion is open. From this central area, you are surrounded by numerous white pillars that tower up to about 100 feet. They support the bottom of a rounded, dome-shaped glass roof, like a huge rotunda; the glass is transparent yet also crystalline in composition, like clear quartz. Standing here (in your visionary body) and looking straight up you can take in its glittering surface as a visual delight.

Although numerous tall thin marble pillars surround the open, central circular area, it also appears that this temple space is divided into 14 divisions like spokes on a wheel; at the hub is the central open area—Zeus' Throne, you could say. From this hub you see 14 equal divisions of the circular space like wedges; at the front of each wedge stands a marble statue of a god (perhaps 30 feet tall) expressed in a specific color, such as lilac or scarlet. When you contemplate or tune into this "statue" for a while, you realize it is not a statue but a hologram of the specific Ray Master, Saint Germain or Master Jesus, respectively, in this case, and it comes alive.

Behind each Ray Master is his or her "wedge" of the Crystal City. Consider this the Ray Master's operational headquarters, teaching areas, and residential facilities. You may alternately (and with equal validity) see each wedge as a Light City itself, or as a magnificent palace of Light with many turrets, mansions, and chambers. Each wedge or chamber is a vast open space with a high domed roof and just below that windows encircling its topmost vertical extent; at ground level, a massive single flame, matching the Ray Master's color, burns on a concave urn.

Within each wedge potentially you may access all those places on Earth and elsewhere in the galaxy (presumably on planets with sentient, higher life forms) where that Ray Master is operational and a supervisor. That means, for example, you could see where all of an individual Ray Master's Sanctuaries (see below) are located on our planet, or on other planets.

Periodically, the Supreme Being (for Judaism, the Ancient of Days; for Norse myth, Odin; for the Greeks, Zeus; the Egyptians, Osiris) visits the 14 Ray Masters. The central open hub is reserved for His visits in which He might appear as a bolt of blinding white light. The 14 Ray Masters, each representing a 1/14th diffraction of that white light, will stand in a circle around Him, like two intermingling rainbows (made of the bright and pale grades of each color) and merge with the source of their own light and enjoy the ecstatic attunement. It is like the 14 severed body parts of Osiris rushing back to join and reassemble his magnificent body of Light.

The Rainbow Bridge, Bifrost, and Its Guardian

Outside the Crystal City lies a rainbow-hued bridge. The Norse myths called this Bifrost which means "quivering road" or "swaying road to Heaven" (from the ON *bifa*, which means "to shake, sway"). Bifrost is also translated as "the fleetingly glimpsed rainbow" or "the multi-colored way;" sometimes it is called *Asbru*, "Aesir-Bridge" (the bridge of the gods, the Aesir of Asgard), while still another term for the bridge connecting Earth and Heaven is Bilröst. It was made by the gods with great skill and knowledge, it is comprised of three colors, it burns with fire, it is the best of bridges, and it will break apart at

Ragnarok (the End-Times or Götterdämmerung, Twilight of the Gods) when the Frost Giants invade Asgard and destroy it.

Bifrost rises from the Earth and terminates in the sky at a dwelling called *Himinbjorg* (ON: "Heaven's castle" or "Heaven protection"), the residence of a formidable giant, the ever-wakeful Heimdall who guards Bifrost for the gods of Asgard. Heimdall keeps the bridge safe and open for them because, as mentioned earlier, every day they ride out of Asgard and across Bifrost into Mitgard (Middle-earth) to assemble for worldly decisions at *Urdar brunnr.*

Heimdall is a singular and enigmatic mythic being, "He who illuminates the world," the "World Brightener" as his name in Old Norwegian attests. Known as the White *As* ("god"), he always wears shining white armor, carries a flashing sword called *Hofud* ("Man-Head"), rides a mighty horse called *Gulltopr* ("Golden Mane"), and bears *Gjallarhorn* ("loud-sounding horn" or "yelling horn").

So who is Heimdall? It may surprise you to learn he is the Archangel Gabriel. Gabriel is Guardian of the Sixth Heaven (in this case, Amaravati), Trumpeter of the Last Judgement (Ragnarok), and the Angel of Revelation and Truth. His prime colors are white and silver. You can see the equivalencies of horn and trumpet, the activity of annunciation and warning, and the colors, principally white; Heimdall is the truth revealer in that he guards Asgard, a prime source of the truth, and allows, or disallows, human entry and thus our exposure to the celestial truth and higher realities.

He has another guise in Welsh lore: Gwyn ap Nudd ("The White One"). Gwyn's otherworldly palace overlaps Glastonbury Tor, the site of a Crystal City. Gwyn is the son ("ap") of Nudd, Lord of *Annwn*, or Heaven, and he possesses a pack of spectral white dogs with red eyes. These are known as the Hounds of Annwn (here Annwn means "Hell" or the Underworld in the folkloric interpretation) or the Gabriel Hounds, and their significance is that once a year Gwyn leads them out into the human world on the terrible Wild Hunt to collect human souls.

European myth tells us that at Yuletide (Winter Solstice eve) spectral horsemen and terrifying hounds ride forth on the Wild Hunt to collect the souls of the living, but the geomantic reality is more benign than this. The horsemen are the Ray Masters and some of their Ray apprentices among the Great White Brotherhood. In effect, they are both horsemen and the Hounds of Hell. The fierceness of the Wild Hunt is perhaps justified in a sense because the GWB's intent is to ride forth from Asgard in search of new *voluntary* recruits for initiation. Also on this occasion, they open the "valves" a bit and allow a larger amount of Ursa Major and GWB Light to flow out of Asgard into our world. If you're in resistance to the Light and truth, it can indeed seem scary and life-threatening to witness the Hunt.

At a certain level, Bifrost is identical with the 14 Ray Masters. It is compounded of the double rainbow spectrum of their Rays, and, more sublimely, it is the Ray Masters themselves that comprise the bridge. Bifrost is an extension from Asgard to Mitgard, our Middle-Earth, enabling our entry into that realm across a bridge of fire.

If you are wary of any aspect of the Wild Hunt, then it will likely be experienced as unpleasant, even demonic in intention, as European myth has encased it; hence the negative valence of the Hounds of Hell (the GWB riders). Somewhat as an insider's joke, the Hounds of Hell reference is also an allusion to Sirius, the Dog-Star, in Canis Major, and its intimate connection with the Great Bear. Ultimately, the horsemen, whether seen as Ascended Masters or galloping, spectral hounds, ride forth on behalf of the great celestial dog, staunch guardian of the galaxy and the GWB Hierarchy. Really, the Hounds of Hell are the hunting dogs of Sirius, hunting us.[3]

In antiquity, the existence of the astral proximity of these Crystal Cities to human habitations was far better known than today, and often the seat of human government was situated at the same place as where a Crystal City was templated on the landscape. For example, in Sumer (today's Iraq), the human city of Nippur was said to be the spiritual home of Enlil and his Mountain House, or *E-Kur*, the "mooring rope" of Heaven. Nearby stood the physical ziggurat (like a flat-topped pyramid) called Duranki ("Bond of Heaven-Earth"), possibly in architectural mimicry of the Glass Mountain. From Nippur, Enlil wielded his authority over the gods and all of Sumer.

Originally, visitation to the Light City was instrumental for cultural and world leaders in forming enlightened policies for humanity and culture. Thomas Jefferson, for example, had a Light City virtually in his Monticello backyard in Charlottesville, Virginia, accessed through the next hill over from his and called Carter's Mountain. It is intriguing, though we may never know for sure, to wonder if he was consciously, bodily aware of this feature or perhaps accessed it in his dreams. His proximity to this Celestial City must at some level have had a benevolent, inspiring influence on him and possibly helped direct his policies for the young United States.

The benefit of human interactions with any of the 108 Light Cities is that it opens up the connection between that spiritual realm and ours. It is not accurate to say human focussed interaction with a Light City activates it; it's already humming with Light and open for business. It is more accurate to say you help create a bridge or conduit for its Light and consciousness to flow into our human material world and into our awareness and our concept of the Earth and to make it easier for others to visit it later and for its reality to gradually ground

---

3.   The "insider's joke" aspect goes yet deeper. Hell is a term commonly used to mean the Underworld, but Underworld actually refers to the realm of created worlds underneath the realm of absolute Light. Sirius is a star in the throat or mouth of the constellation Canis Major, the Greater Dog; myth tells us this dog guards the galaxy, protects the well of stars. Hindu star lore says the fierce god Shiva (in his guise as Rudra) is identical with Sirius, and Hindu art portrays Shiva as a four-armed deity dancing in a ring of fire. This ring of fire is the galaxy seen from the outside; Shiva is the Dog protecting the threshold of our galaxy. To him, this galaxy is the Underworld because it is under, or sequential, in the flow of light into matter. So the Hounds of Hell are the same as the Dogs of Sirius, once you make these links, and they ride looking for recruits for initiation from the outskirts of our galaxy deep into the Underworld, which is our realm.

into our human reality and time period so that by the time we reach 3,000 A.D., the Light City will be *right here* among us.

The Importance of the Light City to Silver Eggs

There is a specific geomantic function for which human access to a Light City is essential. The feature involves a Silver Egg; the Earth has 1,080 of them. When hatched, each Egg—these are massive silvery eggs of light, some 200 feet tall—yields a hologram of Horus, the Egyptian far-seeing falcon-god and a guise of the Elder Christ. Elder here means the original Christ, outside of spacetime and before the Christ entered humanity, became the Younger Christ (i.e., the Christ Child, hatched from each of the 666 Golden Eggs on the Earth) and underwent the five initiations (transformations) culminating in ascension.

The Egyptian myth of Horus is about the Christ depicted as a falcon god. Horus is the Face of Heaven and he has two eyes and two guises. Horus' White Eye (his right) pertains to his guise as Horus the Younger, *Heru-pa-khart*, associated with Ra, the Sun god (and geomantically, the Golden Eggs); his left Black Eye is called *wedjat* and is associated with the Moon and its wisdom deity, Thoth. The *wedjat* Eye is Horus the Elder and is represented geomantically on Earth by the Silver Eggs.

To hatch the Elder Horus and activate his *wedjat* Eye on Earth, you need something from the Light City: it looks like a slender, hollow crystal shank, perhaps two feet long and of a single color, usually gold. You place the shank inside the Silver Egg and Horus eventually hatches, which means, he emerges in our visionary geography. The shanks are stored in a special chamber within the Light City, and to successfully interact with a Silver Egg you must be able to travel there in vision and retrieve a shank and then deposit it like a key or seed in the Silver Egg.

The shank, the Ofanim explain, is "a solidified precipitation of consciousness from another time frame [circa 3,000 A.D.] that when 'melted' by Love from Above [a focussed warm regard enlivened by the Ofanim] helps to hatch the Egg." In effect, Horus needs reassurance from the enlightened future that it's okay to manifest now. Silver Eggs are not hatched in a single day or even directly after the introduction of the colored shank; usually, it takes some time, and often, many humans will have worked on one Silver Egg over lifetimes until the time is ripe and finally somebody fetches the appropriate colored shank from the Light City to finish the job.

For example, in Sedona, Arizona, the Ray Master's Light City is accessed through Cathedral Rocks, a striking rock formation. The Horus Silver Egg is located in the same place as a perhaps 100-foot high rockface next to a church called the Chapel of the Holy Cross. Some years ago during the week of Epiphany (culminating on January 6, the true birthday of Christ on the Earth), I spent a week meditating in this area to help hatch the Silver Egg. More properly, I should say I spent time periodically interacting with the Egg, acting as an interface between the Ofanim, transmitting angelic Love from Above, and the Earth and its myriad Nature Spirits, who would benefit from this Egg being hatched.

When the moment was ripe, I visited the Light City at Cathedral Rocks, found the archives where the golden shanks are kept, took one, came back to the Silver Egg, and dropped it inside like a catalyst. After a while, the eggshell started to dissolve and the magnificent silver falcon inside became visible. Metaphorically, the far-seeing, high-flying falcon is an apt image, as the Egyptians obviously thought, for the Elder Christ outside of spacetime, watching everything in the created worlds.

For individuals, one benefit of a visionary foray into the Light City is to get acquainted with the true seat of world government and its leaders, the Ray Masters. If you do not know which Ray you are aligned with, meditative time spent in the Light City may acquaint you with this for the first time; if you do know or at least suspect which Ray is yours, then you could go at once to that Ray wedge for a potential interview, encounter, or blessing from the specific Ray Master.

Light Cities do not require energization by humans for them to be active, as do other geomantic features. But, as I have emphasized, they do require maintenance.

Here's an example: A Light City sits in the vacant, somewhat derelict, Mayor Frank Ortiz Sports Park in Santa Fe, New Mexico. I interacted with this site for a time, then moved away and 11 years passed, then I interacted some more. During those years, the energy and ambiance of the park had deteriorated from how I remembered it and described it in my field notes. Now it was, in the words of a colleague with me that day when I returned to it, "uncared-for, desolate, trashed, partied." I found the energy dismal, uninspiring, dark, and unwholesome: entropy had claimed it, and the place looked slovenly.

This deteriorated condition had not affected the condition of the Light City, but it did place an energetic roadblock before people who might otherwise have been sensitive to its existence or at least to something numinous there. Improving the energetic vibration of such a place is not difficult, and with my angelic colleagues we introduced what measure of Light was then feasible for the site to hold.

The Ray Master Saint Germain let burn a massive lilac flame across the park and in the center of the Light City. In vision, I descended from the top of the Glass Mountain to the core of the Light City and reiterated the lilac flames. Then I created a circle of 14 blazing pillars of light, each one keyed to a Ray color. It's not that the Light City needed a reminder of its essence; rather, my iteration of its 14 Ray spectrum grounded its reality through the human, planetary realm in a kind of geomantic resonance, inside and outside. The next step was to locate where Bifrost was positioned in the landscape and update it.

The Bifrost of this copy of the Light City left the side of the hill and grounded itself near the Santa Fe River in a park. That probably was where the last systematic human interaction with this Light City had positioned the bridge. To some extent, its position can be altered in a given epoch. We sat in the park by the river (a long sliver of green abutting a usually tiny stream) and recreated the bridge by visualizing its planks—each a vertical flame of one Ray color. Then we chose a color—I chose lilac—and walked the color as if through a roaring river of (lilac) flames up to the front gates of the Light City. Then we walked it back.

This helped to establish Bifrost again as a cognizable, experiencable reality in our time. It also enabled the lights of the Light City to start flowing down into Santa Fe reality like colored streams of consciousness. In this way, a portion of the Ray Masters' different themes of consciousness was able to fertilize the Santa Fe landscape temple (altogether a geomantic terrain of many features). In the months to come, should someone sit in this park and allow themselves a reverie, they might find themselves offered the opportunity to walk along Bifrost and in some form of cognitive interpretation interact with the Light City and the Ray Masters.

How to Interact with the Light City

For a partial list of locations for the Light City of Amaravati, see Table 5. To interact with the Light City, we are talking, initially, about how to get into one. The secret is the bridge. Every Light City has a Bifrost, or Rainbow Bridge of 14 colors, leading like a drawbridge from its front gates down to an earthing point on the landscape. The Bifrosts that I have seen tend to be one mile long or less. The essential fact is that experientially they appear to be made of 14 streams of living fire.

Table 5
Selected Locations of the Celestial City of Amaravati
(also called the Ray Master's Light City or Crystal City)

1. Brown's Hill/Carter's Mountain, near Monticello, Charlottesville, Virginia

2. Cathedral Rocks, Sedona, Arizona

3. Hambledon Wood, near Burley-Oakham at Rutland Water, Rutland, England

4. Tetford, Lincolnshire, England

5. Ile-Ife, Nigeria

6. Hamdon Hill, near Montacute, Somerset, England

7. The Tor, Glastonbury, Somerset, England

8. Salfords, between Reigate and Horley, near London, England

9. Hill of Tara, near Dublin, Ireland

10. Mount Shasta, California

11. Nippur (*E-Kur*, Enlil's City, Sumer), Iraq

12. Panagitsa Hill, Euboea Mountain, Mycenae, Greece

13. Frank Ortiz Park, Santa Fe, New Mexico

14. D.A.R. State Forest, Goshen, Massachusetts

15. The Hague, Netherlands

16. Beacon Hill, Boston, Massachusetts

17. Mount Katahdin, Baxter State Park, Millinocket, Maine

18. Grand Place-Grote Markt, Old City Center, Brussels, Belgium

19. University of Washington campus, Seattle, Washington

20. Uluru, Ayer's Rock, near Alice Springs, Northern Territory, Australia

21. Heliopolis-An, near Cairo, Egypt

22. Mount Mouatahuhuura, Bora Bora, French Polynesia-Society Islands

23. Harney Peak, Black Hills, near Pine Ridge, South Dakota

Table 5
Selected Locations of the Celestial City of Amaravati
(also called the Ray Master's Light City or Crystal City) (Continued)

24. Mount Olympus, Greece
25. Tintagel, Cornwall, England
26. Palm Beach, Florida
27. Machu Picchu, Peru
28. Mount Parnassus, Delphi, Greece
29. Pyramid Lake, Paiute Reservation, near Reno, Nevada
30. Liddington Castle, The Ridgeway, Wiltshire, England
31. Crown of the U.S. egregor, the Eagle, Western Pennsylvania

Say you have identified the earthing point of a Bifrost. It may appear this way: you stand before 14 towering flames of different colors; from left to right, the color spectrum follows the electromagnetic field spectrum of visible light (refer to Table 1). From the far left and moving right, red and pink, then gold-orange and pale orange, rich yellow and pale yellow, emerald green and spring green, cobalt blue and sky blue-turquoise, then indigo and magenta-blue violet, and finally, purple and lilac. You may see these colors, or suspect them, or you may actively visualize them.

Select one color, whichever one draws your attention and interest, and, in vision, stand directly in front of this flaming column of color. Let's say you chose pink. See or visualize the pink flame before you, as perhaps 50-100 feet tall. Enter the flame and immerse yourself in it; now, construe yourself as moving along it as if on an escalator, or actively walking along it as if it is a palpable plank in Bifrost made of fire, yet one that does not burn you and allows your passage. Or concentrate your attention on the pink flame all around you and wait until something changes. What may happen next is you find yourself inside the City.

If you know your color—let's say it's bright rich yellow, Lao Tzu's Ray—visualize yourself standing amidst a towering, all-encompassing bright yellow flame. This is like sending a *Hello!* in the specific color to the Ray Master you wish to meet. Without effort or forcing it, allow your awareness to merge with or be permeated by the specific Ray flame until that becomes for a time your sole perceptual reality. You may find that this Ray visualization inducts you into that Master's wedge and awareness and opens the door for interactions.

By selecting a color that appeals to you (in the first example, pink) or knowing your actual Ray color (in the second example, yellow), you put yourself in resonance with the Master of that Ray. It's like ringing a specific doorbell. You may, or may not, perceive the Ray Master, or some identifying vestige of her presence; if so, this Ray Master may welcome you into her "wedge" of the Light City, which is a larger—*vast*—domain of her Ray. Possibly it may be the start of a long-term introduction and initiation experience for you under that Ray.

When your experience is finished, be sure to retrace all your steps and wakefully return to your physical body wherever you are sitting or standing. I recommend jumping up and down and stamping your feet a few times; this will help bring your awareness and presence back from the Light City and into your body.

4

PHYSICAL RETREATS

In brief: These are physical, deliberately created caves, usually in mountains, shaped into assembly halls, workshops, council chambers, archives, spiritual focus points, Light Ray broadcasters, and other functional features of the Great White Brotherhood; there are 212 on the Earth and human access to these, even in vision, is by GWB invitation only.

Inside the Hermetically Sealed Caves

In information passed on to his student, Godfre Ray King in 1932, Saint Germain explained that in the early days of the Earth the Ascended Masters prepared a series of Physical Retreats inside the Earth. Using specialized powers referred to as "the Flame," the Ascended Masters carved out interior spaces inside the planet, creating or expanding existing caves mostly inside mountains.

It was a kind of ultra-high technology mining operation whereby using advanced spiritual means, the Ascended Masters hollowed out huge subterranean headquarters for their use. They had elementals (Nature spirits, probably gnomes) collect and dispose of the rock debris generated by this mining, and later the Masters disintegrated the remaining material by use of this Flame. It was necessary that these Retreats be entirely secret and undiscoverable by humanity in the outer world because the "Great Light" the Masters wielded on behalf of the Earth needed to have "Indestructible Protection."[1]

For the most part, the identity and location of most of these Physical Retreats is still a well-kept secret. In his series of books from the 1930s, Saint Germain drops occasional references to selected Retreats. He refers, for example, to the Retreat in the Andes Mountains, presumably in Peru, which is the residence of "the golden-haired Masters from the Great Central Spiritual Sun."[2] Frequent mention is also made in King's books of the Royal Teton Retreat in the Grand Teton Mountains near Jackson Hole, Wyoming, as well as the one at Table Mountain, located somewhere in Wyoming in the Rocky Mountains; this one is Saint Germain's own retreat which he calls the Cave of Symbols.

King described his visits to both Retreats—to the Cave of Symbols both in his physical and Light body, and to the Royal Teton Retreat in his Light body only—in his two narratives, *The Magic Presence* (1935) and *Unveiled Mysteries* (1939). King noted that these Retreats contained a great many physical objects which were products of a highly advanced technology; archives of ancient, vanished, or forgotten civilizations; devices that facilitated the ascension process; and great meeting halls into which Ascended Masters from Earth, Venus, and the Great Central Sun would precipitate themselves as if forming their bodies out of the ethers at their own command. From our human viewpoint, it was as if by magic.

King makes a statement, describing the interior of the Council Chamber inside the Cave of Symbols, that could have come right out of the *Tales of the Elders of Ireland*. Recall its frequent mention of bright crystal chairs inside the *sidhe*-palaces. King reports a massive central table made entirely of jade and veined in gold, around which stood 60 chairs of solid gold upholstered in violet velvet. Into this

---

1.   Ascended Master Saint Germain, *Ascended Master Instruction*, Saint Germain Series, Vol. 4 (Schaumburg, IL: Saint Germain Press, 1986):125.

2.   Ascended Master Saint Germain, *Ascended Master Instruction*, Saint Germain Series, Vol. 4 (Schaumburg, IL: Saint Germain Press, 1986):161.

chamber came the Ascended Masters in their brilliant robes (the Irish mantles: auric effulgence). From the brilliant robes of one Master glittered what seemed to be a mass of jewels, but in actuality were "points of Dazzling Radiance" emitted from his body.[3]

King makes it clear that while these Retreats are physical in nature, their entrances are veiled from the public, hidden or phase-shifted from ordinary perception. Saint Germain told King the Ascended Masters had means of hermetically sealing off entrances to their caves for protection and making it impossible for humans to penetrate these Retreats unless invited. "In this way we are able to protect entrances to retreats, buildings, buried cities, mines and secret chambers," Saint Germain told him, adding that many of these had been "held in a state of perfect preservation for over seventy thousand years."[4]

Saint Germain refers unspecifically to a variety of former physical cities on the Earth (in the sense of megalithic citadels, such as what are now the ruins of Machu Picchu in Peru) that were removed from physical reality by being somehow hermetically sealed away inside the Earth. Several of these buried cities, for example, appear to be somewhere in the Amazon region, and King quotes Saint Germain as saying the city structures of Atlantis are still hermetically sealed (and hidden) in perfect condition at the bottom of the Atlantic Ocean.

King also describes a physical visit he made to a Physical Retreat in Saudi Arabia. This one once was on the ground, then it sunk and was deliberately buried and shielded. Almost unbelievably, King says during his visit there the desert floor opened up revealing a metal framed entrance; he travelled through a subterranean passageway for 20 minutes, then descended by elevator for 370 feet and entered a huge chamber with massive columns 300 hundred feet high. This was an ancient Retreat, King was told, "one of our [GWB] principal council chambers."[5]

---

3.   Godfre Ray King, *The Magic Presence* (Schaumburg, IL: Saint Germain Press: 1935): 196-7.
4.   Godfre Ray King, *Unveiled Mysteries* (Chicago, IL: Saint Germain Press, 1939): 114.

The location of the Physical Retreats is closely guarded information, and access to them appears to be entirely by invitation only. King's account gives the impression that one could bodily walk past the physical opening of the Cave of Symbols and never notice it, or if one suspected it there, could never open the door. It reminds us of the scene in *The Lord of the Rings* where the Fellowship of the Ring waits patiently before the Gates of Moria, barely outlined on the cliff-wall (only because the Moon just came out under the right conditions to illumine them) as Gandalf seeks to remember the password that will open the massive stone gates that only now the Fellowship can see at all. Those doors were doubly veiled and protected.

From my own research I can report that the Great White Brotherhood maintains a Physical Retreat inside Santa Fe Baldy, a peak (elevation 12,622 feet) at the southern end of the Sangre de Christo Mountains, about 25 miles northeast of Santa Fe, New Mexico, in the Santa Fe National Forest. I only know this because recently (2005) I was shown a few aspects of the Retreat, by grace, during a visionary (not physical) visit to the site.

Inside the mountain the Retreat is defined and contained by a massive golden citadel. The Retreat has many levels, like a large building at a university. Inside the vast golden domed interior space, in one area the floor opens (or retracts itself) and up rises a golden radar dish with a long spike antenna; my impression was that it is for sending and receiving data across this galaxy and the universe and possibly other universes.

Elsewhere on this floor are numerous file cabinets and tables around which human researchers work; they seemed to me to be an astronomy unit tabulating research data.[6] Also on this floor I find a room of a dozen engineers, both seated and standing, around a conference table covered in papers. Before them stands a model of the Earth's Light grid, perhaps four feet in diameter. Behind them is a

---

5.   Godfre Ray King, *The Magic Presence* (Schaumburg, IL: Saint Germain Press: 1935): 325-6.

blackboard, and a few engineers use this to calculate and display math results.

On the floor below this, another research group works with holographic projections of geometric solids, probably Light grid simulations. On the floor below this, another group of perhaps 15 sit around a worktable dominated by an inverted black cone, ribbed like the underside of a dark mushroom. They study the ridges and ribbing; the cone or mushroom is a scale model of an aspect of the Earth. Nearby is a massive library, stocked with bookshelves, archives, and galactic and star histories; numerous people sit in there intensively studying.

As mine was a visionary visit and not one in the body, as were King's, no doubt much of my imagery is somewhat filtered and approximate, or metaphorical. It is intriguing to note though that in 1994 a remote viewer reported that indeed there is an operation underneath Santa Fe Baldy, but in his interpretation, it is "a Martian base that serves as a center for their planetary operations."[7]

What the Retreats Do for the Earth

The fact that the Physical Retreats are sealed against human intrusion also signifies you are only likely to enter one by invitation, and probably only in a visionary sense if your clairvoyance is up to the task, though King showed us bodily visits can happen too. So the practical question is: what geomantic effect do these Retreats have on our physical Earth?

---

6.   These seemingly physical and even somewhat mundane physical descriptions are not presented as being ultimately accurate, only suggestive. To see a file cabinet in a visionary realm probably means some device for holding and organizing information is before one; to construe it as a file cabinet is convenient as long as we remember not to take it as literal truth, only as suggestive and metaphorical.

7.   Courtney Brown, Ph.D., *Cosmic Voyage. True Evidence of Extraterrestrials Visiting Earth.* (New York: Onxy/Penguin Books, 1997): 323.

For one, each Retreat is a center and focus of spiritual power wielded by the Ascended Masters for the benefit of Earth and humanity. The physical matter of the halls themselves has been impregnated over the centuries with the exalted Light emanations of the Ascended Masters constantly in their vicinity so that the cumulative spiritual charge itself has radiating effects on our physical environment. The mere presence of a Physical Retreat is a blessing on the local landscape. The U.S. has nine "Retreats of the Ascended Host," King reports, and from these "the Power of the Sacred Fire is constantly flowing forth" to consume a portion of psychic discord and the products of destructive activities emanated by Americans.[8]

This gives us a preliminary picture of what the Retreats do for the Earth. They emit Light and beneficial focussed higher consciousness from the GWB.

Here are some examples of other benefits they offer us: On July 1, 1932, according to Saint Germain (quoted by King), "Balls of Light" were sent from the Royal Teton Retreat to selected cities around the world, including New York, Chicago, Alexandria, Hong Kong, and Buenos Aires, as well as to the capital of every State in the U.S. These "Balls" were meant to raise awareness, provide subtle spiritual illumination, and support efforts (by persuasion, not force) by political leaders to act benignly on behalf of human welfare.

In August 1932, an outpouring of Light and a "Mighty Radiance" went out from seven Ascended Masters to "Seven Sun-Centers" in America, including ones in New York City, Chicago, Denver, and Seattle. This radiance included an intensification of the "Mighty Christ Presence." On July 4, 1933, 54 Ascended Masters focussed seven cosmic rays, again from the Royal Teton Retreat, out to numerous "Points of Focus" to be held and distributed for the "Blessing of America." More specifically, the intent was to "strengthen, to bless,

---

8.   The Ascended Masters, *The "I AM" Discourses on America*, Saint Germain Series Vol. 18, Lotus Ray King (Schaumburg, IL: Saint Germain Press, 2001): 279.

and to adjust that activity of mankind which is necessary to their quickening and further progress."[9]

On January 1, 1935, 214 Ascended Masters and 12 Masters from Venus focussed "Great Rays of Light" from the Royal Teton Retreat to Washington, D.C., the capital of each State, and to principal cities of every continent. The "Outpouring of Light" was meant as a blessing and purification of these areas.[10]

Preparing Human Helpers for Geomantic Events

More recently, in November 2004, Saint Germain invited myself and a colleague to have a visionary-body visit to his Cave of Symbols Retreat. We followed Saint Germain through a long dark tunnel which eventually opened into a huge chamber resembling an empty aircraft hangar. The two of us stood on a railing overlooking the floor of the "hangar" where Saint Germain addressed an assembly of perhaps 500 Ascended Masters and their adepts. The group itself was a dazzling presence, illuminating, almost blindingly, the hangar space.

We understood that Saint Germain had brought us into a council chamber within his Cave of Symbols Retreat. The Ascended Masters dispersed, as if the wall of the chamber opened up and they simply walked out of there to different spots across the United States. Each was equipped with a massive lilac flame, and they began to stand as sentinels with that flame at selected locations, the majority of which were west of the Rocky Mountains, and five were in New Mexico, including one very close by.

---

9.   Ascended Master Saint Germain, *Ascended Master Instruction*, Saint Germain Series Vol. 4 (Schaumburg, IL: Saint Germain Press, 1986): 5-6, 83-4, 276.

10.   Ascended Master Saint Germain, *Ascended Master Instruction*, Saint Germain Series Vol. 4 (Schaumburg, IL: Saint Germain Press, 1986): 46.

We briefly observed a few of the Ascended Masters fulfilling their task. One stood at the Plaza in Santa Fe, New Mexico's capital and once known by the Indians here as the Dancing Ground of the Sun. Now something would dance on the Plaza again: a lilac flame. The Ascended Master was perhaps 200 feet tall and stood in the midst of a towering lilac flame whose diameter spanned at least one mile, thereby including the State capital buildings in its radiance. Other locations of lilac flames we observed included Portland, Oregon; Abilene, Texas; and Las Cruces, Alamagordo, and Valle Grande (above Los Alamos), all in New Mexico.

The intent seemed to be to start through the lilac flame of Saint Germain a transmutation process within the United States in areas initially susceptible and open to this change to start burning off some of the dark grid infiltration of the Earth. We could picture this dark grid in energetic terms as pockets of black sludge, dark clouds, greyish smoky areas, of foci of intense atheism, materialism, and negativity, where the good (the Light) in humanity is suppressed, invalidated, or interfered with.

The dark grid is one term of many possible ones to indicate this alternate, secondary layer to the Earth's primary Light grid. The dark grid is a kind of cancerous growth, like a black octopus with 100,000 tentacles inserted like cords into different localities (typically places of political or religious power). It is the planetary embodiment of the Antichrist, the forces in opposition to human cognitive freedom, truth, Light, and the Christ—not so much a "person" but a global condition facilitated by a complex, still-growing, toxic-organic dark network.

The lilac flames established in these locations, and staffed by individual Ascended Masters (more likely holograms of themselves, for like Ray Masters and angels, they are granted multiple manifestations), will exert a steady persuasive pressure on mass consciousness; they will not abrogate human free will to resist the Light or the process, through the lilac flame, of reclaiming it. But they will help it.

To those who accept and welcome the lilac flames, reality will seem lighter, brighter, freer, a delight; for those who resist it, reality may seem more fraught with difficulty, obscuration, impedance, or constant undefined threat, and life will seem edgy, uncertain, uncomfortable. Our planetary reality will consist—to most of us, all of this is behind the scenes of physical consensus reality—of this insistent pressure of the truth and Light to burn off the many layers of lies, distortions, fabrications, sophistries, manipulations, and deceptions, the myriad skins of toxic untruths that blanket the planet and psyche, and especially the U.S., at this time.

In early February 2005, Saint Germain brought us again to this council chamber within his Cave of Symbols to brief us on an upcoming geomantic event. He showed perhaps 100 humans (present in spirit form) how he and his Ascended Master colleagues would implant massive lilac tubes at perhaps 100 locations around the world on February 20 of that year. The tubes would be perhaps a mile in diameter and exert a continuous radiational effect, as if emitting lilac waves in all directions. Each tube, he said, would be a "transmutation focus." My colleague and I were asked to participate (which we did) in the placement of one tube at Frijoles Canyon in Bandelier National Monument, near Los Alamos, New Mexico. This was part of a multiphase energization of this geomantically important site.

In March 2005, on a return visit we made to the Cave of Symbols, Saint Germain offered instruction on applications of the lilac flame. He was monitoring a large demonstration lilac flame, perhaps 50 feet high and wide. He tossed things into it that resembled black symbols, suggesting we do the same. What things? Negative states of mind, tense situations, anxiety, fretting, mental obsessions. Allow these to be represented by a sign, symbol, or glyph, he said, then toss them in the fire. One black symbol Saint Germain tossed in the flames burned white, indicating the flame had taken the emotional charge out of it and rendered it pure and neutral, just energy.

Saint Germain suggested I transmute an emotional state. I chose irritation. To me, this complex of anger and irritation looked like a twisted pretzel shape of molten red lead, heavy and hot. It sizzled and burned in the lilac flame, and the blackness within it started to come off as smoke. I saw pictures and scenes within this pretzel of irritation and assumed they were karmic complexes being released. Finally, only a white shape remained. Saint Germain said this white shape represents my now purified life force, freed from its binding with the negative emotionality, and it was now available for me to reclaim as a source of energy and inspiration.

Saint Germain indicated that this seemingly minute transmutation of a little bit of my personal emotional reality had already lightened the planet and freed others, even if infinitesimally, from the grim pull of their own emotional gravity. The tiniest gesture makes a difference. Lilac vibrates faster than the energies typically accreted in the first five chakras, the seats of the elementally-based emotional body of the human, thus it is not subject to their persuasive gravitational pull and can transmute their contents.

Next, he demonstrated how to use the lilac flame over a house. Over a typical home, clairvoyants may observe a great deal of astral pollution, dark smoke, grey splotches, inimical spirit beings and ill-minded astral creatures, and thought-forms. The lilac flame, set to burn completely around and through the house (or office) acts like an insect fryer for this level of lower astral trash. Eventually, inside the lilac flame, the home becomes a white, purified space, to some extent immune to outside though subtle environmental pollutants as well the effects of the extruded ones of the inhabitants of the home.[11] The

---

11.   The difference between immunity to some extent and total immunity is the degree to which the house residents keep producing more astral content. If the astral space around and in a house is cleaned up, but then the people living there continue with their lifestyles, both psychological-emotional and actual-physical, then soon the environment will resume its polluted condition. If people learn certain psychic tools that are a kind of sanitation and personal grooming approach to astral emissions, then the cleaned-up environment will stay relatively pure and thus one's house becomes mostly or totally immune to toxic energies.

lilac flame, Saint Germain suggested, acts as a kind of constant (astral) air purifier for the life inside and around the house.

At the level of the community, the lilac flame can have beneficial effects. Santa Fe, New Mexico, for example, is a community generally tolerant of alternate lifestyles and persuasions, and it is considered a friendly mecca for gays and lesbians. Recently, a gay male teenager was brutally assaulted by angry heterosexual teenagers; afterwards, a vigil was held for him at the Plaza. The vigil took place within the lilac flame and the Ascended Master maintaining it.

This means that all the people assembled, both for and against homosexuality, were participating in the political event while under the transmutative influence of the lilac flame. For those who on a soul level wished to drop a level of unconsciously held anti-gay "pictures" from their auric field, the lilac flame facilitated their release; for those who held punishment and judgement in their hearts, the lilac flame still had an illuminating effect on them, unconsciously, as it were, singeing the outer bristly "beard hairs" of their unflinching attitudes. Further, the Plaza's lilac flame and the transmutation process under-way as the inner aspect of the vigil radiated out across the city and surrounding New Mexico landscape, affecting a much larger area.

Next, Saint Germain showed us the use of the lilac flame between two geomantic sites, in this case, Frijoles Canyon (Bandelier National Monument, about 50 miles from Santa Fe, near Los Alamos), and Santa Fe Plaza. As mentioned, a massive lilac tube had been installed at Bandelier, and this tube acted like a washing machine in spin cycle, centrifugally dispersing the flame for miles. Its action was also like continuously thumping a big, bright, deeply sounding bell, and the energy currents of this thumping rippled down the "hill" of Bandelier (it's on the slopes of a massive caldera, a collapsed former volcano) towards Santa Fe. The Plaza's lilac flame also sent out light and sound waves in all directions, some of them meeting the incoming waves from Bandelier.

The result was the creation of a new kind of sacred space, a zone of transmutation running 50 miles straight overland from Santa Fe to

Bandelier. Everything inside this zone, Saint Germain said, would start to have the quality of feeling lighter, easier, more fluid—people, animals, the landscape, situations, the nature of reality. People would find it easier to start letting go of things, dropping problems, getting free of emotional weights and psychological obstacles because they would be living in this lilac flame transmutation zone, a sacralized landscape of grace.

Then Saint Germain gave us an example of using the lilac flame on a global level. He brought our attention to the earthquake fault zone in the South Asian area, the site of the December 2004 tsunami-earthquake. There burned a towering lilac flame along the fault line and rising many miles into space. It seared the etheric belt surrounding the Earth and the first few layers of the astral plane, creating another kind of sacralized transmutation zone. This was a vertical bridge connecting the physical through the etheric into the lower astral, and through this zone the dead of the disaster were able to rise out of their earthbound condition and ascend to their designated after-death spiritual place. The flame created a kind of runway for takeoffs for those killed in the event on their vertical ascent into the higher realms.

Even months after the event and, one presumes, after most, if not all, of the dead souls had made their departure from the Earth plane, the lilac flame bridge was still in place there, as a contribution to planetary health. From ground level (that is, if you were in a boat), you could look up into the flame and see numerous faces looking down at the Earth as if from a gallery (i.e., the lower astral plane). That means if you were to meditate in a boat in this zone, you could have a mystical experience and possibly visit the astral realms while getting a transmutation benefit as well. The area had become a kind of positive Bermuda Triangle.

In terms of the human relevance of the reality of the 212 Physical Retreats, one conclusion that seems supportable is that for some people working with the GWB, particular Retreats serve as briefing places for planned geomantic events. Even though most of humanity today has no interaction with these Retreats and is unaware of them, embedded as they are within the physical mass of the planet, surely it is reassuring to know the Earth hosts more than 200 Ascended Masters "hives" and that they are constantly working to expand the Light on humanity's behalf.

5

ETHERIC SANCTUARIES

In brief: *This is a series of about 192 Cities or Sanctuaries of Light situated above the Earth but in reference to specific geomantic features and serving as working, regional "offices" for the Ascended Masters, their adepts, and in some cases, a parallel human lifestream living in Golden Age-conditions prior to bodily incarnation.*

The Golden Etheric City and Other Sanctuaries

Ray Godfre King, accompanying Saint Germain on a physical visit to the Retreat in Saudi Arabia (a Physical Retreat), witnessed aspects of a meeting of about 200 Chiefs from the various GWB Councils distributed around the Earth. The clear impression one gets is that with the Ascended Masters, it is of no matter whether they meet in physical or Light bodies, or in the Physical Retreats or Etheric Sanctuaries, though it is certain these are two separate facilities with different quantities, functions, and locations.[1] No doubt what we construe as

---

1. Godfre Ray King, *The Magic Presence* (Schaumburg, IL: Saint Germain Press: 1935): 340.

huge differences between a physical and etheric retreat or a physical and Light body are far less to their fluidic state of being.

Confusing the picture for us a little more is the fact that some of the Etheric Sanctuaries were once physical but then removed to the etheric plane and rendered invisible somehow, often many thousands of years ago.[2] In some cases an Etheric Sanctuary is situated over a once thriving but now vanished physical city. A prime example is what Saint Germain refers to as the Golden Etheric City of Light now over what we know as the Sahara Desert in Africa; once, that area was a fertile, flourishing green region, he reports through King.

In *The Magic Presence*, Saint Germain explains that about 70,000 years ago a majestic city filled with spiritually advanced people was set in the then fertile, semi-tropical, and lushly green region we now know as the Sahara. Above the physical city, itself the capital of a vast empire, was the Golden Etheric City, "composed of Self-luminous etheric substance." Its inhabitants, the Ascended Masters, watched the progress of humanity and drew into the Light "all who will discipline and make themselves ready."[3] Eventually, the physical city was ruined and abandoned, but the Golden Etheric City remained, and still remains, above that site.

In 1932, Saint Germain referred to the Etheric Cities over the Earth's principal deserts, saying there was one over the Tucson, Arizona, area, the Gobi Desert in Mongolia, and somewhere in Brazil, possibly the Amazonian Mato Grosso region.[4] The Etheric City over the Gobi Desert undoubtedly is the same as Shambhala, the GWB's master Sanctuary for the Earth, operating in conjunction with another City identified over the Sun Temple ruins of the islands of

---

2. "The retreats, once physical on the lost continents of Lemuria and Atlantis, were withdrawn to the etheric plane, reachable only by the most advanced initiates." Mark L. Prophet and Elizabeth Clare Prophet, *The Masters and Their Retreats*, Edited by Annice Booth (Corwin Springs, MT: Summit University Press, 2003): 410.

3. Godfre Ray King, *Unveiled Mysteries* (Chicago, IL: Saint Germain Press, 1939): 59-60.

Lake Titicaca in Bolivia. "These are the two most intense points of Light in the earth," and the Light is that of "Natural Rays" of "Cosmic Fire" focussed onto the planet from above.[5]

In communications to King in the 1930s, Saint Germain frequently referred to the Golden City and indicated its continued use and vitality. The City is located within the "Etheric Belt" surrounding the Earth, an impenetrable band stronger than steel, Saint Germain commented.[6] This City projects "Searchlights or Rays" down to selected locations on the Earth, including America. Its Rays are sent in all directions like wheel-spokes offered in service of humanity. From New Year's Day and continuing for three weeks (in 1932) there was "great rejoicing in the Golden City" as during that time it transmitted "Light and Sound Rays" to the Earth. Saint Germain also said that those in the Golden City, at least that year, were sending forth their "Glorious Radiation" to their human students.[7]

---

4.   This is a massive region of Amazonian rain forest in Brazil and reputedly the location of a mysterious lost civilization and city called Z. Finding it was the focus of Colonel Percy Harrison Fawcett, a British explorer, who disappeared in the attempt in 1925 and was never heard from again. His targeted location for the vanished ancient city was the southern Amazon basin, between the Tapajos and Xingu river tributaries. The European, and especially British, search for vanished cultures and their ruins dovetailed with the earlier Spanish obsession with *el indio dorado*, or Eldorado, the golden-skinned Indian who lived in a fabulous city of gold. It is possible the fables of abundant physical gold might have been a materialization, and thus misinterpretation, of the subtle actuality of Etheric Sanctuaries like the Golden City. Recent archeological expeditions in the Xingu region of the Amazon have uncovered evidence of numerous man-made earthen mounds, pre-Columbian settlements laid out in complicated, geometric patterns, and signs of a massive man-made landscape that could have sustained millions of people. All of this suggests that perhaps "Z" was an actual ancient and once physical city, flourishing as the one Saint Germain indicated in the Sahara Desert and with perhaps an Etheric Sanctuary or some sort of GWB facility above it. See: David Grann, "The Lost City of Z," *The New Yorker*, September 19, 2005: 56-81.

Where the Etheric Sanctuaries Are Situated

From our physical world perspective, it is a little difficult to pin down the actual location of individual Etheric Sanctuaries and Etheric Cities. Generally, the Etheric Cities are positioned *above* a landscape feature while the Sanctuaries are set "on" the landscape but in a different dimension. For example, there is an Etheric City *over* Glastonbury Tor in Somerset, England. It appears to be made entirely of gold, square and squat (one level), and perhaps one mile wide and long. If you stand on the top of the Tor and *look up* you can clairvoyantly see the massive front gates.

About three miles into Frijoles Canyon (from the Visitors' Center) at Bandelier National Monument in Los Alamos, New Mexico, sits an Etheric Sanctuary. It seems to be on the ground. The Native

---

5. Ascended Master Saint Germain, *The "I AM" Discourses*, Saint Germain Series Vol. 3 (Schaumburg, IL: Saint Germain Press, 1935): 46, 204.

6. Presumably, the "Etheric Belt" is a subtle region of the Earth's atmosphere, perhaps contiguous with the upper levels of it. It's easier to get an impression of its function than its exact location in our physical space coordinates. The Austrian clairvoyant and founder of Anthroposophy, Rudolf Steiner, characterized the human etheric body along these lines, and we may reasonably extrapolate these qualities to describe the Earth's etheric body, or "Etheric Belt:" The ether (sometimes called the fifth state of matter) is mobile, fluid, and filled with wisdom and life; it is the bearer and seat of our intellect and filled with flowing, weaving, living thoughts and memories; thinking is its inner activity (like Pierre Teilhard de Chardin's *Noosphere* perhaps). It contains living, formative forces, the finer substances of Man's beings, and spiritual elements from the Sun; the etheric body is rhythmic, cyclic, harmonious, moving in time, like music, and in fact, emitting sounds like music, a kind of humming and singing, perhaps fragments of the Music of the Spheres; and it is filled with warmth, light, and a phopshorescent glow. The etheric body contains the forces of life and vitality and even the body's original blueprint necessary to effect deep healing. This gives us some idea of the "Etheric Belt" and what conditions might be like "up there" for the Etheric Sanctuaries.

Americans once referred to this as the "White Tipi of the Chiefs," understandably as the tipi, and not, say, the Greek Parthenon, would be a familiar architectural form to use to visualize an otherworldly structure. To me, it appeared as a golden square edifice perhaps one-half mile wide with big front gates; inside, there were numerous chambers and council rooms, and a huge central multi-tiered meeting space, like a 19th century European opera house.

To some extent, the differing nomenclature can cause confusion. The Etheric City over the Gobi Desert, which is Shambhala, is in fact the Earth expression of one of the eight Celestial Cities on the slopes of Mount Meru, and it appears to be on the ground under a huge dome. According to the Vedas, this one, in the direction of cosmic West, is called Sudhavati and is ruled by Lord Varuna; in metaphysical lore, Shambhala's ruler is called Sanat Kumara, the Eternal Virgin-Youth and chief of the Lords of the Flame (the GWB), present there for the last 6.5 or 18.5 million years (the estimates vary).

There is but one Shambhala on Earth (it's in Mongolia, in the Gobi Desert, but phase-shifted out of physical visibility), but there are 1,080 different access *portals to it* from various geomantic locations around the Earth with several in Glastonbury, England (see Table 6).

---

7.   Ascended Master Saint Germain, *The "I AM" Discourses*, Saint Germain Series Vol. 3 (Schaumburg, IL: Saint Germain Press, 1935): 26, 35, 192, 216, 322.

Table 6
Selected Shambhala Doorways, Planetary Total: 1,080

1. Church of St. Andrew (churchyard), Aller, Somerset, England

2. Avenue of Cedars, Glastonbury, Somerset, England

3. Hummellfjell Mountain, Os, near Roros, Norway

4. Iao State Park, Maui, Hawaii

5. Guadalupe Peak, Guadalupe Mountains National Park, Texas

6. Chalice Well, Glastonbury, Somerset, England

7. Merlin's Mound, Marlborough, Wiltshire, England

8. Blackhill Spring, Tetford, Lincolnshire, England

9. The Cadmeia, Thebes, Greece

10, Merlin's Cave, Tintagel, Cornwall, England

11. Bardsey Island, Wales

12. Merlin's Hill (Bryn Myrddin), Carmarthen, Wales

13. Mount Kailash, Tibet

14. South Cadbury Castle, Somerset, England

Shambhala certainly gives the impression of a city: it occupies a large area, has many buildings, libraries, council chambers, fountains, parks, and divisions, as well as a host of spiritual beings. Some refer to Shambhala, said to be an oasis in the Gobi Desert, as the Sacred Island, based on the Akashic Records memory that long ago it actually was an island in the Central Asian Sea that filled this area. Theosophical tradition says that around 45,000 B.C., the great "City of the Bridge" was built around the shores of the Gobi Sea, the bridge linked it with the sacred White Island (Shambhala) in the Sea's middle.[8] As with the Sahara, which was once lush and semi-tropical, the implication here is that once the Gobi Desert was otherwise, featuring a fertile island amidst a big sea with a physical settlement topped by an etheric one.

As an Etheric City, Shambhala seems to be *on* the ground but removed from the physical dimension; the one at Glastonbury is *above* the Tor; the one at Bandelier is *on* the ground; and the ones at the Sahara Desert and Lake Titicaca are both *above* the physical landscapes. Experientially, and in terms of psychic access by humans, the location above or on the ground does not matter. It is also clear that some of the Etheric Cities are in fact Etheric Sanctuaries, the difference being size and function. The City over Lake Titicaca, for example, to clairvoyant viewing appears structurally similar to those over Glastonbury Tor and at Bandelier.

The function of these Etheric Sanctuaries or Cities was to tutor, guide, catalyze, and oversee the development of civilizations seeking to incarnate the Light. As Saint Germain explained to King, the Golden Etheric City of Light over the physical city in the Sahara was present as a constant benefactor. Human citizens regularly interacted with the "gods" in the Golden City above, and the physical city's leaders took direction and counsel from these gods. The two realms were congruent.

---

8.   Annie Besant and C.W. Leadbeater, *Man: Whence, How and Whither* (Adyar, India: Theosophical Publishing House, 1913): 102-3.

We might picture such a City or Sanctuary as a Light template subtly structuring the etheric field over a human settlement to make it easier for those embodied humans to follow, even copy, the divine way, based on truth (*rta*). Remember that one of the prime functions of the Seven Rishis was to uphold the cosmic laws (*rta*) and to teach them to humans. The contiguity of a GWB City and a spiritually thriving and evolving human city would be ideal to further this.

Classical Vedic Descriptions of Sanctuaries

The ancient Indian texts, such as the *Mahabharata* and the *Ramayana,* give us occasional pictures of this celestial ideal. The *Ramayana* refers to "all the Celestial Beings, in their aerial chariots as large as cities" parked in the sky to observe the original descent of the celestial Ganges River to the Earth. So many celestial beings irradiated the cloudless sky "it seemed a thousand suns had risen there."[9] This picture suggests two things: some of the Etheric Sanctuaries could be "aerial chariots" of celestial beings; and these cities, if "parked," possibly can be moved elsewhere.

One of the magnificent and opulent cities referred to in the *Mahabharata* was Hastinapura, today believed to have been near New Delhi. It was founded by Hasti II, the son of Bharata, the founder and namer of India—a country originally known as *Maha Bharata,* Great Bharata, the land energized and awakened by Bharata. It was the central and capital city of the Kurus (or Kauravas: the 100 sons of King Dhritarashtra), one of two striving dynasties (the other was the Pandavas, born of five gods) whose exploits, battles, and epiphanies are the epic's subject matter.

Krishna, an incarnation of Vishnu (the Hindu equivalent of the Christ), had a palace built for him by Visvakarma (the cosmic architect of Hindu myth: he built palaces and chariots for many gods).

9.   *The Ramayama of Valmiki.* Vol. 1, Translated by Hari Prasad Shastri (London: Shanti Sadan, 1953): 90.

Called Dwaraka (also: Dvaraka or Kusasthali), originally it was built to shelter the Yadava clan and was situated on an island in the ocean; but this island submerged after Krishna "died," that is, left the human field of action for a time. Dwaraka is believed to have been located at the northwestern tip of the Saurashtra peninsula, near the Arabian Sea, the same place as a physical city still visited by many pilgrims.

The use of the term "submerged" here most likely refers to a period of time in which the Etheric City went into quiescence in terms of human interfacing. The "ocean" it submerged into could be construed as the etheric plane; since this city was already in the etheric plane, it simply receded further into it and became inaccessible.

Krishna's city is mentioned often in the *Mahabharata*: Arjuna saw the "splendid fortress city from a distance, shining like the sun on the horizon." Dwaraka ("Many-Gated") could be reached only by crossing a heavily guarded bridge. This bridge was huge and golden and spanned the ocean that lay between it and the land. The city was encrusted with precious jewels, and arranged symmetrically around the city center were 16,000 white palaces, one for each of Krishna's queens. The central royal palace towered like a white mountain above all the other structures.

The city was girded by a massive fortified wall whose perimeter was 100 miles long, and gods were frequently seen inside Dwaraka "celebrating a never-ending festival." It is the "sacred and eternal city, which abounds in opulence and is always crowded with rishis." Dwaraka's opulence included beautiful lakes with swans and red and blue lotuses, golden archways encrusted with jewels, and numerous white mansions lining the roads along which there would be magnificent processions of elephants, chariots, and worshipping brahmins.[10] The city has flowery parks and pleasure groves, the air is redolent with the sound of swans and cranes paddling serenely in lakes blooming with white and blue lotuses. Krishna's city boasts 900,000 mansions made of silver and adorned with gold, emeralds, and other jewels; his own

---

10. Krishna Dharma, *Mahabharata* (Los Angeles: Torchlight Publishing,1999): 137, 139, 237, 877.

private inner city has 16,000 palaces, one for each of his *gopi* wives. This city was gem-studded and fabulously opulent.

Krishna commisioned Visvakarma to build Dwaraka as his special citadel following his victorious defeat of the son of Jara, the Demoness. Dwaraka, difficult to access, would contain all manner of wonderful things: crystal gateways, gold domes, gold houses with jewelled roofs and emerald floors, swift milk-white horses; it would also feature Indra's famous assembly hall called Sudharma presented to Krishna as a gift, along with many celestial trees, including the Parijata (one of five species of heavenly trees). A mortal meditating under such a tree "does not remain tied down to the characteristics of mortals (viz., hunger and thirst, old age and death, grief and infatuation)."[11] In other words, he would be likely to achieve enlightenment.

Clearly, even with the often-noted Indian penchant for exaggeration, the place described was never a physical city but an opulent Etheric Sanctuary.

The Indian texts mention a third city. This is Indraprastha, built by Visvakarma at Krishna's request for the Pandavas. Visvakarma constructed numerous white palaces and mansions, massive dark gates to protect the city, pleasure temples and innumerable temples to Vishnu and other celestial beings, and schools for teaching Vedic sciences to the brahmins. Indraprastha is considered the forerunner (or original site occupant) to the modern-day city of New Delhi.

Although Indraprastha and Hastinapura are often described separately, sometimes they appear to be the same place at or near today's New Delhi. However, in the *Mahabharata* they were distinguished as being the *two* great capitals of the Earth, one for the Pandavas, the other for their cousins, the Kauravas, both of whom vied for control of the kingdom of Bharata. Contemporary scholars now say Indraprastha was situated about 60 miles southwest of Hastinapura and that

---

11. *Srimad Bhagavata Mahapurana, Part II*, Translated by C.L. Goswami M.A. (Gorakhpur, India: Gobind Bhavan-Karyalaya Gita Press, 1971): 323.

both were situated in the valley between the Yamuna and Ganges Rivers in northeastern India.

In accordance with this interpretation, then, Hastinapura was known as the City of Elephants (literally Elephant [*hastin*] City [*pura*]). Archeologists today locate the ruins of Hastinapura near an old bed of the Ganges, about 57 miles northeast of Delhi in Uttar Pradesh. However, the Elephant City etymology seems a clue to the otherworldly nature of this settlement and a likely reference to Airavata and the other white guardian celestial elephants associated with the *Lokapalas*, especially Indra, thus giving away the show that this was a divine and celestial, but not physical, city. When you have a mention of Airvata, Ganesh (another elephant form), or white guardian elephants, this is a clue the Ofanim (who use elephants as godforms) are involved and thus the location is certainly not physical by any standards today.

Krishna is also associated with Mathura, a town in Uttar Pradesh, India. The *Srimad Bhagavata Purana* establishes Mathura on the banks of the Yamuna River as Krishna's birthplace, yet its description of the place suggests it's more of a celestial city. The entrances are lofty, the gateways made of crystal, and the wide arches and doors of gold, the *Purana* says. Pleasant parks, gardens, and moats abound, and the crossroads are paved in gold. Mathura reverberates with the sounds of peacocks and pigeons, and the inlaid lattice-work of the balconies and turrets are studded with diverse gems. The town itself was strewn with flower garlands, the roads sprinkled with water.[12]

Etheric Sanctuaries as Divine Abodes

Vedic lore speaks of India's four *Dhamas*: these are divine abodes that embody power and spirituality. Krishna's Dwaraka in Gujerat, is one; the others are at Badrinath, Rameswaram, and Puri. Each of the four

---

12. *Krishna: The Beautiful Legend of God, Srimad Bhagavata Purana, Book X,* Translated by Edwin F. Bryant (New York: Penguin Books, 2003): 171.

is strongly associated with celestial beings and sages, and although these *Dhamas* have physical grounding points (extant human cities or known locales), we are observing evidence from a different angle of more Etheric Sanctuaries, situated subtly at or above these locations.

The Vedic description of *Dhamas* gives us insight into the placement and function of the Etheric Sanctuaries. "*Dham* refers to one of the four abodes of sanctity in the cardinal directions for the Indus of the entire subcontinent." Visiting the four *Dhamas* is part of the "merit pattern of religious circulation" and pilgrimage first set forth in the *Mahabharata,* still observed in India today.[13]

Picture an Etheric City, such as Hastinapura or Dwaraka, positioned above a human settlement. Its vibration, energy essence, and the way its Light frequencies cymatically structure space would be like a constant golden shower over the physical city, enriching it with benevolent, higher consciousness. The four Etheric Cities (*Dhamas*) over India occupying the four cardinal directions were situated there as part of a long-term plan for the evolution of the Indian soul in the context of its sacred geography; all of this was awakened, overseen, and mentored by Bharata, that country's spiritual founder and mentor.

Once, human access to these Cities was far more regular, and from our viewpoint today, easier. In the milieu dramatized by the Hindu epics—vastly long ago, the almost unimaginable epoch remembered in myth as the *Satya Yuga* (Time of Truth) or Golden Age—humans came and went so fluidly from Hastinapura, Dwaraka, Indraprastha, and other Etheric Sanctuaries as to make it seem to us today that these Cities surely were physical. The *differences* between physical and etheric spaces were not so pronounced, even radical, then as today; and perhaps the two realms so interpenetrated each other that their boundaries were blurred. We must also factor in that the human body

---

13. Surinder Mohan Bhardwaj, *Hindu Places of Pilgrimage. A Study in Cultural Geography* (Berkeley, California: University of California Press, 1973): 169-70.

and its cognitive-psychic apparatus might have been more Light-filled than ours today, making subtle perception very easy.

Implicit in this observation is another one: the interpenetration of the heavenly model and the Earthly copy or hologram in the visionary geography was seemless *back then*. Today, in most landscapes around the world, we look out upon the land and see little, if anything, to suggest the overlay of a visionary geography. Or if we see something megalithic—a stone circle, standing stone, barrow, tumulus, pagoda, shrine, temple, or pyramid—we see either the monument to a foreign or antique religious view of the world, whose ontological parameters we can barely suspect, or we see an opaque mystery or anomaly from the deep, uncommunicating past. This is a painful degree of entropy and amnesia. Yet *back then*, in the time of the great myths, the overlay of archetype and localized expression was more vivid, palpable, *evident*.[14]

The Vedas tell us these Cities were spiritual enclaves, immense structures made entirely of gold, that is, of Light in its highest, purest expression, and opulent in every sense and detail as they were pre-eminently rich in the Spirit. That's what all the "gold" should signify to us today, that and the abundance of the various classes of higher beings portrayed—rishis, siddhas, gopis, Gandharvas, Apsaras, and the rest.

In fact, we can trust the accuracy of the lush depictions of these beings in Hindu art and iconography, especially when it comes to

---

14. It is potentially still more complex, for in some cases, what is described actually refers to locations exclusively in the spiritual world. The Ofanim, for example, state that the world and events described in the *Mahabharata* were not terrestrial, but of the spiritual realm. "We dictated the *Mahabharata* [to the sage Vyasa]. It means he got out of the way and we gave it [the text's 88,000 verses] to him to explain the workings of the inner worlds reflective of the world and consciousness at that time when it was written. It is reflective of our view of what has happened in the Earth." The text is usually credited to Ganesh, the elephant god, who dictated it to Vyasa; Ganesh is one of the Ofanim's guises in Hindu culture.

their extravagant head-pieces, crowns, and appurtenances, for even a brief clairvoyant glimpse today inside one of these Sanctuaries reveals essentially the same picture. It is a visual smorgasbord of a staggering and delicious range of spiritually advanced beings.

According to visions reported by Elizabeth Clare Prophet, human lifestreams waiting to embody on the Earth live in some of these Etheric Cities. They study in great "Universities of the Spirit" where they learn the higher arcs of music, government, art, healing, and more. This is consistent with the *Mahabharata* and other Hindu texts which describe throngs of adulatory humans welcoming the return of Lord Krishna to Dwaraka; Dwaraka is clearly a divine Etheric City, yet the presence of so many humans (admittedly in a spiritually advanced condition) is otherwise puzzling, until we factor in Prophet's view to the interpretation.

"These waiting souls live and work and serve in situations not unlike those they have left on the planet," Prophet says. "The etheric cities show us what the previous golden ages on earth looked like and how the world can be again in a future golden age." These "great cities of light in the etheric" keep the pattern for what the physical world is intended to be in the next Golden Age.[15]

Once while walking on a small hill behind the Tor in Glastonbury, England, in a part of town known locally as Paradise, I suddenly came upon a transparent sphere, like a soap bubble right against my nose but the size of a baseball stadium turned vertical. Inside were people walking about, hordes of them, happy, Light-filled, self-realized, very different than the mass of humanity today as seen in a typical crowd. It was as if I were looking through a membrane into an alternate or parallel human reality. Possibly, I had a brief glimpse of the "waiting souls" inside a chamber in that great city of light above the Tor.

---

15.   Mark L. Prophet and Elizabeth Clare Prophet, *The Masters and Their Retreats*, Edited by Annice Booth (Corwin Springs, MT: Summit University Press, 2003): 398-99.

What the Sanctuaries Do

The Etheric Sanctuaries are tutors to Earth civilizations. The one over Lake Titicaca in part oversaw the birth and elaboration of the Incan civilization and its foundational omphalos nearby at Cusco, in Peru, as well as the far earlier formative events for civilization at Tiahuanaco also nearby on the Bolivian border. The Etheric City over the now vanished Atlantean continent functioned similarly, and it is still present, hovering like a beacon from the past above the Atlantic Ocean.

The Etheric Sanctuary at Frijoles Canyon appears newly primed for involvement in human affairs in our time, while the one over Glastonbury Tor may have greater relevance in the future when that sacred town, long ago called *Domus Dei* ("God's Home"), embodies the prophecy of being the New Jerusalem.

For the most part, the Etheric Sanctuaries appear similar in their architecture, having been designed and constructed by Visvakarma long ago. They may vary in size and complexity (they may not all have 16,000 white palaces like Dwaraka), but their essential nature seems consistent. Whether they are perceived as being on the ground or above a physical landscape feature is not too important: both perceptions are accurate and illusory. It is probably more precise to say the Etheric Sanctuary is *within* a given landscape.

A view of the planetary array of the Etheric Sanctuaries, as seen clairvoyantly, shows them to be above the Earth hovering like stationary Motherships as often portrayed in science fiction movies. Curiously, the first time I saw an Etheric Sanctuary (mentioned above: the one over Glastonbury Tor) in 1984, it created this impression as I looked up at it. I wrote of it then: "I see a tremendous grey outline occasionally flushing golden and sparkling. It is radically huge, like a dodecahedral spaceship hovering silently, like fabulous architecture from another world about to land with twelvefold intention; like a mile-wide apparition laying the whole of Glastonbury under its divine shadow...."[16]

In my recent viewing of their array, the spaceship-like Etheric Sanctuaries appear set within a series of 120 interlocking equilateral triangles of light at whose three tips is another GWB feature called Temples of Light or Color Temples (see below). In communications with Saint Germain, I had the impression there are 120 stationary Etheric Sanctuaries set in the center of the 120 triangles but another 72 moveable ones located at the GWB's discretion. The smaller Sanctuaries can be likened to "scout ships" sent out from the great Mothership (the major Etheric Sanctuary) to settle in smaller, more specific areas overshadowed by the Mothership. These may be relocated as needed, although from a human perspective, such relocations happen only rarely and only over great periods of time; and memories of such relocations could be the basis of the tale of Krishna's Sanctuary being submerged.

The 120 Etheric Sanctuaries can raise or lower themselves with respect to the Earth's surface as appropriate, consistent, at least metaphorically, with the Vedic description of the gods' massive aerial chariots the size of cities. These Sanctuaries can be "lowered" to be closer to or even on the ground, most typically during times of high activation and human-GWB interfacing in that area. While stationary high above the Earth, these Sanctuaries can illuminate an entire area, like turning on massive, brilliant floodlights for a few seconds. They can also release a shower of golden rain as a kind of celestial fertilization to the Earth. India's ancient tales often tell of the gods, observing events on Earth, responding favorably with a shower of rose petals or flowers or sometimes the sound of kettledrums and conches.[17]

How to Interact with an Etheric Sanctuary

Bear in mind that the GWB Etheric Sanctuaries are specialized "field offices" of the Ascended Masters. While in general they welcome human interaction, at times they might not wish visitors at their

---

16.   Richard Leviton, *Looking for Arthur. A Once and Future Travelogue* (Barrytown, NY; Station Hill Openings/Barrytown, Ltd., 1997): 340.

Sanctuaries. In other words, human access to a Sanctuary is at their discretion.

As to the technique of reaching an Etheric Sanctuary, we can take a clue from the marvellous vision from 1872 that Black Elk reported. He was nine years old and was summoned to visit the Six Grandfathers in the spirit world. He said that two men came down to him from the clouds, "headfirst like arrows slanting down;" each carried a spear that emitted jagged lightning. They told him the Six Grandfathers (GWB members) were waiting for him and he should follow them. Black Elk started to follow the men with the flaming spears when a little cloud came down very fast, scooped him up, and took him to the middle of "a great white plain with snowy hills and mountains" high above the Earth.[18]

Here's how we can adapt Black Elk's "method:" When you are in the proximity of a known Etheric Sanctuary, stand and surround yourself with a towering lilac flame on all sides, rising up from inside the Earth and and to a point high above you. State your intention to visit the Sanctuary and ask that, if it is appropriate, one or two GWB representatives come "down" to meet and escort you into the site. How you perceive their means of conveyance is variable and up to you.

---

17. In one mystical account, a spiritual adept named Dhruva Maharaja was traveling through the solar system in his visionary body and saw "all the demigods in their airplanes showering flowers upon him like rain." In the Vedas, you find frequent mention that "the Devas [gods] will shower down flowers on great personalities, especially at the time of great victories or other glorious events." Richard L. Thompson, *Alien Identities. Ancient Insights into Modern UFO Phenomena* (San Diego: Govardhan Hill Publishing, 1993): 287.

18. Nicholas Black Elk, *Black Elk Speaks*, Edited by John G. Neihardt (Lincoln, NE: University of Nebraska Press, 2000): 17-18.

Shambhala as the Premier Etheric Sanctuary

Let's come back to Shambhala with all this in mind. As the GWB's premier Etheric Sanctuary or City, Shambhala is well-known in metaphysical circles, and even something of its numinous reputation has permeated exoteric culture. James Hilton's 1933 classic *Lost Horizon* about a paradaisal Shangri-La of wise, blissful immortals nestled in a secret mountain valley somewhere in the Himalayas certainly enhanced or possibly seeded Shambhala's legend in Western culture.

Shambhala was recognized in Russian and Tibetan Bön (pre-Buddhist) traditions, and has had names such as Belovodya ("White Waters"), Imperishable Sacred Land, the Indestructible *Vajra* Continent, the Land of the Turquoise-Winged Cuckoos, Olmolungring, Sacred Island, Treasure Continent, Shraddhavati, Sudavati, Sukavati, and the White Island, among others.

The name Shambhala comes from the Sanskrit and means "the Source of Happiness." It is generally equated with Sukavati (also Sanskrit: "the Blissful"); it is called one of the most important of "Buddha-fields" (a realm dominated by Buddhas, or Awakened Ones). The place is said to be flooded in radiance, filled with exquisite fragrances, wondrous flowers, and trees of jewels; the sound of rushing water is music; and all souls here cleave to the Truth (Dharma, *rta*) until they reach nirvana.

The Ray Masters' Light City and the assembly of the Great White Brotherhood are considered an aspect of Shambhala. As suggested above, Theosophical tradition holds that Shambhala was founded on Earth long ago when representatives from the spiritual worlds and planets at a higher level of development (notably Venus) established their base here. The Ofanim note that they have several representatives at Shambhala "working on particular development projects."

The Ofanim note that to reach Shambhala, you must be able to pass through the abyss or chasm that looms between the relative truth and Truth, and that Shambhala as a zone of consciousness exists in between this abyssal doorway and the source of the Absolute Light (the Supreme Being). This doorway (in Qabala, it's called Daath, a secret, extra Sefira [a sphere or vessel of Light] on the Tree of Life) "is the connection to *Ain-Sof* [the Absolute Light] and is the highest point that human consciousness can appreciate." Shambhala "exists on another plane. It is present, has been, and will be, and is not influenced by Earth activity though symbiotically it is related to Earth with a degree of intercommunication when and where necessary."

As mentioned, the Earth is equipped with 1,080 portals to Shambhala. Glastonbury and environs in England at the present time offer the easiest and most available access to Shambhala through a doorway; at least four portals may be accessed in and around Glastonbury. One is a little up the road past Chalice Well, a lovely, angelically-infused public garden in the center of town. This doorway appears as a pillar existing between the fourth and fifth dimension; you walk through the pillar, pass through an etheric tunnel, and arrive at Shambhala. Another entrance is at the yard of the Church of St. Andrew in the village of Aller, near Glastonbury.

The basis for the location of the Shambhala Doorways is precise, based on the array of dome caps from a dome and the implicit spirallic pattern linking them. Where two dome caps (a dome can generate up to 48 smaller versions of itself called dome caps) intersect, forming a vesica piscis or almond-shaped overlap, there is the doorway. That point of intersection, in turn, is determined by the mathematics of the Golden Mean, or phi, involved in the unfolding of the spiral pattern linking the dome caps.

Since Shambhala is the premier Etheric Sanctuary, it may take a little perseverance to pass through the portal. If you are consciously working with a Ray Master, you may be given an initial visit by grace and from this gain an understanding of how to make it there on your own. Once you have mastered the protocols of entry, usually it is easy to make return visits. Of all the Etheric Cities, it is probably best first to try to visit this one since, as a Celestial City with numerous doorways, it was set up for human visits.

The other Etheric Sanctuaries are generally visitable, but due to their specific locations around the Earth and their prior involvement with Light centers and high civilization nodes, their focus is somewhat specialized. Shambhala, global in nature and responsibility, is thus more generically suitable for open-ended, "fact-finding" human visits.

Why go to Shambhala? In my experience, it was my first introduction to the residences of the Ascended Masters and where I first became aware of my initiation involvement with two Ray Masters and one Ascended Master. Each of them presented me with teachings and symbols of which no doubt at that time I perceived only a little. They acquainted me with my "Book of Life and Karma," a holographic record of all "my" past lives, each page like a full-length movie. I also received auric field and being-body purification in Light showers, rainbow fountains, and baths.

It is important to remember that for about 99% of embodied humanity, one cannot access Shambhala physically. It exists in another dimension, not as remote from our realm as Mount Meru, yet still accessible only by clairvoyant means and travel in one's Light body. The vibrational gradient you have to surmount bodily is too arduous for almost all of us. Strenuous overland treks through Tibet and Mongolia in search of Shambhala are likely fruitless; yet paradoxically, it is fairly easy to get there psychically. After all, it is one of the eight Celestial Cities templated in the Earth's visionary geography for the benefit and edification of humans interested in visiting it.

How to Get to Shambhala

To get to Shambhala on a visionary level, you need a sword, which is an expression of focussed psychic insight (expressed through the sixth chakra at the brow) and a poised mind. When your insight is sufficiently refined and you can see the pattern behind the apparent (as in the Sword in the Stone process), then the sword of insight can open the doorway. The Shambhallic portal exists between the fourth and fifth dimension; it may resemble a pillar which you enter then you move through a structure like a broad pipe used for channeling and transportation. You may encounter a few challenges of your *bona fides* along the way, possibly including a lion guardian at the entrance. With the sword you pass through the lion's brow chakra to move forward into the Celestial City. When I first went to Shambhala in vision, I arrived at the edge of a precipice overlooking a vast plain with a massive dome sparkling in its center. That dome encases, energizes, and protects Shambhala, and you'll have to enter it to interact with this sublime Etheric Sanctuary.[19]

On another visionary expedition there, I arrived in a Light fountain arising out of a huge reflecting pool whose water seemed silvery-light blue, spuming columns of different colors. It was ringed by flowering fruit trees, notably ones bearing golden apples; beyond this pool was a corona of majestic white-marbled temples, though one was markedly golden and to me bore a resemblance to the Lincoln Memorial in Washington, D.C. I entered one building: it appeared to be a library filled with people. Another building, possibly part of the seat of government, featured a massive golden throne set atop six vividly sculpted, almost real, lion's heads.

On a subsequent outing, I discovered a potentially easier way to get there. I say potentially because it requires a certain dexterity in Light visualization based on having gone through an angelically-taught, 10-step sequence called the Christed Initiation in the Buddha Body. In one of the steps you reconfigure your energy field as an octahedron of glass (an eight-sided shape, made of two four-sided pyramids stacked base to base, their points in opposite directions). Then you surround this shape with the 14 flames of the Ray Masters (this is Bifrost) to create a rainbow glass body effect.

---

19. For a longer description of the Shambhala visit, see: Richard Leviton, *Looking for Arthur. A Once and Future Travelogue* (Barrytown, NY: Station Hill Openings/Barrytown Ltd., 1997): 563-567.

Assuming you are positioned at a Shambhala portal, you may then likely find yourself transported (in vision: your body will remain where you are seated) to Shambhala. The specific arrival place is intriguing because it appears to be that same large, silvery-blue reflecting pool, except now you have brought your own spuming fountains of different colors. The pool seems to be a kind of landing pad.

6

TEMPLES OF LIGHT

In brief: *These are specialized etheric temples situated high above the Earth and dedicated to the emanation and distribution of individual Ray colors and to the potential experiencing of these Rays by human visitors through visionary immersions.*

Sitting in the Ray Flame

This feature, seemingly a well-kept secret, appears to be directly associated with the Ray Masters. In the 1930s, as part of his communications with Godfre Ray King, Saint Germain referred, very sketchily, to a series of what he called Temples of Light. He mentioned five, including a jade, green, violet, ruby, and crystal Temple of Light, adding that they are situated above the Earth's atmosphere in the "Etheric Belt" surrounding the planet.

These Temples appear to be administered by selected Ascended Masters, working in conjunction with the Ray Masters, and also by certain Devas, which we may understand to be angels or highly accomplished beings of Light. For example, seven Ascended Masters act from the Violet Temple of Light and send forth "Mighty Rays, commanding obedience to the Inner Activity of Divine Forces acting everywhere on the physical plane," said Saint Germain in the 1930s. One Deva works from the Jade Temple to quicken the "Inner Activity" of humans on Earth. A "Mighty Deva" works through the Green

Temple to spark inner spiritual activity towards "a certain definite action" in students, cities, and even the U.S. [1]

Saint Germain advised his students through King that if they wished to visit a Temple of Light they could command the "Mighty I AM Presence" within (essentially, the Higher Self) to take them to it in their dreamtime and later help them remember what they did in the Temple. In response to our request, Saint Germain brought two of us in the waking state (but in a visionary state) into the Blue Temple of Light for a look around.

It is likely that one's first visit to a Temple of Light (or perhaps more descriptively, a Color Temple) will be in accordance with their predominant Ray. This is the Ray one's soul originally and consistently incarnates through. Saint Germain introduced me to the Blue Temple. It appeared square in shape, situated somewhere high above the Earth, and inside its space was dominated by a massive dark blue flame burning on a horizontal crescent urn. The walls were of the same blue (lapis lazuli) as the flame but seemed to be studded with crystalline knobs throughout their surface, like blue Christmas lights.

The point of visiting a Temple of Light is to sit in the flame. I sat in the blue flame and felt myself being grounded sideways through time back to "my" beginnings, when as a soul "I" first entered the Blue Ray. You get grounded back to your soul essence expressed by a color Ray, and in the process, at least temporarily, everything "you" have been and accreted since is stripped away. The blue flame burned off, in terms of my present identity—let's say eclipsed for the moment to give me a broader view—all the obscuring definitions and conditionings "I" had accumulated over the eons of incarnations. The experience is more than a purification: it is also deeply energizing, healing, strengthening, and fortifying. It steels you for another round of living and insight.

---

1.   Ascended Master Saint Germain, *Ascended Master Instruction*, Saint Germain Series Vol. 4 (Schaumburg, IL: Saint Germain Press, 1986): 131, 143.

Visiting the Temple of Light that accords with your soul Ray is the first step. Then you could sample the others, because each Ray and its gradation (e.g., dark blue and light blue, scarlet and pink) has valuable information for you and will contribute to different levels of purification, fortification, and insight. For example, Saint Germain said the Blue Ray is good for disintegrating the coarser or lower elemental aspect of being human and stimulates the electron activity in the physical body; we already know the lilac flame is excellent for transmutation of negative states and energies.

In the King books, Saint Germain advised his students to "use" the Rays like spiritual tools and to experiment with combinations as one Ray may contain the activity of another. The rose-pink Ray of Love, as he called it then, may be touched by the Violet Ray of Power for better effect, or you can edge this same Ray with gold on one side, violet on the other, to produce a trinity of love, wisdom, and power.

He noted that when students gained understanding and familiarity with the Rays they could try more combinations as situations required or inspired. Saint Germain meant this in terms of wielding the Rays while wakeful in the physical body, but you can also experiment with or at least sample the different colors by visiting different Temples in your visionary state.

Thus the Color Temples can school you in various practical applications of the Rays. For example, Saint Germain recommended to me to visualize a wand with the lilac flame burning on its tip then to use this to anoint each of the major chakras, from crown to groin, so that for a while they burn with the lilac flame. This will start a purification and transmutation process in one's subtle energy centers and possibly free one from a layer of foreign or unpleasant personal energies and thoughts.

Distribution Pattern of the Color Temples Over the Earth

The distribution of the Temples of Light seems based on a triangulation pattern. Seen from space, the Temples of Light appear positioned at the vertices of a complex array of contiguous equilateral triangles surrounding the Earth like a lace doily. This is the same pattern as mentioned above under Etheric Sanctuaries. At each vertex sits a different Color Temple, and each broadcasts its Ray down like a broad spotlight to a section of land. As mentioned above, in many cases, but not all, inside the space of a triangle sits a golden Etheric Sanctuary.

The triangulation array is formed by another geomantic feature called Oroboros Lines. These are 15 primary energy tracks that encircle the globe, major ley lines that oroborically join together, the tail in the mouth, the end meeting the beginning. These cross the planet and intersect at 62 places; altogether their crossings and intersections create 120 equilateral triangles. This is the triangulation matrix into which the Temples of Light were placed.

Technically, the Oroboros Lines are close to the Earth's surface while the Temples of Light are high above in the Etheric Belt; but functionally, and as seen from space, the Etheric Sanctuaries and Temples of Light appear to be embedded in the Oroboros Line array and at the same plane or level as the equilateral triangles. At the least, the triangulation array determines the placement of both features, and one does not have to go physically to a specific landscape feature to access the Temples of Light. If you believe it's possible, you can do it from your home. The only "rule" is: If you can do it, you can do it.

In a triangulation array of 120 equilateral triangles, there are only 62 *different* vertices because 298 of the possible 360 overlap and thus are duplicates. At each vertex, then, there could be a Temple of Light, or 62 in all. However, due to the amount of Earth's surface area given over to oceans, and thus no human settlements under them, only 49 of the possible 62 slots have been filled with Temples of Light (leaving 13 empty). The seven primary colors are represented, and each gets seven Color Temples, thus 49 in total.

The intensity of the colors may be modulated to produce darker or lighter shades of each color, thus effectively representing the 14 Rays. The Temples are arrayed so as to produce different color combinations across the triangulation pattern, such as an orange, blue, and violet blending together. At each of these 62 vertices you also have an overlapping of differently "flavored" Oroboros Line energies. These 15 lines transmit the energies of the twelve zodiacal signs plus three from stars in the form of a solar (Sirius), lunar (Canopus), and neutral (Polaris) energy.

In most cases, three different Oroboros Lines pass through a vertex. These Lines, incidentally, are typically less than one-quarter mide wide. A Temple of Light's inherent color broadcasting is intermeshed with the specific Oroboros Line zodiacal influence, making a rich mixture. Further, their color emanations complement the emanations from the Oroboros Lines. That means a given landmass within the area overshadowed by a triangle may receive emanations from three different Color Temples and three different zodiacal influences (which, by definition, are also color-vibration frequencies).

The presence of specific Color Temples over a region has long-term effects on life, consciousness, and the quality of culture in that locale. One may even be drawn to live in a certain place (or to be born there) that has, for example, the spotlight of a Blue Temple focussed on it. This effect is not as concentrated as when you immerse yourself in the flame of a Blue Temple, but still, a Blue Ray's diffused focus over a region subtly will effect all aspects of your life there.

How to Interact with a Color Temple

Picture a square building, like a box, with you inside it. Assign a single primary color (one of the seven rainbow hues) to this box; if you know your soul Ray color, then you might wish to select this; if you don't know it, select a color that appeals to you. Picture a massive central flame of this selected color burning in an urn in the center of the room. If you choose scarlet, for example, you will have a scarlet flame burning in a scarlet chamber.

Enter the flame and immerse yourself in the redness of the flame for awhile. Simulating your presence in the Color Temple will help you actually be there. Ask the Ray Master of that Ray to assist you in being there; to facilitate this, redo the Bifrost flame meditation, presented above, align with that Ray, then return to the Temple.

7

RAY MASTER SANCTUARIES

In brief: These are specially dedicated sanctuaries, 1,080 in all (443 are active today), for individual Ray Masters, most often situated in proximity to a physical landscape feature such as a hill or mountain or overlapping a human-made ritualized space such as a temple, shrine, or oratory. The chief characteristic of each is a flame in the color of the Ray burning in an altar at the center of the sanctuary.

1,080 Sanctuaries Originally Assigned to the Earth

The 14 Ray Masters have been allocated individual meeting places easily accessed within Earth's visionary geography. I call them Ray Master Sanctuaries. Originally 1,080 were assigned, but in present time, due to a marked lack of human interest (and even awareness of these Sanctuaries), only 443 are active. The other 637 are temporarily dormant or in a sense, closed to the public. Assuming an equal division of the extant 443, then each Ray Master today has about 31 Sanctuaries, compared to the full allocation of about 77 per Master.[1]

What is the purpose of this feature? First, it anchors the energies of the Great Bear on Earth as well as the Ray differentiation of each Master. Second, it offers a dedicated initiation space for individual

Ray Masters to meet with their students and in the past to be honored by their devotees. It's not that the Ray Masters want devotion or public adulation, but in terms of mass consciousness, even in classical times, this was how the non-psychic public related to them. What I call Ray Master Sanctuaries were then "temples of the gods" for deities like Hathor, Aphrodite, Hephaistos, or Apollo, ritualized encounter spaces or places to mark their birth (manifestation) in the world.

Their places of "birth" are Sanctuaries where their energy enters the world. The Egyptian love-goddess Hathor was honored by a temple at Dendera called *Ta-ynt-netert* ("She of the Goddess-Pillar") and her Ray Master Sanctuary overlaps the physical structure, even though the latter is now in ruins. Delos was once a prime ceremonial center for Apollo, marked by an Apollonian Sanctuary and sacred precinct and numerous temples on the island's northwestern side, near the harbor; annual festivals and games called the Delia were held to honor his birth there. In Glastonbury, England, an obscure part of town called Beckery retains the memory (and archeological proof supports this though the ruins are gone) of a chapel there dedicated to Brigit (or St. Bridget: she was both a goddess and a saint); that memory is true as there is a Ray Master Sanctuary maintained there by Ray Master Lady Nada.

The classical descriptions of certain sanctuaries of the Olympian gods give us further clues to the sites' uses. People consulted the sanctuaries of Apollo at Delphi and Mount Ptoion for oracular guidance on worldly and spiritual affairs. At the Ptoion sanctuary, oracular

---

1.   When the Ray Masters were first assigned to work with the Earth, only 12 were allowed to manifestly interact with the planet. Of course, the other two Ray Masters existed (Ray No. 2, Master Nada and Ray No. 13, Master Maha Chohan), but their activities for a while were subsumed within Ray No. 1. Thus the original allocation of the 1,080 Sanctuaries would have been 90 per Master; then when the spectrum was expanded to allow all 14 to operate, each Master would have had about 77 Sanctuaries. In practical human terms, this was so long ago that for most of our human history of interacting with Ray Masters, the 14 have been available.

utterances were made in front of or inside a cave that contained a spring, and Apollo Ptoios was known as *ennychos*, the one whose advice was sought in the dark, i.e., in the cave. At Delphi, Apollo, as the son of Zeus, "knew his father's will. His prophetic utterances reached men through the mouth of the Pythia," the trained psychic priestess who administered the oracle. Here Apollo "counselled them on their actions and conduct, and taught them, to meet their destiny by acting 'moderately,' within the proper limits 'which always exist.'" The Delphi dictum said, Know Thyself, which practically meant use self-knowledge to take advantage of one's capacities.[2]

The Delphic oracle was consulted by ordinary citizens as well as rulers. Most came for advice on matters small and great, personal and of the State. Apollo was honored for his ability to resolve conflicts while teaching the oracle-seekers morality, prudence, and tolerance. The *Homeric Hymn to Apollo* praised him for his "unerring" counsel to humanity, while the philosopher Heraclitus said Apollo gives signs, even though, paradoxically, it seems he says nothing and conceals nothing. The Delphic oracle directed colonists in their quest to settle new lands, advised rulers on political decisions, constitutions, and war conduct, and even selected lists of Attic heroes.

Some of the central Virgin Mary apparition sites, such as at Lourdes, France, and Fatima, Portugal, are overshadowed by Ray Master Sanctuaries. Sites of key mythic events attributed to single gods, such as Delphi, Greece, the oracular shrine of Apollo and the place where he "killed" the dragon Python, or the Parthenon on the Acropolis in Athens, dedicated to the city's patroness, Pallas Athena, are in fact Ray Master Sanctuaries maintained by those named "gods."

The geomantic reality of other Sanctuaries has been eclipsed in popular or mythic awareness until recently: the Sanctuary of Ray Master No. 8, Hilarion (pale green) at the St. Joseph Oratory on

---

2.   Athina Kalogeropoulou, "Delphi: the Sanctuary of Apollo," in *The Greek Experience. A Companion Guide to the Major Architectural Sites and an Introduction to Ancient History and Myth*, Edited by Evi Melas (New York: E.P. Dutton, 1974): 64.

Mont-Royal in Montreal, Quebec; the Sanctuary of Lao Tzu, Ray Master No. 5 (rich yellow) on, over, and within a peak overlooking Zephyr Cove on the shore of Lake Tahoe, Nevada; the Sanctuary of Ray Master No. 2 as Mary Magdalene, at the conspiracy-burdened French village of Rennes-le-Chateau. See Table 7 for a partial listing of locations of Ray Master Sanctuaries.

Table 7
Selected Locations of Ray Master Sanctuaries
Planetary Total: 1080, 443 currently active

RAY 1	RAY 2	RAY 3
•Lesbos, Greece: Hephaistos' birthplace	•Lourdes, Grotto of Masabielle, France (Virgin Mary-Master Lady Nada)	•Accra, Ghana, Retreat of the Goddess of Justice, focussed over Freedom and Justice Arch
•Mount Etna, Sicily, Italy		
•Ponte Vecchio, Florence, Italy	•Jasna Gora, Czestochowa, Poland (Virgin Mary-Master Lady Nada)	•Liberty Bell, Independence National Historical Park, Philadelphia, Pennsylvania
•Rotterdam, Netherlands		
•Banff, Lake Louise, Alberta, Canada	•Paphos, Cyprus (Aphrodite)	•Colorado State Capitol Building, Denver, Colorado
•Staples Center area, Los Angeles, California	•Erice (Eryx), Sicily, Italy (Aphrodite)	
•Gethsemane, Jerusalem, Israel	•New Bedford, Massachusetts, The Rose Temple (Master Lady Nada)	•Potala Palace, Red Hill, Lhasa, Tibet (Chenrezi)
•Vatican City, Rome, Italy	•Bridget's Chapel, Beckery (Bride's Mound), Glastonbury, England (as Brigit)	•Sphinx, Giza, near Cairo, Egypt
•Biblioteca Nacional de la Republica Argentina, Buenos Aires, Argentina		•Beacon Hill, Boston, Massachusetts
•Rameswaram, Tamil Nadu, India	•San Damiano, Italy (Virgin Mary, Master Lady Nada)	•Awali, Island of Bahrain, Persian Gulf
•Banares, India		•Naples-Cumae, Italy
•Hagia Sophia, Istanbul Turkey	•Fatima, Portugal (Virgin Mary-Master Lady Nada)	•White House, Washington, D.C.
•Ramkot, Ayodhya, India	•Dendera, Egypt (Hathor)	•Goetheanum, Blood Hill, Dornach, Switzerland
•Govardhana Hill, Mathura, Uttar Pradesh, India	•Kildare, Ireland (St. Bridget)	•St. Paul's Cathedral, Ludgate Hill, London, England

Table 7
Selected Locations of Ray Master Sanctuaries
Planetary Total: 1080, 443 currently active (Continued)

•Rennes-le-Chateau, France (Mary Magdalene)	•The Tor (above it), Glastonbury, England
•Palace of Fine Arts, San Francisco, California	
•Central Park, New York City, New York	
•Kremlin-St. Basil's Basilica, Red Square, Moscow, Russia	
•Maidan Nezalezhnosti ("Independence Square"), Khreshchatyk, Kiev, Ukraine	
•Medellin, Colombia	

Table 7
Selected Locations of Ray Master Sanctuaries
Planetary Total: 1080, 443 currently active (Continued)

RAY 4	RAY 5	RAY 6
•Bodh Gaya, India	•Zephyr Cove, Lake	•Mount Rose, Califor-
•Dead Sea-Salt Sea,	Tahoe, California	nia
Israel	•Rampart of the War-	•Anapurna, Nepal
•Church of San	riors, Cashel of the	•Tepeyac Hill, Mexico
Francesco, Assisi, Italy	Kings, Cashel, Tipper-	City, Mexico
•Mount Omei,	ary, Ireland (St. Patrick)	•Medellin, Colombia
Chengdu, Sichuan	•Hill of Uisneach, Rath-	•Quito, Ecuador
Province, China	conrath, Westmeath	•Banff, Alberta, Can-
•Shigatse, Tibet	County, Ireland	ada
•Dal Lake, Srinagar,	•Giant's Causeway,	•Avila, Castile, Spain
Kashmir, India	Bushmills, Ulster	•Mount Elbert, Rocky
•Artemision, Ephesus,	County, Northern Ire-	Mountains, Colorado
Turkey (Artemis)	land	•Buenos Aires, Argen-
•Cynthian Temple,	•Croagh Patrick, Con-	tina
Mount Cynthus, Delos,	nacht County, Ireland	•Lookout Mountain
Greece (Artemis)	•Yungdruk Gu Tseg,	("Chatanuga"), in both
•San Christobal, New	Nine-Storey Swastika	Tennessee and Geor-
Mexico	Mountain (Mount Kail-	gia, near Chattanooga,
•Bear Butte, South	ash), Tibet	TN
Dakota (Lakota-Chey-	•Cerne Abbas, Dorset,	•Hokkaido, Japan
enne)	England	

Table 7
Selected Locations of Ray Master Sanctuaries
Planetary Total: 1080, 443 currently active (Continued)

•Tien-Tai Mountain, "Celestial Terrace," Zhejiang Province, China
•Deluun Boldog, Burhan Haldun-Hangai Mountains, Mongolia
•Mount Marcy-Lake Tear of the Clouds, Adirondacks, near Lake Placid, New York
•Denali (Mount McKinley), Alaska
•Upward Cave of the Alchemists, China (exact locale unknown at present)
•Monticello, Charlottesville, Virginia
•University of Rochester campus, Rochester, New York

Table 7
Selected Locations of Ray Master Sanctuaries
Planetary Total: 1080, 443 currently active (Continued)

RAY 7	RAY 8	RAY 9
•Primrose Hill, London, England	•St. Joseph Oratory, Mont-Royal, Montreal, Quebec, Canada	•Le Chateau de Liberte, Rhone River, France
•Gurla Mandhata, Tibet (near Mount Kailas)	•Mount Pelion, Thessaly, Greece	•Naples, Italy
•Bodh Gaya, India	•Mount Pholoe, Pylos, Greece	•Florence, Italy
•Tiger Hill, Darjeeling, India	•Mount Dicte, Crete, Greece	•Vatican City, Rome, Italy
•Empire State Building (above it), New York City	•Mount Eden Park, Auckland, New Zealand	•Lincoln Cathedral, Lincoln, England
•Shigatse, Tibet	•The Plaza, Santa Fe, New Mexico	•Verona, Italy
	•Novosibirsk, Siberia, Russia	•Eleusis, Greece
	•Amsterdam, Netherlands	•Thebes-Luxor, Egypt
	•Rotterdam, Netherlands	•Memphis, Egypt
	•Dubuque, Iowa	•Kalighat Temple, Calcutta, Bengal, India
		•Knossos, Crete, Greece

Table 7
Selected Locations of Ray Master Sanctuaries
Planetary Total: 1080, 443 currently active (Continued)

RAY 10	RAY 11	RAY 12
•Cumae, Italy (Apollo) •Delphi, Mount Parnassus, Greece •Didyma, Miletus, Turkey (Apollo) •Temple of Apollo, Corinth, Greece •Vale of Tempe, Mount Olympus, Thessaly, Greece •Pagasae, Greece •Delos, Greece (Apollo's birthplace) •Darjeeling, India, Temple of Good Will (Master El Morya) •*Brugh na Boinne*, or *Oenghus an Brogha* (House of Oenghus), Newgrange, Ireland •Almu (Hill of Allen), Leinster, Ireland •Megara, Greece •Dome of the Rock, Jerusalem, Israel •St. Peter's Basilica-Piazza San Pietro, Vatican City, Rome, Italy	•Luxor, Egypt •Athens, Greece •Mount Phicium (Mount Phaga-Sphinx Mountain), Thebes, Greece •Sphinx, Giza Plateau, Giza-Cairo, Egypt •Brockway Beachhead, Lake Tahoe, California •Santa Fe Baldy, near Santa Fe, New Mexico •Serapeum Temple, at Alexandria, Egypt •Saqqara, Egypt •University of California campus, Davis, California	•Parthenon, Acropolis, Athens, Greece (Pallas Athena) •Hisarlik Hill, Troy, Turkey •Ka'aba, Mecca, Saudi Arabia •Mount Neriton (Anogi), Ithaka, Greece •Summit House, Mount Holyoke, Hadley, Massachusetts •Ochaine Mountain (*Sliab Tuath*), Plain of Murtheimne, Ireland •Nürnburg, Germany •Mycenae, Greece •Brazen House, Sparta, Greece •Temple of Athena, Assos, Turkey •Temple of Athena, (Paestum-Poseidonia), Pesto, Italy •Wearyall Hill, Glastonbury, England •Santa Fe County Line, I25, Santa Fe, New Mexico

Table 7
Selected Locations of Ray Master Sanctuaries
Planetary Total: 1080, 443 currently active (Continued)

•Winnipeg, Manitoba, Canada
•New Orleans, Louisiana
•Arnhem Land, Northern Territories, Australia
•Hill of Uisneach, Ireland
•Fountain of Barenton (Belenton, or Bel-Nemeton, Bel Sanctuary), Brittany, France

Table 7
Selected Locations of Ray Master Sanctuaries
Planetary Total: 1080, 443 currently active (Continued)

RAY 13	RAY 14
•Fajada Butte, Chaco Canyon, New Mexico •Prague Castle, Prague, Czech Republic •Gerona, Spain •Safed, Israel •Rodruban *sidhe*, Hill of Tailtiu, Navan, Ireland •Croagh Patrick, Ireland •Wawel Hill, Cracow, Poland •*Tor Conaind* (Conann's Tower), Glass Island, Tory Island, Ireland •Dragon Hill, The Ridgeway, Wiltshire, England •Tintagel, Cornwall, England •Dinas Emrys, Caernarvonshire, Wales •Grand Canyon, Arizona •Hermopolis-Khmun (Khemnu), Egypt	•Mount Etna, Sicily, Italy •Four Corners Monument, Utah-Arizona-New Mexico-Colorado border •Sylene, Libya •Arc de Triomphe, Paris, France •Lanchid-Chain Bridge, Budapest, Hungary •Baghdad, Iraq •Temple of the Maltese Cross, Carpathian Mountains, Transylvania, Romania •Victoria, Vancouver Island, British Columbia, Canada

Through the Sanctuaries, individual Ray Masters can transmit and ground their portion of the total Ursa Major reality (the 14 Rays) in multiple locations on the Earth. Each Ray Master has a primary reality field in the galaxy, yet each of their Sanctuaries is a hologram of that; or perhaps by analogy we should say the Ray Master's primary reality field is a "Mothership" and her "scoutships" are the Sanctuaries.

All the scoutships or Sanctuaries are connected by lines of light (specific to the Ray color) to the Mothership, or Ray Master's primary reality field. Periodically, the Ray Master pulses their Ray reality through this network and the Sanctuaries light up. Humans living under the influence of a Sanctuary will potentially experience a heightening of their personal reality during the pulsing.

Thus Ray Masters *feed* the network of their Sanctuaries and the landscape zodiacs affiliated with them with their portion of the Ursa Major spectrum, and they feed the entire galaxy with their $1/14^{th}$ filtering of the Ursa Major totality. This way the Ursa Major energy gets fed into the galactic system and its Earth holograms in both a widespread and local way. The Great Bear's responsibility to the galaxy is to continuously nourish all its stars, constellations, solar systems, and planets with Light, as well as all its affiliate holograms such as the array in the Earth's visionary geography. It is after all the great *Mother* Bear of the galaxy.

A Visual Description of a Sanctuary

What does a Sanctuary look like to psychic perception? We must allow latitude for and grant validation of individually filtered perceptions, so let's say as a general visual guideline it may look something like this:

Picture a tall, very narrow rectangle or split pillar that acts as a doorway between the worlds. On the other side of this is the Ray Master's domain of one color, and it may appear as a spherical realm or perhaps as a globular amphitheater with living images of all the Ray

Master's activities, guises, incarnations, and residences presented as a holographic resume.

That's one possibility. Here is another:

You're sitting on the sandy beach at Zephyr Cove on the shore of Lake Tahoe. Across the road and through the woods and up the rocky face of the bare peaks one prominence in particular seems numinous. In the *same place* as this peak but in the next dimension is a temple of white marble. It has a central domed rotunda and two long wings or extensions on either side. Inside is a central urn some 100 feet across, and upon it burns a massive and brilliant rich yellow flame.

Around the edge of this urn are seats and there are more along the walls; various humans in spirit form and other spirits from different evolutionary life-streams are present before the flame. Present also is a single majestic male human of genial nature dressed primarily in fine yellow robes and resembling a royal figure from classical China. This is Ray Master No. 5 in one of his guises as Lao Tzu, the founder of Taoism, author of the *Tao de Ching*, and master of this Sanctuary.

How did I get into this Sanctuary? Obviously not in my physical body. As part of a geomantic workshop I conducted at Lake Tahoe, I arranged for a group to visit this Sanctuary. It was not necessary to physically climb the peak and sit on the top. We sat within view of it, probably a mile at least overland from it. That was close enough. My angelic colleagues the Ofanim transported our group in our visionary bodies into the Sanctuary and there Lao Tzu welcomed us all and gestured for us to enjoy his yellow Ray flame. (Often, if you cannot physically reach the approximate location of a Sanctuary, or other geomantic feature, the angelic realm, especially the Ofanim, can get you there by way of "higher technology"—transportation in their designated meeting space, a Rotunda of Light. Part of your awareness is bilocated so you can perceive events at this new locale while remaining present in your physical body.)

Once you have visited a Ray Master Sanctuary in this way, the second visit is easier. You may return in memory; you may send a *Hello!* to Lao Tzu and request a return visit; picture yourself in the yellow flame and be there again. Don't worry about a Ray Master being too busy with more important galactic affairs to give you any time. Each of the 14 Ray Masters is capable of 1,746,000 simultaneous manifestations—they can be in that many places at the same time, including ten minutes with you when you genuinely wish it.

With these introductory comments in mind, let's now review the selected Sanctuaries and Ray qualities of the 14 Ray Masters, starting with Ray 1, scarlet.

Sanctuaries of Ray Master Jesus of the Scarlet Robe

Although Judeo-Christian culture identifies Jesus exclusively with Christianity, as a Ray Master he has influenced many other cultures and religions and taken or inspired many guises. In India, he has been the carrier of the Rama and Krishna[3] manifestations, yielding his Ray Master's form to the Christ (Vishnu) to create the composite spiritual figures of Rama and Krishna. Both are regarded as among the principal manifestations or "descents" (*avatars*) into form by Vishnu.

Yielding oneself up and surrendering are key aspects of Ray Master Jesus's Ray. He refers to it as the "scarlet flame of surrender," because this color is most malleable to surrender, to one becoming an empty vessel. Many of Ray Master Jesus' mythic guises have been as a celestial smith, the forger of metals, the master of the smithy fires, creating numerous objects and devices from gold.

The scarlet flame of surrender softens, almost melts, the hard metals, so they willingly surrender their forms, their rigidity and self-definition, their identity, to the smith who then shapes them according to the inspirations of the Logos (Christ-Vishnu). The Scarlet Ray prepares matter for that giving over of itself to the Christ-Logos so that

---

3.   Some texts, such as the *Srimad Bhagavata Purana*, present Krishna as an expression of the Supreme Being which would place him, in this interpretation, above the rank of Ray Master.

the Father (the Supreme Being, God) may enter them. The Ray prepares the metals to release their resistance. On a bodily human level, we may functionally equate the metals with the chakras, which also need softening. Traditionally, esoteric teachings associate the metals with the planets and their bodily correlates, the chakras. So this Ray and its Master applies its heat to soften the metals of our energy centers so that ultimately they may all be converted into gold containers for the higher Light.

You can sense this flame of surrender at Rameswaram in Tamil Nadu, in the southernmost part of India. Rameswaram is one of India's four *Dhamas*, the cardinal sacred abodes of Vishnu, this one representing the South. Rameswaram is regarded as holy today because long ago Rama stopped here in his pilgrimage throughout India. His actions are detailed in the classic epic, the *Ramayana*, in which he, Hanuman (the Monkey-God: the Ofanim in another guise), and their retinue sought to regain Rama's consort, Sita, captured by Ravanna, a ten-headed demon, who held her at Lanka.

It was at Rameswaram that Hanuman constructed a massive, 800-mile long bridge to link India with Lanka, generally equated with Ceylon, now Sri Lanka.[4] On his successful return from Lanka, Rama performed *puja* here (a ritual ceremony) to thank Shiva (one of Hinduism's trinity of gods, with Brahma and Vishnu) and to purge himself of contamination for having killed Ravana.

That's the outer story of why Rameswaram is holy and a *Dham*. The inner is that above the city in the ethers is an operational Ray Master Sanctuary maintained by Ray Master Jesus (Rama); it is one of the 443 still active ones. It sits over Rameswaram like a massive scarlet

---

4.   But probably mistakenly. The old texts say Lanka was set atop Trikuta Mountain, but according to the *Srimad-Bhagavatam*, another very old Hindu text, Trikuta is 80,000 miles long and across and is situated beneath the Ocean of Milk, and thus high above our world. All this clearly disqualifies it from being physically in the country of Sri Lanka. Richard L. Thompson, *Vedic Cosmography and Astronomy*. (Los Angeles: The Bhaktivedanta Book Trust, 1989): 48.

citadel, like a crown over the devotional ardor of the countless generations of pilgrims and spiritual aspirants whose willingness to surrender their individuality to the purifying, transcendental flames of
Rama is expressed as a tableau of thousands of upraised arms and
cupped hands. Inside the Sanctuary in a central urn burns a massive
scarlet flame, 100 feet across and high.

Although the Lanka in the *Ramayana* is usually equated with the
island of Sri Lanka, it is in fact a Celestial City. It is described as
golden Lanka set atop Trikuta Mountain; it was originally Kubera's
golden citadel, and Kubera was one of the eight *Lokapalas*, Guardians
of the Directions, his being North. Geomantically, it is probably
closer to the reality of things to construe Rameswaram as a Ray Master Sanctuary (and *Dham*) operating in proximity to a Celestial City
known as Lanka, acting perhaps as an embarkation point to the larger
citadel called Lanka, not the country of Sri Lanka per se, but a glittering heavenly domain.

Ray Master Jesus, in his guise as Rama, maintains another vital
Sanctuary above the Ramkot citadel complex in Ayodhya in Uttar
Pradesh, one of India's seven sacred cities (a list that includes Dwar-
aka, mentioned earlier). Here is Rama's birthplace and the center of
his holy kingdom, so Hindu legend says. During *Ramnavami*, or
Rama's Day, in April, hundreds of thousands of pilgrims converge on
Ayodhya from all over the north of India to celebrate and worship
Rama.

The *Ramayana* describes Ayodhya as the capital of the kingdom of
humans, ruled over by King Dasarath, yet its description makes it
seem more a celestial residence than an earthly one. Ayodhya was
built by Manu, a son of Surya (the Sun-god); the city was 100 miles
long and a red stone paved highway ran through it; above the city cir-
cled the golden "airplanes" (*vamanas*, which could also mean aerial
chariots) of the celestial Apsaras; Dasarath's opulent golden hall, with
gold seats, silk tapestries, and massive marble pillars, was said to rival
in splendor the assembly hall of Indra himself.

It is difficult to conceive of this level of fineness and opulence today in our physical world, but at the time this story took place, the Earth was flourishing in the *Satya-yuga* (the Golden Age), a time basically the opposite pole of reality expression and Light permeation we have today (called the *Kali-yuga*: Black or Lead Age). King Dasaratha, at the time of the story, had already ruled for 60,000 years, so the Vedas claim, so clearly he was not a mortal in any sense we recognize today; more likely, he was a member of the Great White Brotherhood presiding over a region of India or perhaps a floating divine city.

Ayodhya was a physical city yet ethereal, or we maybe we should say its astral model overlapped its physical manifestation, like a well-fitting glove of Light. So the two realms, physical and subtle, expression and ideal, interpenetrated each other. Then there was so much Light and truth in reality, *rta* was so much the order of the day, that the city appeared golden; it could not have appeared any other way or in any other hue. Gold was its truth and unalterable reality.

Above Ayodhya gleamed the scarlet citadel of Rama's Sanctuary, which to Valmiki, poet of the *Ramayana*, "resembled a mass of white cloud…[or] the peak of a white cloud." Rama's palace was "filled with cheerful men and women and resembled a lake filled with lotuses, visited by innumerable happy birds."[5] Incidentally, here we have another viable psychic description of aspects of a Sanctuary. In keeping with the sacrificial surrender aspect of the scarlet Ray, King Dasaratha would step down and install his son, Rama, as the new regent.

Also relevant is the fact that Rama, beheld by a charioteer, was seated on his golden couch in his palace, his body smeared with sandal-paste, *red* as blood. True to the spirit of surrender, Rama has to give up his immense wealth, power, and authority to wander the wilds of India as an ascetic for fourteen years as a fulfillment for an old vow his father made to one of his wives who now forces him to honor it.

Ayodhya was Rama's birthplace because here his energy and Ray consciousness is always available, ready to be birthed in and incar-

---

5.   *The Ramayana of Valmiki.* Vol. 1, Translated by Hari Prasad Shastri (London: Shanti Sadan, 1953): 171.

nated through individuals seeking it. Rama's scarlet Ray of surrender with its insistent rich fullness is always ready to flame up in the hearts of his devotees, and Ayodhya is an excellent, well-prepared place for humans to access this quality, similar in function to Tintagel in England, where the celestial King Arthur is always available to be born within us.

A global picture starts to emerge regarding the distribution and function of the Ray Master Sanctuaries. It appears that to some extent individual Ray Masters specialize in particular cultures and sacred geographies—as we'll see below, Master Portia with Tibet, Pallas Athena with Greece and Ireland, and as we've just observed, Jesus-Rama with India. Through multiple Sanctuaries, they subtly direct and inspire the unfolding of the specific soul qualities of that culture and its corresponding visionary geography and the landscape angels and egregors who maintain the congruence between the peoples' soul intent and the prepared landscape qualities.

Another aspect to this picture is that Ray Masters may be assigned to administer other major geomantic features. In the case of Ray Master Jesus, in his guise as celestial smith he appears to be in charge of the Earth's 144 Sun Centers (also called Mithraea, [singular Mithraeum], from the Mithras Sun rites: one of the eight Celestial Cities). That means the specific Ray Master will also likely be in charge of human visits to or initiations in such temples. One example of a Sun Center administered by Ray Master Jesus is at Mount Etna in Sicily (see below).

The Sun Center is dominated by a massive central spherical flame comprising thousands of Solar Angels called Agnishvattas. These Angels, technically, are the flames, the mighty fires of the smith's forge. Their essence pertains to building self-aware substance, to creating the pure Ego or mental body.[6] The smith helps shape this essence into numerous forms, and he does this at the Sun Centers. That is, from our viewpoint. In actuality, each of the 144 Sun Centers is a hologram of the singular reality of the Great Central Sun, a kind of cosmic omphalos for the forging of forms to hold the Christ Consciousness.[7]

The Greek myth of Hephaistos parallels this geomantic reality nicely. Inside Mount Etna, the Olympian fire-smith god, Hephaistos, toils at his forge, creating implements, thrones, shields, even palaces for the other gods. These are containers of all sizes for the Solar Logos, represented by the fires, and may range from the Periodic Table of the Elements to sublime "equipment" used by the GWB.

Hephaistos is assisted by three Cyclops, from the Brotherhood of Etna, as Virgil called it in the *Aeneid*, a fraternity of 100 Cyclops who live in caves on the slopes of Etna. The Cyclops (literally: "Round-Eyed Ones") are human-like expressions of the angelic order called Elohim, who early in the life of Earth took giant form for a time; the single round eye represents their unfaltering divine, unitive vision, their constant focus on the Supreme Being's plans which are always foremost in their sight.

---

6. The Agnishvattas, according to Alice Bailey, are the Fire Devas, Fire Dhyanis, the Solar Pitris of the mental plane that pertain to humanity's essential nature and creative power. "The work of the Agnishvattas (the self-conscious principles, the Builders or constructors of the egoic body on the higher mental levels)...is to unite the atma, buddhi, and manas [aspects of Man's higher being bodies] with the lower three, the physical, astral, and lower mental body, and form the middle principle." Alice A. Bailey, *A Treatise on Cosmic Fire*. (New York: Lucis Publishing Company, 1962): 680-1.

7. The Great Central Sun is a term found in some metaphysical sources, including those from Saint Germain. It is generally understood to mean the Sun behind the Sun, or the true and ultimate Sun at the heart of the galaxy or even the cosmos. As such, it is not a sun or star in any conventional sense we may have of such celestial bodies. Saint Germain likens it to the Christ Consciousness. He further notes that Surya, known in Vedic myth as the Sun-god, is in fact an Ascended Master and a great intelligence from the Great Central Sun, a representative of what Saint Germain calls this mighty and tremendous reality.

The Elohim-Cyclops assist Hephaistos, as Ray Master Jesus, an agent of the Solar Logos, in creating suitable incarnational containers for the Solar Logos and Christ Consciousness; as celestial smith, Hephaistos monitors and supports the life of the God-aware solar fires in all created things.

At the same time, let's think of this also in terms of the smith constantly softening and smelting down the metals of our energy centers (the interior planets) within the searing flames of the Agnishvattas who will imbue these metals (the chakras), possibly even recast them as an alloy, with the roaring heat of God-awareness.

At Mount Etna, Ray Master Jesus has positioned one of his Sanctuaries in working proximity to the raging forge-fires of the Sun Center. Here, elegantly, the physical features of the volcano mirror the overlapping celestial template, the roiling, often erupting lava matching the inferno tended by the Solar Angels.

The Sun Center is an interactive temple and workshop based on the spiritual reality of the Great Central Sun, and to an extent, our own local Sun, Helios. Even to consider some of the physical facts of our Sun gives a vivid impression of the Sun's awesome power.

To start with, our solar system of planets lives within the vast aura and stormy atmosphere of the Sun estimated to be 7.3 billion miles across (the solar system diameter), participating in its spiritual and physical aspects. A coronal mass ejection, for example, which is the eruption of a huge plasma bubble and electrically charged gas from the Sun's outer atmosphere, can travel from one to five million miles per hour and assume a diameter of 30 million miles, and with a mass equal to 100,000 battleships creating an impact equivalent to 100,000 hurricanes. A solar flare is a sudden explosive release of built-up magnetic energy with the comparable force of 10 million volcanic eruptions in a few minutes or of millions of hydrogen bombs exploding.

Let's not overlook the Sun's extreme heat either, as the original of Hephaistos' volcanic hot forge under Mount Etna: at its core, it's 29,000,000° F and 10,000° F on the "surface" or photosphere, though the corona, which extends for millions of miles above the photosphere and away from the Sun, reaches temperatures in the millions of degrees. "In a sense we are actually *in* the outer reaches of the solar corona."[8] Wherever we stand on Earth, we're in the solar wind, "howling" past us at a speed of 10 protons and electrons per cubic centimeter per 500-700 kilometer/second and at a searing temperature of 200,000 K. The Sun "constantly seethes with activity," generating the cosmic equivalent of tornadoes and hurricanes.[9]

These physical qualities of our local Sun suggest the extreme potency of the solar Light at the level of the Great Central Sun, which the Sun Center embodies. These are the fires over which the great celestial smith Hephaistos has mastery. Here are some impressions of being inside the Celestial City of the Sun, or Sun Center:

There is a huge central ball of Sun-fire on an urn, surrounded by attendants, then an outlying city of orange-gold, with dozens of chambers for meetings and work. The Sun Center appears one level high, sprawling though orderly. From outside it looks a bit like the Pentagon, though not that shape, but in the sense of a huge ground-level structure with many inter-connecting parts, all golden orange, with a central ball of fire. The ball of Sun-fire, seen inside, is comprised of the Solar Angels, the *Agnishvattas*—thousands of them stand like Sun-fire stalks inside the flame. They are the flame. There is no ground floor inside this either; it is more like being in the center of a fully-opened dandelion gone to seed. You are at the center of a sphere of angelic fire. Many beings from all over the cosmos are here for study, immersion, or because this is the center of things and everything else is entropic.

Ray Master Jesus administers the Sun Centers, though he does not always have a Sanctuary adjacent to them as at Mount Etna. The

8.   James B. Kaler, *Stars* (New York: Scientific American Library, 1992): 116-117.

9.   Michael J. Carlowicz and Ramon E. Lopez, *Storms from the Sun. The Emerging Science of Space Weather* (Washington, D.C.: The Joseph Henry Press, 2002): 8,13,76.

Agnishvattas are the fires that the divine smith tends, and Jesus walks right into the forge, into the flaming sphere of fire, to interact with the Solar Angels. They are the builders (and source of) *self-aware substance*. The forge is the fiery heart of self-consciousness, the pure Ego, self-aware substance, and this is the heart of that self-awareness. Substance is aware of itself and knows that it is God. The Sun center is the inferno of this awareness built into all substance. The rest of the Celestial City comprises the smithy's workshops for casting self-aware substance into forms. That is the smith's job.

Ray Master Jesus is involved with three regular geomantic events each year, starting with the Epiphany, January 6. This is the traditional, and correct, birthday for the Christ Child on Earth (before it was moved back to December 25), still observed in the Greek Orthodox segment of Catholicism. On this day, the Christ sends a focus of Christ Consciousness to the Earth via a selected geomantic node (the location varies each year). Ray Master Jesus assists this Christ focus to ground in the Earth.

He is also involved in the spring equinox as Rama, and the fall equinox as Balder. For the spring equinox, in his guise as Attis, the dying son of the Great Goddess Cybele, he (and the Great Mother) blesses the Earth with Light. At the autumnal equinox, Ray Master Jesus in his Norse guise as Balder (Odin's son, and the first god to "die) enacts a ceremonial return to his highest spiritual home called Breidablikk, and he brings human souls with him to reboot their spiritual grounding for the year. From Breidablikk he radiates his full magnificence of Light to the world. In brief, in the spring, he brings the Light of Christ *into* the Earth; in the fall, he brings the Earth (through its inhabitants) *up to* the spiritual home of the Christ Light.

The Scarlet Ray's Complement—The Rose-Pink Ray of Master Nada

Ray Master Lady Nada in all her guises is the Ray complement—"consort"—to the primary scarlet Ray of Ray Master Jesus. She is Sita to Rama, Radha to Krishna, Mary Magdalene to Jesus, pink to scarlet—in color terms, they are a "natural" pair, a match made in Heaven, the perfect couple.

Nada's name means "Sound" as in mystic sound or subtle sound accompanied by an effulgence, and she is associated with music in many of her cultural guises: as the Vedic rishi Narada, inventor of the *vina* and musical instructor to the Gandharvas, the celestial musicians; as the Egyptian cow-goddess Hathor, mistress of music, dancing, and the sistrum rattle; as Aphrodite, sea foam-born goddess of love, eros, and beauty. All these qualities and attributions are descriptive of Ray Master Nada.

Nada is Sanskrit for "Sound," but in the sense of inner sounds "that become audible when the network of psychoenergetic currents (*nadi*) has been duly purified."[10] Nada is considered in Hindu yoga to be the second level of manifestation of the Absolute in the guise of sound, and it has various forms ranked by degree: like the sound of a conch, a thundercloud, a mounain waterfall. Alternatively, it is like the sound of the ocean, a thundercloud, kettledrum, or waterfall (the first degree); the second degree of Sound is like a big drum or bell; the third like the sound of a small bell, a bamboo flute, a lute, or bee. Nada is also a sounding, droning, roaring, like a roaring bull, for Nada also means "bull," but bull also means God, for the Supreme Being has often assumed a monstrous-magnificent white cosmic bull guise.

Hence, the Hindu mystics used the term *Nada Brahma*, meaning Sound is God (Brahma), or God is Sound. Brahma, or its abstract

---

10. Georg Feurstein, *The Shambhala Encyclopedia of Yoga* (Shambhala, Boston, 1997): 192.

principle, Brahman, is "the inner consciousness of man and of all living things, so *Nada Brahma* means God is Sound" and also that Creation, the cosmos, and the world are sound. "Nada Brahma is one singularity: the primal sound of Being. Being itself."[11] The different nuances to sound, sound at all levels, these different inner sounds, then, suggest some of the esoteric side of the musical associations of this Ray Master.

When it comes to music, dance, and sound, we should interpret this reference a little more deeply than is conventionally done. For sound, let's think in terms of primary seed syllables, differentiations of the *Word* into *words*, into a sea of mantras and primordially creative sound currents which Nada administers. To say Aphrodite was born of the sea-foam is a way of pointing to her mastery of this vast sound ocean of mantras, the seething reservoir of fundamental sounds, of sound syllables that are *seeds* for reality, matter, and consciousness.

As Ray Master Jesus embodies the *Word* or Logos (the Christ), so Nada embodies the *words*, the proliferation of the Word into innumerable sound forms.

Ray Master Nada, as a "female"-appearing Ray Master, is also an emissary of the universal Great Mother, the feminine aspect of the Supreme Being, the unfathomable, mysterious maternal womb out of which all Creation proceeds. "I am about surrendering to the Mother," Nada says. "I can expand myself to transmit Her." Through Nada one can behold aspects of the Great Dana, the Great Mother (Dana, Danu, An, Anu) of the Tuatha de Danann (the Irish GWB) and the Anu or An of the Anunnaki, as it were, singing through the sea of sounds, through Nada.

As the Master of the Scarlet Robe, Jesus leads one through the Christ to the Father, and as the Master of the Pink Robe, Nada conducts one to the threshold of the Divine Mother, the "Goddess of the

---

11. Joachim-Ernst Berendt, *The World Is Sound. Nada Brahma. Music and the Landscape of Consciousness*, Translated by Helmut Bredigkeit (Rochester, VT: Destiny Books, 1987): 17,18.

Beginnings" in her widely variegated guises and depictions. These include, in part, Dana, Danu, Anahita, Anu, Anna, Tanit, Tanaïtis, Anna Parenna, Cybele, and more recently, Theotokos, the Mother of God, whom we know as the Virgin Mary—the "vast Mother…suffering and glorious…lady of all origins and servant of the Lord."[12]

Ray Master Nada says she is the "soft landing, the parachute" for one who has surrendered through the scarlet flame. She helps to remake one after the life-changing surrender under the auspices of Ray Master Jesus, after the great metals meltdown in the smithy and the surrendering of the separate identity grounded in the chakras. She also "softens one" in preparation for beholding an aspect of the Great Goddess.[13] It is possible, while clairvoyantly visiting one of Nada's Sanctuaries and after immersion in her Ray flame, to pass through that realm into another.

Here the predominant shade of red is darker, cadmium red, blood-colored. Her temple appears vaster, emptier, featuring only a massive 200-foot tall living "statue" of the Great Mother. She presents so many forms all at once she appears almost shapeless; she is so vast and protean she appears almost obese, like those steatopygous Paleolithic depictions of the universal Mother (the Irish *Sheela-na-gigs*), with huge drooping breasts, a gaping vagina, and no facial features. She is scary and ugly, benevolent and maternal—the fourfold Goddess in a single form.

Her body is the cosmos, the immeasurable sea of sounds, mantras, vibrations. The Gandharvas are the singing cells in her colossal form. Her emissary, Ray Master Nada, binds the newly self-aware solar sub-

---

12.   Jean Markale, *The Great Goddess. Reverence of the Divine Feminine from the Paleolithic to the Present.* (Rochester, VT: Inner Traditions, 1999): 39.

13.   In her guise as the Irish goddess Brigit (later condensed by Christianity into St. Bridget of Kildare), she was a daughter of the Dagda, lord of the Tuatha de Dannan, the Followers of the Goddess Danu. As a Tuatha, she was by definition an emissary of the Great Mother, here known as Danu or Dana.

stance her consort Jesus the Smith works with in his forges to the universal sound currents and words. That is the ultimate expression of Eros (Aphrodite's child), and it is also the Christ Child, the progeny of the rose-pink and scarlet Rays, Jesus and Magdalene, but in the initiation sense of a second birth, born within, a spiritual regeneration.[14]

As an emissary of the Great Mother, Ray Master Nada is one of four female-valenced Ray Masters who participate in the Virgin Mary apparitions. Participate in this sense means they, either singly or collectively, generate the apparitional form of the Virgin Mary so frequently reported since the mid-1800s. All Marian apparition sites are not necessarily Ray Master Sanctuaries, but at least four are, including the famous Lourdes in France and Fatima in Portugal.

Ray Master Nada is also involved in human initiation into Arthurhood. Here King Arthur, as the Solar Logos, is understood to be a position in consciousness that can be attained over time by dedicated and embodied human individuals. Certain geomantic features, notably one I call an Ixion's Wheel, facilitate this. An Ixion's Wheel (360 are on the Earth) usually looks like a sarcophagus in the form of an equal-armed cross or a sword with pommel. You lie inside it (in vision) as the Arthur stream in the form of a sharp sword infuses you, although it may also seem like an impaling. Ray Master Nada supervises this catalytic initiation by the Solar Logos sword.

---

14. This subtle relationship has been literalized and overly materialized in the popular though misleading works of *The Da Vinci Code* (2003) and its essential conceptual bedrock, the earlier *Holy Blood, Holy Grail* (1982). Whether a physically embodied Jesus and Magdalene had a physical child and thus engendered a blood lineage is not the point and is seductively irrelevant as well as "misplaced concreteness" as Alfred North Whitehead would say; the point is that the fullness of that Ray (with its two parts, the "marriage" of scarlet and rose-pink) births the Christ Child within any human who wants the experience. To focus on a postulated singular *outer* bloodline of these two Ray Masters diverts the spiritual attention from where it belongs: on the process *within* oneself of birthing the new Christ Child.

I first encountered Ray Master Nada at an Ixion's Wheel at Beckery, a neglected part of Glastonbury yet one of prime geomantic importance. Nada has a Sanctuary there, commemorated exoterically by what archeologists agree are the ruins of a former chapel dedicated to the Irish Saint Bridget, who once lived here. My first visionary impression of her reminded me of a celestial figure from J. R. R. Tolkien's Middle-earth mythos: variously called Varda, Elbereth, Tintalle, Gilthoniel, Elentari, and Lady of the Stars, she made the stars and filled them with Light.

I had just entered the white chapel (it's a Light temple) at Beckery and noted it was illuminated by four golden candles set in tall holders, one at each corner of a golden sarcophagus whose contours seemed to match perfectly those of the human body. Behind the sarcophagus on the wall hung a bas-relief in gold of a rearing dragon. Then a woman entered the chapel. Her smile seemed to straddle multiple dimensions. Her dark hair was tied in a chignon under a Moon-white bonnet with slender chin straps. Her gown was white and long, and lapped at her ankles; it was sequined with thousands of twinkling stars. A gold crown glittered on her head.

Her eyes were wise, deep, loving, almost more than I could see or bear to see without glancing away. Beautiful. I thought I was seeing something Elven out of Tolkien, which I later realized is amusing because when the Hobbits beheld something numinous, such as an Elven queen, they would typically feel they had just encountered something liminal and almost unbelievable out of an old story or Middle-earth legend.

I didn't know it was Ray Master Nada at the time, but I knew at least she was the real figure behind the attribution of Saint Bridget, Saint Bride, the goddess Brigit, the Bee-Keeper of Beckery Island, and the other names used for her over time. She gestured for me to lay down in the sarcophagus, which I did, staring at the ceiling. Years later, when I revisited this experience, I saw I had been impaled by King Arthur.

Portia's Sanctuaries of the Orange Ray

Ray Master Portia's (Ray No. 3, orange-gold) focus is discrimination and discernment in the process of transmutation and the disassembling of the body and life of illusion. She works closely with Ray Master Saint Germain (No. 14: lilac), and in fact the two are principals, along with the Archangel Michael and the Ofanim, in the long-term project to reinvigorate the Earth's Light body and midwife its change. Her portion of the Orange Ray involves the rigorous alignment with the truth (*rta*, the cosmic laws the rishis are commissioned to uphold and teach), transcendental insight into the true nature of matter, consciousness, and reality, and the sublime mysticism of name, form, and emptiness.

She has at least two Sanctuaries within the United States. She has one over the Liberty Bell at Independence National Historical Park in Philadelphia, the U.S. capital from 1790-1800 and home of Benjamin Franklin, one of her incarnations. We must be subtle and fluid in conceiving of Ray Master incarnations; Portia showed me a long stream of life images and pictures from thousands of human lives she has touched, influenced, participated in, permeated, or deeply overshadowed, to a greater or lesser degree. Franklin was a partial incarnation.[15]

Even though, from our linear viewpoint, Lady Portia *was* Benjamin Franklin, she kept her Sanctuary over Philadelphia open during his lifetime. At night, whether he was in Philadelphia or anywhere

---

15. Ray Masters may participate in human lives to a greater or lesser extent, along a continuum of permeation so we must approach this subject carefully. Ray Master Jesus, for example, deeply influenced two simultaneous lives, Desiderius Erasmus of Rotterdam, the Netherlands, and Leonardo da Vinci of Florence, Italy; they were both influential contemporaries though working through two different cultures. It is correct to say both that Jesus incarnated through those two individuals at the same time and that he focussed a "spotlight" of his own Ray and essence on both of them at the same time, retaining most of his presence above in his Ray Master Sanctuaries over both cities.

else in the world, Franklin could visit the Sanctuary in his spirit form for information and encouragement. Portia's Sanctuary is like an archival museum of artifacts, treasures, books, artwork, and numerous reference libraries off in the wings. Franklin would go there for ideas for statecraft.

Wings is more than poetical license: the Sanctuary in fact is shaped like a golden eagle (the U.S. national logo and the form of its egregor or National Watcher Angel), its wings outstretched over Philadelphia, its eyes directly over the Liberty Bell in the Park below. Franklin after all was one of America's Founding Fathers, and this responsibility had spiritual underpinnings, including frequent, easy access to Portia's Sanctuary and America's egregor.[16]

The second Portia Sanctuary is situated over the Colorado State Capitol Building in Denver, Colorado. Denver, as Saint Germain commented in 1932, is one of seven "Sun Centers" in America (including New York, Chicago, and Seattle) "to which Seven Great Beings are this day pouring out a Mighty Radiance."[17] The Sun Center at Denver is about two miles in diameter. The Capitol sits in the center of this geomantic vortex and Portia's Sanctuary resides above it. Even though Ray Master Jesus is the smith always found at Sun Centers, other Ray Masters may have special working assignments with individual Sun Centers, such as Portia at the Denver one.

Another Ray Master Portia Sanctuary is situated over the Potala in Lhasa, Tibet. There she was known to Tibetans and their high lamas as Chenrezi (Avalokitesvara in India), the one-thousand armed, eleven-headed Bodhisattva,[18] the Lord Who Surveys or the Lord Who Looks Down. The name is also translated to mean "He Who Hears the Sounds [Outcries] of the World" or the "Sound [*isvara*] That Illu-

---

16. America's egregor, in the form of a golden eagle (in Light form or astral form), overshadows an area of western Pennsylvania, and as a geomantic feature, has numerous correlation points on the land.

17. Ascended Master Saint Germain, *Ascended Master Instruction*, Saint Germain Series Vol. 4 (Schaumburg, IL: Saint Germain Press, 1986): 83.

mines the World." One of "his" epithets is Great Compassion. To the Tibetans, Chenrezi (*sPyan-ras-gzigs*: "Looking with Clear Eyes") is the patron, father, and protector of the Land of Snow (Tibet). Portia's Sanctuary at Lhasa is about one mile in diameter, situated above the Potala on Red Hill in the western section of the capital city. The original palace, Kukhar Potrang, was established on this hill by Songsten Gampo (circa 620 A.D.), the first Tibetan ruler and believed to be an incarnation of Chenrezi (which means Portia was Songsten Gampo). It burned down and was replaced by the present Potala whose construction began in 1645. Red Hill, which dominates the city, and its Potala, were dedicated to Chenrezi. The Potala Palace has been the official home in Tibet of the last 9 Dalai Lamas (which again implicates Portia as Avalokitesvara).

In the same pattern as exhibited later with Benjamin Franklin in Philadelphia, Ray Master Portia was on hand for consultations and guidance with Songsten Gampo (paradoxically an aspect or partial incarnation of herself[19]) and other Tibetan leaders over the centuries, including His Holiness the 14th Dalai Lama, also said to be an incarnation of Avalokitesvara, as were the previous 13.

---

18.   The term Bodhisattva means "Enlightenment Being" and is central to Buddhist belief. A Bodhisattva is a being on the way to total Buddhahood and who embodies and manifests wisdom and compassion and delays the definitive entry into nirvana (leaving the universal field of action for good) until all sentient beings and lifeforms are liberated, that is, brought into self-knowledge and enlightenment. That is a long commitment indeed, one all the Ray Masters take.

19.   Paradoxical, perhaps, only to the Western mind. Hindu belief maintains that it is possible for a deity to remain in their celestial abode and at the same time produce an incarnation for Earth that embodies a portion of their full essence, attributes, or powers. Such partial incarnations are called *Amsa* or *Amsa-avataras*. A full incarnation of the deity is called *Purna-avatara*; and an inspirational incarnation, the third category, in which still less of the deity is present in the embodied human, is called *Avesa-avatara*. Thus a Ray Master may manifest in Earth culture in any of these categories, with a greater or lesser amount of their fullness.

Avalokitesvara-Chenrezi is associated with the Diamond Sutra (the *Prajnaparamita*), a series of chanted verses pertaining to how consciousness gains insight and from this gains wisdom into the inherent emptiness of all forms (*shunyata*), considered by Buddhists to be the true nature of reality. Thus Portia's orange-gold Ray through her Sanctuaries over Philadelphia, Denver, and Lhasa, transmits to all interested this transcendental, liberating wisdom about the nature of reality.

Ray Master Portia's involvement with the Earth involves at least four different geomantic features. First, she works with the labyrinths, specifically the Hall of Records type (there are 12 copies of this on the Earth)[20]; second, she works with energy funnels and the star-temples found at the end of them (2.8 billion copies: many of them parallel stone or tree avenues); third, she superintends the 72 national egregors and the omphalos points for the landmasses they oversee.[21] Fourth, Portia maintains the 72 Heads of God (Crowns of the Ancient of Days), enwrapping them in her Ray flames; these Crowns are geomantic expressions of the Supreme Being as a vast white head found at 72 locations around the Earth.

Regarding her work with the 72 national egregors, Ray Master Portia says, "I calibrate the relationship of the egregor and its ethnoscontents [the soul essence of, for example, the Irish] with the divine signature of the Name [of God] registered there." Each of the national egregors is grounded at a site in a given country that acts as

---

20. The Earth has astral forms of 9 different labyrinth designs, such as a 7-turn, 9-turn, and 11-turn, and for each there are 12 copies (108 labyrinths in all). One of these types is known as the Cretan Labyrinth which in actuality is at least 10 miles across; another is the Hall of Records type, perhaps 1/2 mile across, generated by domes.

21. In the Earth's original design, 72 significant landmasses were designated; these were areas smaller than continents, and to each a people, omphalos, and protector landscape angel (egregor) were assigned. The egregor looks after that grounding and interacts with the people and processes the experiences of that country's numerous landscape angels as accumulated over time.

its navel; here celestial energies are mixed with terrestrial and distributed across that landmass through an arterial-capillary type network.

For example, the navel or omphalos point for Ireland is the Hill of Uisneach; the national egregor for Ireland is called Eriu, according to Irish myth, and that landscape angel works through Uisneach for all of Ireland, even giving the country its original name, Eriu. Each of the national navel points also has a global function in that it represents one of the planet's 72 minor chakras and also one of the 72 Names of God that work through them.

What Ray Master Portia means by "calibrate" is that she adjusts the dynamic between, for example, the Irish national protector angel, the history and soul life of the Irish (ethnos-contents), and the specific Name of God grounded at that navel point. Portia maintains a massive orange-gold Ray flame around each of the 72 egregors of Earth all the time, but when its turn comes for the Name to be sounded through the national omphalos point it protects, then Portia amplifies the flame and makes herself more keenly present to the egregor to provide it counsel and affirmation. "I adjust or fine-tune the Name the egregor sings to the people once a year."

During the course of a 360-day year, all 72 Names of God are sounded on the Earth, one at a time, through one navel point-minor chakra at a time, and for five days, until after 360 days all have been sounded. During the extra five days of the year, Ray Master Portia amplifies her Ray flame around all 72 egregors and is simultaneously present with all of them during the tumultuous completion of the Name; at that time, the complete Name of God, the *Shemhamforesh* of 216 letters and 72 permutations of three Hebrew letters each, reverberates around and through the planet.[22]

This event is called Heaven on Earth Day, and it runs from midnight December 21 to midnight December 25. During this period, the complete Name of God is sounded continuously across and through the planet, a phenomenon that has the additional effect of illuminating the Earth's Light body. The complete Name reverberates like lightning flashes in the planet's Light body, illuminating all its celestial contents—the entire array of visionary geographic features. The event is called Heaven on Earth Day because the totality of the Earth's Light body is a virtual copy or living hologram of all the levels and contents of Heaven, and during these five days, it is revealed to the Earth.

Ray Master Portia oversees activities and developments at a site of global significance from her Sanctuary above a prominent hill called the Tor in Glastonbury, England. This area, which has 60+ geomantic features, including a large landscape zodiac that will be among the first on Earth to be illuminated, is the outer heart chakra, or *Anahata*, for the planet. Its own folklore describes Glastonbury as Avalon, or the entrance to it, and as the Summer Country, esoterically understood to mean essentially the same as Avalon—the realm of Light.

Celtic prophecy sees Glastonbury as the future site of the New Jerusalem, but this is understood to mean not a replication of the actual physical Temple of Jerusalem, but a massive temple of Light gradually emerging out of the ethers, "lit by the radiant glory of God" that "glittered like some precious jewel of crystal-clear diamond," a city of "pure gold, like polished glass," and "beautiful as a bride dressed for her husband," as John of Patmos, the ecstatic poet of *Revelation*, proclaimed so long ago.[23]

Portia is known in Celtic myth as Avallach, King of the Summer Country, a name highly similar to another of her guises, *Avalok*itesvara, the Hindu-Buddhist Bodhisattva and Lord Who Surveys or Looks Down, just as Portia does from her Sanctuary high above the

---

22. In Judaic tradition, once the high priest of the Temple of Jerusalem was able to correctly pronounce the *Shemhamforesh*, and he did this once a year on the Day of Atonement (Yom Kippur, usually late September to mid-October, the 10th day of Tishri: in October 2006 it's at sunset October 1). Judaic lore says that once every seven years the Jewish sages were permitted to teach the Name's secret pronunciation to select disciples.

23. Revelation (21:3, 11-12, 17-18, 23), in *The Jerusalem Bible* (Garden City, NY: Doubleday & Company, 1966): 450.

Tor. She is Avallach, she is Avalokitesvara. The height above the Tor indicated in this image pertains to dimensions: Portia views and oversees the merry Avalonian phantasmagoria of the heart chakra at Glastonbury from the realm of pure mind and adamantine truth, called Dharmakaya in Buddhism, or one of the Upper Worlds as described in Qabala (either Beriyah or Atziluth).

Appropriately, through the Indian and Tibetan Buddhist perception, we find another of Portia's guises, this time as a Dharmapala ("Dharma Protector"), the wrathful six-armed deity called Mahakala, the Greak Dark One. Avalokitesvara is said to have 11 heads: 10 are compassionate, one (Mahakala) is wrathful. A Dharmapala protects the Dharma (the ultimate cosmic truth, the Vedas, *rta*, *maat*, *asha*, and the other similar names for the laws and operating principles of the universe the rishis safeguard) against all enemies, such as evil spirits, demons, inimical influences, or entropy. More subtly, Mahakala's dark hue bespeaks her ability to transcend all form and name and to absorb everything into it, just as black absorbs all other colors.

At the Glastonbury landscape temple, you have Portia as Avallach, King of the Summer Country, surveying all activities (dimensionally) below in Avalon, and you have Portia as Mahakala, the wrathful Dharmapala, out at the periphery of the landscape temple protecting all activities within from outside interference. She safeguards the Light temple from above and at ground level against the enemies of the Light. The Mahakala emanations are interspersed with towering lilac flames, representative of the cooperative presence of Saint Germain, who also takes the form of the Tibetan Heruka (a wrathful deity) Khorlo Demchog, a four-headed, 12-armed blue-black deity who transforms [transmutes] hate energy to wisdom.[24]

Portia indicates that as Master of the Orange Robe she is commissioned to oversee activities of the archetype of the heart chakra and its expression at all levels, including its geomantic templating at different levels across the Earth. In Qabalistic terms, the heart chakra is equivalent to the Sefira (a sphere or container of Light; 10 Sefiroth are described) called Netzach ("Victory"), which is linked with Venus, imaginative fluidic forms, and the vision of beauty triumphant. This suggests that as Ray Master of the Orange Ray Portia superintends the passage of the Absolute Light (Qabalists call it *Ain-Sof*) through the Sefira of Netzach, that is, a complete dimension of being that receives then passes on this level of Light to the next lower domain.

Sanctuaries of the Master of the Pale Orange Robe

Portia's complementary Ray Master within the Orange Ray is generally known as Kuthumi. His incarnations have included John the Baptist and St. Francis of Assisi and will include the future Maitreya Buddha. Kuthumi (a contraction of Koot Hoomi Lal Singh, his name in his last known human life, as a 19th century Himalayan adept and co-sponsor of the Theosophical Society) is the revealer of arcane spiri-

---

24. A Heruka is a semi-wrathful type of Dharmapala, or Dharma protector. Sometimes, the term Heruka is used exclusively to refer to Khorlo Demchog, known in Sanskrit as Chakrasamvara, which is translated variously as "binder of the chakras" and "supreme bliss of the wheel [chakra]". A Dharmapala (Tibetan: *Drag-ched*) is a high spiritual being who removes all interferences and bestows the optimal conditions for the pure practice of Dharma, which is a Buddhist way of saying adhering to the truth of reality and the purity of mind (as in higher consciousness). Heruka (Tibetan: *tRak-thung*) is a Sanskrit word and suggests a being (usually masculine) or state of mind that is founded in the union of emptiness and bliss, which means recognizing and abiding in the inherent emptiness of all forms and phenomena. In the Tibetan explanation, the Heruka is a blood-drinker, at least metaphorically, in which "blood" refers to doubt, dualistic confusion, and self-cherishing. The Heruka embodies the radiant, selfless, blissful qualities of pure, awakened mind. In the case of Glastonbury, the Dharma being protected is the seed of the Earth's singular and future New Jerusalem as well as the entire geomantic architecture of the global heart chakra and the ability and freedom of human souls to interact with this complex system without undue outside interference.

tual knowledge and guardian of the gate to the higher mind and transcendent knowledge, plans, and purposes of the Supreme Being.

The majesty of this range is suggested in two of Kuthumi's Buddhist guises: as Vairochana, one of Buddhism's five transcendent Buddhas, and as his complement, the Bodhisattva Samantabhadra. Vairochana, whose name means "He Who Is Like the Sun," is often depicted as making the ritual gesture (mudra) of supreme wisdom and holding his two prime symbols, the *Dharma-chakra* (symbolizing the teachings about true reality, or Dharma) and the Sun. As Samantabhadra ("He Who Is All-Pervadingly Good"), he is the protector of all those who teach the Dharma, and he rides a six-tusked white elephant to signify the power of wisdom to surmount all obstacles.

Kuthumi is the fearless quester for transcendental knowledge of God, and you can see this quality in three of his mythic guises: as the Greek hero Perseus, he assists (Ray Master) Pallas Athena in "killing" the Gorgon Medusa whose gaze petrifies all those who face her; as Durga (a Hindu female warrior goddess), he is given powers from all the gods (Ascended Masters) to "slay" the Buffalo Demon, Mahishasura, a monster of cosmic proportions and activities; and his Egyptian guise as Sekhmet, the powerful and terrible lion-goddess who belches fire, who with the Sun-disc on her head is the warlike expression of the Sun scorching and devouring Egypt's enemies.

Kuthumi's role as John the Baptist who baptised people in the River Jordan as a preparation for the ministry of Jesus the Christ is congruent with this. The formidable monsters that Kuthumi "killed" were not all inherently monsters. It is somewhat a matter of perspective. Rather, we could better construe Gorgon Medusa, the Buffalo Demon, and the enemies of Egypt as expressions of the transcendent nature of God (in Buddhism, the Dharmakaya or absolute Truth realm), admittedly scary from our reduced human self viewpoint. To everyday reality, surely this face of divinity is monstrous because it is so real and true; Ray Master Kuthumi introduces us to this realm, baptises our awareness in it, and helps us through it. At the same time, he helps us (the the galaxy and cosmos) resist or become neutral to certain inimical, entropic, or disruptive energies (personified as monsters, possibly like the Buffalo Demon).

It is the Self, the Christ, and the higher mind knowledge of God, that Kuthumi reveals. As a John the Baptist or Sekhmet, he is the great desert scorcher, the high solar wind burning off all resistance to the immanance of the Christ, preparing (baptising) the ground of consciousness for the advent of the cosmic Christ.

He doesn't slay the cosmic monsters; rather, he makes them available to humanity for they are not monsters at all but tantric expressions of sublime truth and absolute reality as befits his identity as Vairochana, one of the transcendent Buddhas. Some of the formal names given to the Lord of this Ray (this includes Portia) suggest this: The Great Connector, The Divine Intermediary, The Angel with the Flaming Sword, the Guardian of the Door, The Keeper of the Secret.[25]

Above Bodh Gaya, India, site of the Buddha's enlightenment, Kuthumi maintains a Sanctuary to keep the Buddha flame alive until the Maitreya (the next Buddha, [Kuthumi]) arrives. As did Ray Master Portia with her incarnation as Benjamin Franklin in Philadelphia, so did Kuthumi keep a Sanctuary active above the city of Assisi, Italy, for his guise as St. Francis of Assisi. At Ephesus in Turkey, he shares his Sanctuary with one of his adepts, Artemis, whose cult (animals and hunting) was honored for centuries in the temple called the Artemision. You can easily notice the similarity between Artemis (the Roman Diana) and St. Francis of Assisi in their relationships with the animal kingdom, essentially as protectors (not hunters).

Lao Tzu's Sanctuaries of the Yellow Ray

Lao Tzu, the founder of both Taoism and Bön (Tibet's pre-Buddhist shamanic culture), is the master teacher in the weaving between conflicting opposites. His Ray is about stillness in motion, non-moving

---

25. Alice A. Bailey, *Esoteric Psychology. Vol. 1, A Treatise on the Seven Rays* (New York, NY: Lucis Publishing Company, 1962]: 77.

concentration in the midst of dualities, or as Alice Bailey worded it, Harmony through Conflict, the Ray of Struggle. The important nuance here is *harmonizing*. This Ray is about achieving harmony, balance, the middle ground between opposites, the peace behind the warring energies of existence, the synthesis of conflicting tendencies such as the fundamental dispositions to inertia and activity. This Ray threads between the breaths for the view of both and beyond; this Ray unifies environmental forces, both gross and subtle.

In terms of his activities and incarnations, Lao Tzu's concerns appear to be concentrated in Asia, including China (where he has 12 Sanctuaries), Mongolia (where he was Chinggis [Genghis] Khan), and Tibet where he was Tonpa Shenrab Miwo, the founder of Bön. But he had a deep impact on Catholic Ireland as the 5th century A.D. Saint Patrick.

Nature is certainly the theater of warring tendencies and opposites, so Lao Tzu instructs those interested in effective ways of working with Earth energies. Through his Bön and Taoist teachings, too, one learns the ways of working with and accommodating the panoply of Nature Spirits, protector beings, and spirits of the landscape. We see this in Ireland where legend says St. Patrick subdued all the snakes of the land and drove them out of the country; he also overcame a dragon-like monster named the Caoranach (or Corra) inside Croagh Patrick in County Connacht: this is Ireland's holy mountain subsequently named after their patron saint.

In a parallelism, Tonpa Shenrab Miwo had to overcome a female demon called Khyabpa Lagring who sought to destroy Shenrab's teachings and who continually interfered with them; later, Khyabpa Lagring became his disciple. Converting an indigenous spirit of the land to become an ally is the key fact to Lao Tzu's Ray.

The "snakes" of Ireland, the Caoranach, and the "demon" Khyabpa Lagring may be better seen as expressions of the autochthonous spirits of the landscape. Geomantically, St. Patrick did not actually drive physical snakes from the land; rather, he worked with the land's protector spirits and local deities through the country's omphalos at the Hill of Uisneach, the home of Eriu, the national landscape angel for that country. There he tutored Eriu in how to manage the diversity of landscape angels and landscape protector beings on behalf of Ireland. He also harmonized the geomantic relationship of humans and the landscape to the Nagas at Croagh Patrick.

Croagh Patrick is the site of a minor dragon (one of the Earth's 1,053 third tier dragons) and a Celestial City that I call Naga City (Vedic name: Raksovati). This includes many snake-like but highly sentient golden spiritual beings called Nagas (their torsos are serpentine and sinuous from energy currents), sometimes called Serpents of Wisdom; their dragon king is Sesa-Ananta. St. Patrick managed these spirits and arranged for the periodic and orderly release of their energy into all of Ireland; this was like "slaying" the dragon to release the healing waters. It is more correct to say St. Patrick opened up Ireland's access to the Naga mentors and their valuable wisdom, allowing it to periodically flow and enrich the country.

Lao Tzu is the spiritual world "stage manager" for the Celtic quarterly feast day called Samhain on November 1 every year. Traditionally, Samhain, which means "summer's end," was the Celtic New Year, marking both the end of summer and the start of the new year. The peak of the event is actually on Samhain Eve, roughly dusk to midnight, October 31 (the traditional Halloween [Hallowmass]). Across the planet, spiritual doors are opened wide and humans are invited to cross the threshold to join what appears to be a massive banquet, massive in the sense that the banquet table seems to stretch entirely around the Earth. The banquet has much in common with the prophecied Messianic Feast or eschatological banquet where at the end of time the "righteous" (the spiritually illumined) will eat the "flesh" of pure Light, derived from Behemoth and Leviathan, two primordial creatures. Decoding these mythic figures we find Behemoth is a guise of the Ofanim, Leviathan a guise of the cosmic dragon, Sesa-Ananta.

The banquet table is set inside what appears to be a subtle ring of light encircling the planet, much like the rings of Saturn. Classical

Vedic thought called this Earth ring Jambudvipa, the "Rose-Apple Tree Island;" it is the innermost of seven subtle concentric rings (each an "island" or *dvipa*) encircling the planet at the equator with the cosmic Mount Meru rising up in the center of them all.

Lao Tzu is the tour guide for those interested in traveling psychically with him to subtle locales including the civilization inside the Earth (the legendary Hollow Earth domain [sometimes called Agartha] accessed through climb-down stairways, or emergence points, called *sipapuni* by the Native Americans); a Hidden Valley (a hidden paradaisal land phase-shifted out of normal physical perception) in Tibet; and an aerial etheric sanctuary (on the order of an Etheric City) above the Earth.

Lao Tzu's method of inducting one (or at least how he inducted a colleague and me) into one of his arcane realms is fascinating and instructive. After aligning ourselves through the crown chakra with his Ray color, Lao Tzu appeared in vision and took us in vision to one of his Sanctuaries in China. It sat over one of those unusual vertical finger-type pinnacles you see in China. Inside his Sanctuary, we passed the massive flame burning in the urn then entered a chamber that had French doors at one end. Lao Tzu opened these, revealing a large classroom, full of students, perhaps fifty feet below us. We descended to ground level and mingled with the students, presumably his apprentices from all over the world, also here in their spirit bodies.

The wall behind the teacher's stand looked like a huge flat-screen TV on which a bas-relief projection of his yellow Ray has been painted or projected in layers to create texture. Yet I saw the flame is a hologram revealing a movie, or a moving image of a location. This seemed to be our beacon. We passed through the flame and headed towards the indicated scene. At first, we hovered high above a sage green, slightly misty, mandorla-shaped valley. We descended slowly, seeming to pass through a membrane, were greeted by numerous air spirits who are aerial protectors of the enclave below, then settled at ground level at the far end of a long, slit-like valley. This expedition turned out to be an introduction to one of the fabled Hidden Valleys, a place like the legendary Shangri-la.

On another outing, which would take us into the Hollow Earth to visit a community there, we started again at one of Lao Tzu's China Sanctuaries. What before had seemed a TV screen and a huge painted yellow flame bas-relief, was now more simply a holographic map of the planet. He pointed to numerous locations that seemed to twinkle and indicated these were areas he oversaw.

They are "cultural reserves or arks," Lao Tzu told us. He meant archival places protected as alternatives for Earth, like seeds of culture for the future, for more exalted expressions of how to ground spirit in matter and have it flourish, in case the present topside Earth reality fails. This seemed quite similar to what the High Lama (in James Hilton's *Lost Horizon*) of Shangri-la explained their function to be: to maintain examples of high culture for a time after the reign of barbarity on the planet. "'Here we shall stay with our books and our music and our meditations, conserving the frail elegancies of a dying age, and seeking such wisdom as men will need when their passions are spent," the Lama told Hugh Conway, a vistor chosen to succeed him.[26]

Then Lao Tzu took us to one. We seemed to head over the northwestern tip of Italy where it meets France at the Riviera, possibly in the area of Monaco. I saw a tall, broad, smooth cliff-face, perhaps 500, maybe 1,000 feet high, rising straight up from the sea. We hovered about half-way up its height and, as it turned out, waited for a hidden door to open in the rock face. When it opened, we passed through, then proceeded down a long, dark tunnel deep into the planet to emerge at a precipice.

Looking over it, we saw it was a tall open shaft inside the Earth, perhaps several miles high, maybe one-quarter mile across. Up through it, like a spuming fountain, continuously rose a beam of light. We descended to visit the Hollow Earth community. Afterwards, we understood Lao Tzu is what we would call the administra-

26.   James Hilton, *Lost Horizon* (New York: Grosset & Dunlap, 1933): 191.

tor of Hollow Earth initiatives and general patron-deity for their existence.

Kuan-Yin's Sanctuaries of the Pale Yellow Ray

As the color consort to Lao Tzu, Kuan-Yin decidedly prefers the highest elevations for her Sanctuaries. Her Ray color is a pale, electric, almost silken yellow, and access to her level requires a higher or more finely tuned clairvoyance than with some of the other Ray Masters. Her guise as the Hindu Parvati, daughter of Himavat (or Himalaya), "Owner of Snow," and consort to the god Shiva, and her attributes as Adrija and Girija (both mean "Mountain-Born") support this higher frequency aspect.

Kuan-Yin generally is regarded as the compassionate goddess of mercy, especially in her Buddhist- and Tibetan-filtered guises as the Green and White Tara or Dolma, but she is also the provider of the high and sublime view, the mountain-top perspective, the exalted, high altitude vista over and through the realm of opposites, divisions, and polarities. She provides—*she is*—the perspective that transcends and dissolves the conflict between opposites—she is the harmony. She says, "I provide the view," the big picture, the majestic, sweeping view above all conditioned forms.

Many of her Sanctuaries are situated above very high elevations, some barely accessible, such as the Nepalese peak Anapurna and Mount Elbert, Colorado, the highest peak in the Rocky Mountains. Elsewhere, her penchant for the heights—she is the true and original Lady of the Peaks—is reflected in the commemoration of her presence in a Sanctuary high above a landscape site by hillside statues of angels or the Virgin Mary such as outside the city limits of Buenos Aires, Argentina, and Quito, Ecuador. With Ray Master Nada, Kuan-Yin is often part of the benevolent apparitional essence of the Virgin Mary, in the guise of the compassionate mother.

Another nuance to her attribution as Mountain-Born pertains to her role as the tutor for humans in the use of the 8th chakra, situated a few feet above the top of the head. The 8th chakra in fact is the Mountain, and Kuan-Yin is our "mountain-climbing" teacher. The 8th chakra is a transpersonal meeting place, seemingly high above the Earth and its geometric Light grid; it is also relatively high above the body and its concerns, accessed from the crown chakra. Seen from the crown looking up, it resembles an opalescent pearl set in a concave shallow basin; the inside of the 8th chakra is like a broad open chalice with fluted or faceted, upward-curving pale yellow walls. It is like a ribbed sphere with the upward-rising ribs spaced about four feet apart. It reminds one of a plump peony blossom about one-half unfurled, except you are standing in the center of the petals.

The human 8th chakra is like a chalice, Kuan-Yin says during a visit I made to her Sanctuary in my 8th chakra, and "into it I will pour my Yellow Ray which will dribble down upon your crown chakra." At first, she appeared in her sublime Bodhisattva guise, a manifestation of the Higher Mind, then she assumed a more human-like appearance, somewhat the way the Chinese have depicted her, with layers of beautiful yellow robes and scarves and a gentle vibration and manner.

Through every curved vertical facet of the 8th chakra you can see Kuan-Yin, or rather, her presence is uniformly distributed through the perhaps 100 vertical facets. Looking upward, you sense the places throughout the galaxy where she has more Sanctuaries, and looking downward to the Earth, the floor is like a viewing screen and you can focus on different Earth areas where she is active. I looked up again, and this time had the impression that where a roof ought to be was actually open or transparent and porous, and a kind of yellow rain was falling through it. I examined a droplet: it seemed to explode in slow motion, opening up to reveal numerous Cherubs (an angelic order) with trumpets. Their sound is a reality-shape in a landscape that when seen from above (and that means above the 8th chakra), looks like a surging, wave-rich yellow sea.

I gradfually realized this yellow sea was ontologically high-end real estate. Kuan-Yin showed me pictures to illustrate its pedigree: this is the place the Buddha went in meditation, where his beatific smile comes from. This is the sea of God's grace and love, the endless "snow" of Himavat, Kuan-Yin's celestial "Father." This sea has the sensation of levitation, buoyancy, of floating without effort; saints come here to be suspended luxuriously upon the sea far above the cares of the world. In fact, the sea is like Kuan-Yin's vibration: gentle, soothing, subtle, pre-rational, like a soft breeze, a warm mist. Floating in this peaceful sea is a great healing, the ultimate sanctuary, a continuous blessing as you float and bathe and drift in the sea of grace.

Djwhal Khul, Tibetan Master of the Green Ray

This Ray appears as a rich, sparkling emerald green with an infusion of yellow, and its Ray Master is the Ascended Master known to students of Alice Bailey's voluminous metaphysical works as The Tibetan, or Djwhal Khul—DK, for short. In most of Bailey's 24 books, from the 1920s to 1950s, DK is credited as the spiritual-world source of the information, and he comments that he was the mentor and information source for H.P. Blavatsky's monumental work, *The Secret Doctrine* (1888).

Appropriately, DK notes that he overshadowed and "permeated" the great scholar of metaphysics, Henry Cornelius Agrippa of Nettesheim, Germany, whose *Three Books of Occult Philosophy* (1531) is still considered the foundation text for Western Occultism and magical lore and practice.

DK is the metaphysical scholar's Ray Master. He takes you deep into universal systems and their operations; he is the universal systematizer and analyzer, the geographer of the Higher Mind, the cartographer of cosmic law. His Ray Master Sanctuary (at least the one near Mount Kailas, in northwest Tibet, above Mount Gurla Mandhata) is a treasury of documents, papers, books—a scholar's well-equipped library, even if disappointingly to a bookworm, book hoarder and underliner like myself this wondrous library is, alas, intangible.

From this particular Sanctuary, DK fulfills one of his prime commissions from the Supreme Being: the development of a new world religion (in its literal meaning, as the protocols to link and bind Heaven and Earth) that combines the impulses and revelations of the Christ and Buddha, Love and Wisdom. Part of this occurs in his overseeing the Wesak Festival during the five days around the first full moon of the astrological month of Taurus (about April 21-May 21). Wesak has no fixed date within Taurus; it purely depends on when the first full moon takes place each year.

The reason for the Taurus full moon is that in Buddhist legend the Buddha attained enlightenment on this full moon while meditating at Bodh Gaya in India. Buddhists contend that on this same full moon each year ("Buddha's Birthday"), the Buddha returns to Wesak Valley in Tibet for eight minutes to bless the Earth and humanity, this blessing being transmitted through the Christ, also present there.

On this occasion, the Christ and Buddha both infuse the Earth in real time through authentic visitations and offer fresh encouragement for the unfolding of higher spirituality. They ground this in a physical valley near Mount Kailas. One of the prime results is the "rebooting" of a geomantic condition called Buddha-Lands or Pure Lands. This is a condition of immaculate purity and high spiritual vibration in which the residents of the higher spiritual worlds, known in Buddhism as *dakinis*, bliss-beings, and the innumerable Buddhas, permeate the physical landscape and its etheric layers. There is no veil between realms, and the spiritual underpinnings of reality are utterly apparent, revealed in their pure truth—*naked*. A Buddha-Land is a condition or place characterized by total wakefulness and awareness without objects—a realm of pure and total awareness without content: Buddha Mind. This awakened state is the condition of matter here, of environment and reality, of the ground of being.

In practical terms, this means that wherever you are or look, you are within this revelation of the Buddha Mind—the plethora of enlightened beings from the most accomplished realms of existence all in the same place as a given physical landscape. There is no separation of land and spirits; it is singularly a Pure Land.[27]

This Ray, then, is about assimilation and synthesis, the ability to reach, understand, and articulate the Higher Mind, its contents and structures as well as its non-content—the pristine empty awareness. In his "own words," through Alice Bailey, DK calls this Ray the one of Active Intelligence (or Adaptability) and the Higher Mind (or Universal Mind).

A person on this Ray will tend to be an abstract thinker, a philosopher or metaphysician, and be one with a highly developed imaginative faculty. Here the researcher may "uncover the thought of God," see "objective significances," and "illumine all the spheres whereon God works." The Lord of this Ray, DK says, is The Keeper of the Records, The Interpreter of That Which Is Seen, The Builder of the Foundation, The Illuminator of the Lotus, and The Universal Mind.[28]

---

27. Here are more impressions of a Buddha Land, Pure Land, or a blissful land permeated by the Buddha's enlightenment: Sites are sacred because "each features a primordial, naturally appearing celestial palace in which resides an assembly of emanated deities." What creates a Pure Land? "They appear because this supreme, original Buddha pervades all things," thus making it a Buddha Land. "This sublime area called Tsadra [a portion of Tibet] represents the mind of enlightenment...." Another location is "a fortress of great liberation and a majestic celestial palace of all buddhas." These descriptions refer to the numinous aspects of actual terrestrial landscapes; at Wesak, the archetype of the Buddha Land in the spiritual world is the stage for the Buddha's blessing. Ngawang Zanpo, *Sacred Ground. Jamgon Kongtrul on "Pilgrimage and Sacred Geography,"* (Ithaca, NY: Snow Lion Publications, 2001):174, 177, 179, 190.

28. Alice A. Bailey, *Esoteric Psychology. Vol. 1, A Treatise on the Seven Rays* (New York, NY: Lucis Publishing Company, 1962): 67, 68, 204, 419.

Ray Master Hilarion of the Pale Green Ray

I began to understand how this Ray works one day while gardening. The Ray Master Hilarion suggested to me that I englobe my newly planted squash hills with a pale, spring green sphere. This would provide an energizing and nurturing field for the seeds during the time of germination and possibly afterwards as the tiny cotyledons struggled to grow. I realized this was a functional and metaphorical description for this Ray.

The pale, spring green Ray has to do with vitality, nurturing and stimulating growth, and quickening new buds, especially in the areas of expanding consciousness and culture. The Ray, as typified by its englobing, fructifying function just mentioned, is a sustenance field for the seeds of higher awareness. It is fitting that one of Hilarion's human guises was the Apostle Paul, whose famous conversion from atheist-doubter Saul to evangelical Paul was sparked by a vision on his journey to Damascus of the risen (ascended) Christ. Ray Master Hilarion leads people to this same conversion experience, when the seed of belief sprouts, and then helps them nurture it.

You can see this nurturing-mentoring focus in one of Hilarion's earlier, mythic guises. He was Centaurus, the father of the centaurs, the fabled race of creatures with a horse body and human head. The most famous among centaurs was Cheiron, tutor to many Greek heroes. With the exception of Cheiron and another centaur called Pholos, who were cast benignly, the Greeks gave the creatures a bad press, attributing bestiality and violence to them, but this was a mistaken perception.

It's easy to see the original purity of the guise in the far earlier Vedic form of the Asvins, the twin horse-headed gods, Nasatya and Dasra. These were the fair, strong, and beautiful sons of the Sun, Surya; they were unequalled in bliss and lived in glory in the sky as weavers of light, hero-helpers, and physicians of the gods. Asvin, which means "possessed of horses," derives from *Asva*, "pervader," an epithet commonly used for Vishnu, one of the Hindu Trinity (equivalent to the Christ-Logos). The Asvins appeared in the sky just before dawn in a golden carriage drawn by horses, or perhaps they were the horses drawing the Sun's chariot.

Surya, the Hindu Sun-god (like the Greek Helios) was portrayed as a horse (even Vishnu had horse attributes and epithets, as typified in the epic Asvamedha [horse] sacrifice), and thus the two Asvins were depicted as golden horse-headed charioteers. Clearly they were luminous deities, but what qualified them to be the physicians of the gods, another of their epithets, was their comprehensive knowledge of the secrets of plant life, as in the fructifying powers of the pale green sphere to support higher spiritual life, and of the etheric body of human and planet, the Etheric Belt, as mentioned earlier. Rudolf Steiner equated the human etheric body with the entire plant kingdom, saying this is where plants "live" in and comprise the human.

Ray Master Hilarion explains that he created the guise of the centaur, and even inhabited the "personality" remembered as Cheiron (some of his GWB adepts assumed centaur guise as well, and still do when appropriate), to mentor early humanity. If you visit (in vision) his Ray Master Sanctuary at Mount Pelion in Thessaly, Greece (the legendary original home of Cheiron), you may possibly still see Hilarion and his adepts in their centaur guise as those thoughtforms were strongly imprinted in the ethers there. In fact, this is equally possible at many of his other Sanctuaries, including the one at Santa Fe, New Mexico, situated over the Plaza.

The centaurs, or in their sublimer form as the Asvins, were the front-runners—the chariot-pullers—for the Christ-Logos in the Great Central Sun (where Surya dwells). It is apt to conceive of them as the horses that pull the Sun's chariot for they teach humanity the approach to the ineffable Sun; they are the fleet-footed conveyors of consciousness to that realm and the experience of the always-risen Christ. Reversing the image, they teach humanity the approach to the Sun's chariot as if the horses face it and you ride them on the way *to the chariot* and its Sun-charioteer. It is less the case that they pull the chariot as lead you on horseback (on their backs, through their teachings) to it.

The centaur guise is metaphorically, even heuristically, apt: it shows us how to use this Ray to ground the higher mind and spirituality in human consciousness that rests bodily upon its animal antecedents and foundations (represented by the centaur's horse form), and how to move in this dual mode towards the Great Central Sun, or the coming dawn (in us) of the Christ awareness. This is all demonstrated in Saul's vivid conversion experience, when the Christ awareness dawned in him.

Hilarion's centaurs also school us in the mysteries of the Eucharist, the ritual consuming of the Christ-Logos, the inexhaustible wafer of the Word. You can see this through the earlier Vedic form of a mass for Christ known as the Asvamedha. This was a year-long horse sacrifice ceremony conducted by a king under conditions of staggering opulence. But since the horse signified Surya and Vishnu, the sacrifice was truly a Eucharistic feast: everyone ate some of the divine horse, whose "flesh" was Christ.

The pale green Ray creates the dedicated sanctuary space—the holy wafer, the body, the horse form with celestial head—that contains the Sun or Christ and conducts one to it (on "horse-back"). Students of the centaurs learned how to consume the Christ through these representatives, how to enter the Christ presence through the centaur guise, and to travel with them across the galaxy and cosmos fleet of foot, which is to say, with full, wide-awake cognition flush with the Christ Consciousness. Perhaps it's easier now to see how Saul's vision of the ascended Christ and his conversion experience illustrates this, how his awakening itself, as a fact and a story, points to the risen, whole Christ, and how it is a nurturing, mentoring example for us to reiterate this profound perception.

Perhaps the ultimate origin of the horse symbol is the Vedic Uccaihsravas, the White Horse that arose, amidst other treasures, when the gods churned the Ocean of Milk. Later in cosmic history, Vishnu's 18th Descent or Avatara into worldy existence was as Hayagriva, the horse-headed Protector of the Scriptures. We might usefully think of the White Horse as compounded of all the sacred utterances, invocations, mantras, and sound currents that create and sustain the cosmos, all the reality-generating permutations of the Word. In this sense, the Horse (as Asva, centaur, Hayagriva, or Uccaihsravas) is the Word made flesh and *mobile*, galloping fleet-footed through all cosmic reality.

Ray Master Hilarion's Ray is about healing at all levels, for it embodies the Christ Sun, transmitting it to (or transporting one to it) all realms of created life. Hilarion and his centaur-Asvin adepts are the officiants and priests of the continuous rite of the assimilation of the truth and reality of the eternally risen Christ.

The Cobalt Blue Ray of Divine Will and Power

The Master of this Ray is generally known as Paul the Venetian, owing to a recent human life as the Italian Renaissance painter, Paolo Caliari Veronese (1528-1588) of Verona, Italy. He lived and worked in Venice for 33 years. The color is a dark, rich, almost smoky, cobalt blue, and the energy is still, serene, deep, and focussed. In the Ray categories of DK through Alice Bailey, this is the Ray of Will and Power. Whose will and power? The Supreme Being's.

Perhaps the salient question to ask is: What does this will and power do? It strips away the falsehoods of being to reveal the virginal diamond core of truth. It is about the divestment of the lower self, the ego or personality; it is the force of God expressed as a wind that rips off all the garments of selfhood; and it is the initiatory confrontation with the power and will of God and the realization that this is a death experience, a disrobing of the veils of separateness and identity.

Some of Paul the Venetian's godly guises illustrate this. He has manifested as the Hindu Kali, the Black One, the black-faced, frightening apparition of the creative and destructive power of time. Kali is dark-skinned, unclothed, gaunt, four-armed; she devours all beings and her darkness is the negation of day, yet like the night it is also the seedbed of potentiality for new life. Kali wears a garland of human skulls and a skirt of chopped arms, and she brandishes weapons of death and dismemberment as she dances in the cremation grounds. She is meant to be deeply scary.

Fierce Kali is the aggressive, even assaultive, face of this inexorable divine power and will as pictured in terms of how its destructive impact is registered on the lower self and its will.[29] For the mortal personality, Kali is very frightening. She personifies time's creative and destructive power; old herself, she devours all beings, and her darkness dissolves individuality and bodily identity; using the severed head she teaches the transience of life; her nakedness suggests the stripping away of entangling illusions and the granting of pure perception—to the unprepared, it's a potentially shocking experience, a graveyard for the worldly personality.[30]

In Egyptian myth, Paul the Venetian made a form for himself as the funerary god Sokar who was believed to reside in the necropolis of both Memphis and Thebes-Luxor. Both locations outwardly had burial grounds, but inwardly, in terms of their geomantic templates, they were Underworld entrances. Part of Ray Master Paul's function at these locations, and in fact at all the other 1,746 Underworld entrances, is to serve as psychopomp to the *Duat* (the Egyptian name for the Underworld, initially meant here in its limited sense as the

29. This usage of the phrase "power and will of God" must be differentiated from the similar language used by militant, fundamentalist Christianity and to an extent, the Catholic Church. In terms of the Ray, this will and power transmits no judgement, punishment, invalidation, condemnation, anger, vindictiveness, or any other negative, heavy-handed and spiritually elitist attitudes attributed by these groups to the Judeo-Christian Yahweh, presumed by believers to be God. Rather, the Supreme Being, as the ultimate source of the will and power, is more like a neutral strong wind that by its sheer force of truth rips off falsehoods from the psyche exposing what is true and real beneath.

30. Anna L. Dallapiccola, *Dictionary of Hindu Lore and Legend* (New York: Thames & Hudson, 2002): 108.

after-death realm) and the soul's passage through its 12 stations after death. In a sense, Paul as Sokar is the implicit narrator of the Egyptian "Book of the Dead" (an after-death manual read to the deceased as a guide of passage through the Underworld: a more recent and accurate translation renders the title as the "Book of Coming Forth into the Day").

Similarly, Paul supervised the death initiation Mysteries at Eleusis in Greece as reflected in the story of Persephone and her abduction into the Underworld by Hades. She was forced to live part of the year "underground" with Hades, the rest "above-ground" (i.e, in the higher spiritual realms, the Upper World) with Demeter, her mother. In effect, during the four or six months she stayed with Hades, Persephone was the Queen of the Dead, and she was regarded by mortals as a dreaded, awful goddess of death.

Persephone was also known as Kore which means "The Girl," a name suggestive of virginity and innocence. But the correct nuance puts the meaning of virginity and innocence at a higher level than the body or sexuality. The Blue Ray strips away all the encrustations upon the pure inner self, which has been depicted as like a glittering diamond or a beautiful virginal girl of high purity (i.e., the soul). As Mazdean mysticism of classical pre-Islamic Persia put it, this is the apparition of Daena, "a heavenly Maiden whose beauty surpasses all imagination." The Daena is the earthly human soul's celestial counterpart, "the Soul of Light or Angel," the "celestial Self, the light-Self of that soul," the "Angel [or one's Higher Self] in feminine guise."[31]

Mazdaism says a human encounters the Daena, an image of the purity of the immortal soul, at the entrance to the Cinvat Bridge (*Chinvatperetu*, "The Bridge of the Decider"), the narrow bridge that links the world of the living with that of the dead. This is a discerning bridge that widens or narrows to a razor blade's width according to

31.   Henry Corbin, "Cyclical Time in Mazdaism and Ismailism," in *Man and Time. Papers from the Eranos Yearbooks*, Bollingen Series XXX.3, Edited by Joseph Campbell (Princeton, NJ: Princeton University Press, 1983): 123,137,143.

the degree of righteousness (karmic purity) of the person about to cross it. It is generally believed that you may cross this bridge only when you are physically dead (after the severance of the silver cord) and are about to enter the Underworld (or afterlife). In a sense, the Cinvat Bridge has a similar function to the Three Judges of the Dead in Hades that the soul encounters in its after-death passage; both involve a life review and assessment.

You get a picture of part of this in the common phenomena reported in Near-Death experiences where the person reviews their life. Although the NDE usually exposes one only to events that took place in the daytime (i.e., normal waking consciousness) and not the nighttime (i.e., astral [un]consciousness), clearly the experiencer is the true and final judge of their life events now under review.

Let's tie some threads together. Paul is Persephone in her role as Queen of the Dead, but he is the supervisor of the death initiation Mystery whereby the embodied ego meets the Light-filled soul (Daena, Kore, the Virgin or Girl, and thus Persephone also) and here he is not Persephone. It depends on the place. It's important to construe the Underworld in large terms: it is not only the realm of the Dead for that is but the antechamber to its full extent. The bulk of the Underworld is actually the entire galaxy understood as a realm for the living (in any form, however subtle) and thus mortal (and eventually dead); only beyond (or above, or before) the Underworld (i.e., in the Upper World) do the eternals, like Demeter, live. So Persephone demonstrates the "fate" of spirits entering incarnation at any level, yet through her own initiation below-ground, she becomes tutor to all others.

Ray Master Paul the Venetian is the guide to this experience and the revelation of the individual's encounter with God's will and power and its aftermath.

Shiva, Kali's mate, is the guardian of the galaxy and functionally the King of the Dead and Hades. Shiva is the Hound of Hell, the Dog who guards the vast house of the stars—Shiva is the star Sirius within Canis Major, the Hindus said—who defends the galactic door to the Underworld of the Milky Way galaxy. Paul's role as psycho-pomp reprises all this: in his different guises, he guides the human soul through the Underworld, the stations of the *Duat* (or *Bardo*, in Tibetan lore; he is also like Dantes' Virgil in *The Divine Comedy*), preparing them for the final divestment of the veils of selfhood; this is the requisite for meeting the King of the Dead (i.e., the created, con-ditioned, and thus mortal ones), Shiva, at the doorway into and out of the galaxy (Underworld).

From the viewpoint of what the newly dead experience, the Cinvat Bridge with the Daena meeting is equivalent to negotiating the Halls of the Dead and the Three Judges, which includes Minos, former King of Crete and master of the Cretan labyrinth, as well as Sokar.[32] In either case, the ego, divested of the body, now confronts one's own Higher Self. Minos is a guise of Ray Master Paul: he is chief Judge of the Dead; the other two Judges, described in Greek myth as his broth-ers, are his adepts. Walking the Cretan labyrinth (a geomantic feature that measured more than 20 miles across, built under the sponsorship of King Minos) was a rigorous death preparation (even for those who would remain living for a while), as one made oneself ready to meet the Minotaur, an aspect of the Supreme Being, as both Zeus and Shiva had manifestations as glorious, fierce white bulls. Here is God-awareness where *your* head used to be.

In keeping with his involvement in the Mysteries, Ray Master Paul the Venetian supervises what is called Scorpio Illumination Day, October 22. This occurs just after the start of the "month" or cycle of Scorpio each year and involves the 100 Mystery Pyramids (huge tetra-hedrons of Light) positioned across the planet. One for example occu-pies about two-thirds of the surface area of Lake Tahoe, which

---

32. Sokar, called the Lord of the Mysterious Region (Netherworld) and depicted as a falcon-headed god, raised the deceased pharoah up into his *henu barque* to transport him into the Duat. Here the *henu barque* serves the same function as the Cinvat Bridge and the Judges' antechamber of the Halls of the Dead. Sokar was also known as "He of Rosetau," the necropolis entrance to the Underworld.

straddles California and Nevada; another overlays Santa Fe Baldy Mountain, near Santa Fe, New Mexico. In a visionary sense, each Pyramid has thousands of Eyes of God on the inside walls; each Eye is a portal to an experience of a particular cosmic mystery. You ask a question, then the appropriate Eye gives you an answer by way of a mystical experience, with Ray Master Paul the Venetian presiding as your mentor for this.

Apollo, Master of the Pale Blue Robe

This Ray appears as a pale sky blue suffused with a trace of turquoise and silver; it is the subtler, more rarified expression of the Blue Ray of Will and Power represented by Paul the Venetian.

Apollo is well-known from Greek mythology where he is one of the Olympian gods, a son of Zeus, the father of all the gods. In Theosophical tradition, he was known as Master El Morya, one of the (temporarily) embodied Ascended Masters with whom H.P. Blavatsky consorted in the mid-1800s. In Ireland, he was called Nuadu of the Silver Hand (*Nuadu Argatlam*, "Silver Arm") who for a time was a leader of the Tuatha de Danann and notable for bringing the Sword to Ireland from Findias.

Findias is one of the four spiritual or "magical" cities described in Irish myth. However, in truth Nuadu-Apollo did not bring what became known as the Sword of Nuadu anywhere; rather, he conducts prepared humans to Findias to observe the Sword and possibly, later, to wield it. The sword was one of the Four Treasures of the Tuatha de Danann brought to Ireland long ago (the same bestowal is recorded in Tibetan-Buddhist lore); it represents, in part, the purity, potency and mental focus of the air element. The wrong use of this Sword was called the Dolorous Stroke in the Grail mythos, and it maimed the Rich Fisher King and precipitated the Wasteland, a condition in which we still live, so the Sword must be respected and only used after rigorous training. The Sword, really, is more of a process or protocol than an actual object; the Sword symbolizes this process.

Beltaine, the Celtic quarterly feast day on May 1, is one of the year's prime events that introduce people, if they wish it, to the Sword of Nuadu. Beltaine is an Irish-Gaelic word that means *Bel-tinne*, the fires of Bel: Bel is Apollo, the *tinne* or fires are his Ray flame in dynamic expression. Traditionally, bonfires (mimicking the fires of Bel) were lit on hilltops on May Day Eve (April 30), and continued through the night; on the next day, livestock were driven through these fires to purify them of contagion and as a protection against "witchcraft" and baleful influences. The fires of Bel have an inner, geomantic aspect of keen importance to humanity and the Earth.

On May Eve, Ray Master Apollo rekindles or amplifies numerous of his Ray fires around the world which burn at Dedicated Outposts (see below); these are landscape nodes where his pale blue Ray burns perpetually on an urn. These are astral fires of course, but they offer Beltaine psychic participants the chance to immerse themselves in the flames to experience firsthand aspects of this Ray and some of the Mysteries Apollo oversees.

As this Ray is about the will and power of God, Apollo is the representative, guardian, and psychopomp of this revelation, correcting a person's misidentification of the source of action (thinking it's one's own solar plexus chakra and individual ego) to realize the true and ultimate source of all action is the Supreme Being. Apollo prepares the space, both psychological and geomantic, for this encounter and understanding, then he conducts us to the Mystery of the will and power in the form of Nuadu's Sword.

Picture yourself standing in a towering pale blue fire; it burns all around you. You may see spirits in the flames; these are adepts of Apollo and affiliates of the Ray. The Ray flames transport you to a new space that is a pure white flushed with patches of pale blue; among crystals, this color is embodied in the gem called aragonite. This new space may appear, for example, initially as a statue in purest white marble of a human-like figure. Inside the statue is an aragonite-like space, and the blue flushes in the white marble are actually an angelic order, the *Hayyoth ha Chodesh*, known in Judaic lore as the

Holy Beasts or Holy Creatures. This is an arcane angelic order of vast numbers, one not given to much human interaction; they are the four Divine Faces between the wheel spokes in God's Chariot, the *Merkabah*.

This aragonite interior may also resemble an architecturally structured space, suggestive of the magnificent European Gothic cathedrals. It is very still, peaceful, and blissful in this space and it exudes a sense of gathered power. Consider this an etheric sanctuary, whose vibrational quality is maintained by the Supreme Being. This is the *Beth-el*, the House of God, from the Hebrew *bayt*, which means container or God's dwelling; in Qabalistic lore, *bayt* (Hebrew's second letter) was the first of 22 fire letters or primordial energies used by the Supreme Being to create the universe. Afterwards, the Supreme Being used *bayt* as a dwelling for what was later called a House of God.

Now as if turning itself inside out or dissolving into empty air, the aragonite "cathedral" space becomes a vast golden square, miles across, an ethereal, magical city.

This square golden city seems only one story high, but it has a domed center. At floor level, inside the city and under this domed roof (or rotunda), stands a massive sword, positioned sword tip up, its handle on a pedestal that slowly turns. Behold the Sword of Nuadu! This sword has a big mythic resume: it is the Sword of Nuadu of the Silver Hand, the one he brought from the spiritual city, Findias, which is where we now stand. It is the sword of the giant Goliath, taken from him by David and given to his son, Solomon, and later sent on the Ship of Time to King Arthur's Camelot. It is the baleful sword that produced the Dolorous Stroke that turned the Rich Fisher King into the Maimed Fisher King, and a pristine Earth into the Wasteland; and it is the same sword destined to heal the Wounded Fisher King when wielded by the Christ-prepared Grail Knight. (In the Arthurian stories, Galahad gets Solomon's sword.)

This mighty sword is an expression of the Supreme Being's ontological puissance, the embodiment of His will and power that Apollo's Ray transmits. It is the mystical Word-Sword, Logos-made,

Christ-wielded, capable of creating and destroying worlds—not a sword to be used lightly or without extreme preparation, yet, surprisingly, it is offered to humanity to use once again under Apollo's guidance.

From our vantage point, it is the shattered sword, the sword that was broken, for humanity fragmented it through ill-advised, disastrous misuse long ago. It is the "creative principle (Word) of the Universe," implanted in humanity through the faculty of speech and mantric, magical utterances empowered by kundalini; it is the Sword of God protruding from the mouth of Man as a sharp blade, as focussed world-creating, world-changing spoken words. It is what injured the Fisher King (an expression of the collective psyche) and various world-conqueror manques: "He sought to use the magical powers inherent in the word for destructive motives to incite hatred, division and enmity among men."[33]

As Nuadu of the Silver Hand, Apollo (the Greeks dubbed him similarly Lord of the Silver Bow) escorts us to Findias, the golden spiritual city, to view the Sword. That is one of the revelations of his Ray, revealing God's Sword, the active expression of the Supreme Being's power and will available to us when we're ready. Apollo was lord of prophecy, oracles, and divination, and the Greeks saw one of his major functions to be the revealing through prophecy (psychic access, telepathy, channeling, intuition) the will of Zeus and how he planned to use this power. In Christianity, the same is expressed as "Thy will be done." We may loosely or informally correlate God's will with this Sword, thunderbolt, *vajra*, hammer, lightning strike, and the other forceful expressions found in myth for God's will in action.

So Apollo creates and protects this spiritual space in which we might experience the Supreme Being's puissance as a truth of reality and behold the Sword, unbroken and adamant, in the golden city of Findias. In Judaic, lore this was the original Jerusalem and also the

---

33. Trevor Ravenscroft, *The Spear of Destiny. The Occult Power Behind the Spear Which Pierced the Side of Christ* (York Beach, ME: Samuel Weiser, 1982): 181-2.

forthcoming New Jerusalem, for as the shaper of this meeting space, Apollo has been Solomon, builder of the Temple of Jerusalem (from David's designs) and the Apostle Peter (Petras), the Rock upon which the original and pure Catholic Church of Jesus Christ was constructed.

On Beltaine, everyone on the planet (not just in Celtic lands where memory of this Ray Master festival is preserved, if sketchily) may pass through the fires of Bel, purifying themselves of the contagion and "witchcraft" of egoic misperception and self-willed, power-based applications that make us forget the true source of action, power, and will. We are the cattle passing through the purifying flames, but this is not demeaning to call ourselves cattle, for in Buddhism, one's absolute Self nature is expressed as an ox (the famous Ox-Herding pictures which symbolize the stages in attaining enlightenment), and, as previously mentioned, Zeus, Shiva, and Osiris (executive expressions of the Supreme Being) all have white bull forms.

Ray Master Apollo transmits the power and will of the Supreme Being in His ability to *heal* (Apollo is the father of Asclepios, the master physician); *express* (Apollo is *Mousagetes*, Leader of the Nine Muses [poetry, music, dance, recitation]); and *excel* (Apollo was the founder of the Pythian Games, a forerunner of the Olympic Games).

Apollo also seems involved in the process of recovering archival memory of the ancient cultural-planetary epoch called Hyperborea. Greek texts talk about how Apollo spent about half of every year in the Far North called Hyperborea; also that he was born on the Cycladean island of Delos to which came two sets of two Hyperborean maidens, Opis and Argis, and Laodice and Hyperdoche, all four of whom were later buried on Delos in the Theke and Sema tombs, respectively. These are veiled references to a geomantic feature called a Hyperborean Time Library (456 on Earth); these are memory records of the Hyperborean civilization and their epoch, and it appears Ray Master Apollo is a Hyperborean emissary to all subsequent generations.

Apollo has created and supervises a geomantic feature widely duplicated across the planet called Arcs of Expanding Consciousness. There are 174,060 of these on Earth. The Greeks called Apollo the Archer, the Far-Shooter and said he always carried a quiver of silver arrows. The Arcs are these silver arrows (at least one of their nuances), making a parabolic, arrow-shot curve across a landscape, typically ten miles long or so, with a grounding and crowning point. An Arc looks like the silver Arch of St. Louis laid on its side across the landscape: you walk through it like a well-lit tunnel to its end; the experience of doing this suggests walking through the parted waters of the Red Sea, as if you walk in a middle curved space in between physical reality, as if a strip of reality has been pulled aside like a curtain. As you walk through the Arc, your consciousness expands parabolically in accordance with the energy steps of the Arc.

An Arc of Expanding Consciousness that is well-defined and easily accessed is available in Somerset, England, and it runs from Glastonbury Tor (the crown) overland in a parabolic curve to a place the local maps call Lugshorn (the grounding point). To look at it today, it is but an empty farmer's field in a village; however, at Lugshorn, you will encounter a towering Fire of Bel, one of Apollo's Dedicated Outposts on which burns his pale blue-turquoise flame. This is the start of the Arc. It continues overland through Butleigh, Park Wood, and Ponter's Bal, and terminates at the Tor, a queerly-shaped hill in downtown Glastonbury.

If you walk this span physically or follow it clairvoyantly, you will likely experience essentially the same event as at Beltaine. First, you are immersed in the pale blue Ray flame; then, as you proceed through the Arc, you enter the aragonite structured spiritual space, the cathedral or sanctuary; then (at the Tor), you may glimpse Findias, the glorious, golden, spiritual city; finally, within Findias, you may have an audience with the Sword.

With 174,060 copies of the Arc of Expanding Consciousness available on the planet, potentially every day is Beltaine and every Arc a walking chance for us to behold the whole, not shattered, Sword, in its original God-given state.

There is a liminal scene in Apollonius' *The Voyage of Argo* (*The Argonautica*) in which Jason and the Argonauts are on route to Colchis for the Golden Fleece. It is early morning, and they perch near the harbor of the lonely isle of Thynias when suddenly Apollo streaks across the predawn, barely lightening sky on his way from Lycia to some place north. "The golden locks streamed down cheeks in clusters as he moved; he had a silver bow in his left hand and a quiver slung on his back." As he streaked across the sky, the island quaked and the sea rushed in high on the shore, almost as if Apollo were like a Concorde flying close to the land, creating similar terrestrial turbulence. The Argonauts were awe-struck: heads bowed, none dared face Apollo and "meet his lovely eyes" as he passed through the air like a shooting star.[34]

In the spirit of this wonderful scene, during a recent Beltaine, Ray Master Apollo conducted myself and another with him as he streaked across the global sky like a silver arrow shot from his own bow of intention and assignment. We touched down briefly at numerous sites he maintains to strengthen and enhance his Ray flames. Our landings (The Greeks called him the god of embarkations and happy landings.) included Bedloe's Island in New York harbor with its Statue of Liberty; Lincoln Park in San Francisco; a place in northcentral Siberia; Avebury in Wiltshire, England; Atlantis under the Atlantic Ocean; and Socorro, New Mexico, home of the famous Very Large Array.

At this latter site, he has a Sanctuary, and we entered it and his Ray flame. Inside were numerous spirits and Ray adepts, and Apollo appeared to us mostly as a burning form, bright, vibrant, powerful, like one of J. R. R. Tolkien's Balrogs except unfallen and angelic. He is a figure of flame, and whatever Apollo's body shape is, it's eclipsed by the flames. We also stopped at a temple in Nepal where Apollo's

---

34. Apollonius of Rhodes, *The Voyage of Argo (The Argonautica)*, Translated by E. V. Rieu (New York: Viking Penguin, 1959): 91-92.

pale blue-turquoise Ray flame burned behind a statue of a golden Buddha; inside the flames were numerous Hanumans, the Hindu monkey-god and helper to Rama. The Hanumans jumped up and down in place with vigor and enthusiasm, even merriment, shaking marimbas.[35]

Serapis Bey, Egyptian Ray Master of the Indigo Robe

According to classical Egyptian texts, the full name of this Ray Master was Osorapis or Asar-Hapi. He was understood to be a blend of Osiris (Asar), the high god, and the Apis Bull (Hapi), an expression of Osiris; scholars say that therefore Serapis was a hybrid, syncretic, even invented deity. His cult center, as found in Alexandria and Saqqara, was known as a Serapeum at which he was equated with the Apis Bull. He was "the greatest god of Egypt during the first centuries of Christianity," often depicted as a serpent, an image meant to denote him a "Dragon [or Serpent] of Wisdom," an old initiation term from the Mysteries.[36]

Ray Master DK describes the Indigo Ray (a very dark blue, like the midnight sky) as the Ray of Love and Wisdom, the Ray of all the Buddhas and great teachers who combine tremendous wisdom with compassion and love. According to DK, a person on this Ray is an inveterate, tireless scholar with an insatiable quest for knowledge and understanding, a desire for absolute truth and the heights of knowl-

---

35. This somewhat incongruous image of the multiple Hanumans with a Mexican-flavor is typical of the antics of the agents of this disguise. Hanuman was one of many cultural forms assumed by the Ofanim, and one of their prime characteristics is amusement, having fun, putting on antics like this for the fancy-tickling of anyone watching them. It's also their way of saying they work with the particular Ray Master in question, Apollo.

36. H.P. Blavatsky, *The Theosophical Glossary* (Los Angeles: The Theosophy Company, 1892 [1990]): 296.

edge still unscaled; such a person continually seeks ever higher attainments of knowing, wanting to plumb what is beyond and that which remains unknown, so as to share this wisdom and teach it out of love for others.[37]

Obviously, Ray Master Serapis Bey is not a made-up deity, though he uses the Apis Bull and other bull guises (such as White Buffalo Maiden to the North American Lakota) to signify the enormity, magnitude, and virility of the revelation of God he superintends. Serapis Bey similarly uses the guise of the Sphinx as a way of testing the preparedness of the initiate to engage this stupendous vision and revelation.

Often, his Ray Master Sanctuary is situated where sphinxes, either in legend (such as at Mount Phicium above Thebes in Greece) or as statuary (Giza, Saqqara, Luxor-Thebes in Egypt) reside. Sometimes, absent any physical signs, the Sphinx is present nonetheless as an astral geomantic fixture, for Ray Master Serapis Bey is in charge of the Mystery Pyramids. These appear as massive, four-sided pyramids of Light situated around the Earth. They are paramount Mystery revelation theaters, the originals upon which the physically manifest stone pyramids of Egypt were patterned. At Giza, the Great Pyramid occupies the same space as a tetrahedral Mystery Pyramid. Similarly, where the stone Sphinx perches enigmatically in the desert is a Ray Master Sanctuary for Serapis Bey, and when he likes he appears in his querying Sphinx-form to evaluate candidates for admission. Almost amusingly, the Sphinx *is* the question: What am I? What is consciousness? What is this form consciousness has taken? What is human?

Serapis Bey says to his students and potential visitors to the Mystery Pyramid: "As the Sphinx, I test the worthiness of those to enter the temple. Do you have the wisdom to handle the revelation offered?" He adds that through time spent in the Pyramid (one translation from the Egyptian has it meaning "The Light") one grows wisdom. It's not the easiest thing in the world to get inside this temple

---

37. Alice A. Bailey, *Esoteric Psychology. Vol. 1, A Treatise on the Seven Rays* (New York, NY: Lucis Publishing Company, 1962]: 203.

for it is situated in the 5th dimension or 5th layer of the Earth's visionary geography (the bulk of the geomantic features are in the 4th dimension or 4th layer), and thus it requires heightened clairvoyance to decode the experience into sensible, daytime terms.

Serapis Bey maintains a Sanctuary at Santa Fe Baldy, a 12,000-foot high mountain in the Sangre de Christo Mountains near Santa Fe, New Mexico. This Sanctuary fronts a Mystery Pyramid that overlaps the considerable girth of this peak. The city of Santa Fe is overlaid by a 10-mile wide landscape zodiac, and about this Serapis Bey suggests that the initiation sequence has one first transit the starfields and Houses of the Zodiac down there then enter the Mystery Pyramid up here which lies outside the zodiacal wheel and probably at a higher spiritual level too.

Also present at Santa Fe Baldy, somewhat below and behind the Pyramid, is a Celestial City, or what I call a Naga City. Classically, this locale was known as Bhogavati, meaning "City of Pleasures" or "Full of Treasures," as well as *Naga-loka* or Patala (said to have 14 levels), and Raksovati. Bhogavati was described in the Vedas and Puranas as an immense voluptuary realm full of Nagas (usually known as celestial Snakes): handsome, golden, effulgent, humanlike spirits with a serpentine torso; sometimes of enormous size, they sport large earrings, many jewels, and towering golden crowns.

In actuality, the Nagas are spiritual beings whose lower torso is sinuous, almost riverine (from activated, flowing kundalini), and whose upper torso and head are human-like, emanating enlightenment. Each is surrounded by a bubble of pale gold. They are known as the Serpents of Wisdom or Snakes, but in truth they are Arhats or Adepts, Dragon Kings, very wise tutelary Dragon Spirits. The snake attribution is metaphorical.

Ray Master Serapis Bey monitors and sponsors their activities, which once earned him the epithet Great Naga (or Great Adept) in his guise as the Buddhist philosopher *Naga*rjuna, said to be one of the "four suns" that illumine the world.

He likens the Nagas' role to that of archivists of the Ray. Since this is the Ray of Wisdom, the Nagas are the custodians and teachers of this wisdom. Humans might visit a Naga City in vision to receive individualized training by a designated Naga tutor. "It's a school for higher wisdom," Serapis Bey comments.

Tutorials in the Naga City are also preparatory for a successful, wakeful experience in the Mystery Pyramid. As an introduction under Serapis Bey's sponsorship, I was introduced to a Naga tutor who conducted me into a golden sphere; it seemed hollow or empty but had protruding knobs on the walls. Somehow, the knowledge and wisdom are within (or encoded) and accessed through these "knobs".

Here is a glimpse of the experience afforded by one "knob:" I stood at the center of a vast spherical gallery full of many thousands of spirits. I understood these spirits to be the innumerable past selves my soul has sponsored anywhere, anytime, in any dimension or universe. I created the Indigo Ray to burn around me in towering midnight blue flames, then perhaps a dozen spirits stepped through this wreath of fire. These were past life selves with wisdom to offer me on a particular topic of interest to me in this life. The Indigo Ray acted as a winnowing device, facilitating the stepping forward of the selves with experience and wisdom relevant to my query.

Making the geomantic set-up richer is the fact that this Naga City at Santa Fe Baldy rests upon one of the Earth's 1,053 minor dragons. Its crowned head sits in the middle of the Naga City at about floor level so that the Naga City surrounds it the way a setting on a ring surrounds the jewel in the center. Each of the minor dragons is the first generation progeny of one of the Earth's 13 primary dragons, and these are emissaries or holograms of the original cosmic dragon, Sesa-Ananta, described in Vedic lore as the repository of ancient knowledge and energy. This dragon is replicated at a global level as the singular planet-encircling Mitgard Serpent.

Apparently, this arrangement is copied elsewhere in the Earth's Light grid, where you have the combination of Ray Master Sanctuary (sometimes in Sphinx form), Mystery Pyramid, Naga City, and coiled dragon. Two examples of this pattern include the Giza complex in Egypt and at Lake Tahoe in California-Nevada (this dragon, called the *Ang* by the Washo Indians, is one of the Earth's 13 primary ones). We encounter another aspect of Serapis Bey's role as psychopomp to the Mysteries in his annual involvement in the summer solstice festival. While traditionally the outer world (at least in Europe) was setting great bonfires on hills and rolling burning wheels down their slopes, initiates under Serapis Bey's direction were traveling in vision to the Great Central Sun[38] to bake their causal bodies[39] for three days in the tremendous solar fires of the cosmic Bull. I visited this "baking" during the three-day summer solstice ceremony (June 22-24); it was like a sweatlodge or pickling brine for thousands, perhaps millions, of spirits, seeking to reshod, refortify, revarnish, and re-equip their causal bodies for the coming year. I sent a part of my awareness to reside in the baking oven and, fascinated, to observe what the others were doing.

During the positive "wake" of the summer solstice saturation-immersion experience, the Earth's 144 Sun Temples (each a hologram or microcosm of the Great Central Sun) engorge with Light from the Bull. This is the original template for the Earth's Sun Temples or Sun Centers, and as mentioned earlier, the Great Central Sun

---

38.   We touched on this mystery earlier in the book. The Great Central Sun (also called Central Spiritual Sun and Eternal Sun Abraxas) is a spiritual Sun or level of consciousness behind our physical Sun. Theosophical lore places it in the Pleiades within the constellation Taurus (the Bull), and says it is Alcyone, the brightest Pleiade. Saint Germain, in his 1930 writings through Godfre Ray King, says it is the natural residence of the "Christ Radiance" and is presided over by the Hindu Sun-god, Surya, a "Great Intelligence" of this domain. The Christ correlation is congruent with the ancient Scandinavian name for the summer solstice, as Balder's Balefires (Balder being a guise of the Christ). H.P. Blavatsky wrote of it: "In the shoreless ocean of space radiates the central, spiritual, and *Invisible* sun. The universe is his body, spirit, and soul; and after this ideal model are framed ALL THINGS." H.P. Blavatsky, *Isis Unveiled, Vol. I* (London: Rider & Co., no date (original:1877)]: 302.

pertains to Surya (the Vedic Helios), Agni (Fire God), and the Christ Radiance; hence the applicability of the Norse term Balder's Balefires for the bonfires lit on hills on Midsummer's Eve (the last night of this 3-day wake-bake, is apt, for Balder was the Norse conception of the Christ ([for them, the first god to die]).

Serapis Bey oversees the immersion "baking" of the initiates in this rich solar energy. It's as if these souls are loaves being baked in the great fire ovens or they are metals being tempered in the celestial smith's forges or even horses (signifying the soul) being reshod with golden shoes.[40] Then approximately at midnight on Midsummer's Eve (June 23), they fly out of the solar kiln, golden and sparkling, and return to their various worlds, including our human realm. Their departure from the Great Central Sun forge enables Light to flow out with them from the Sun Temples like a solar wind into the Earth's Light grid as a nutrient and a blessing.

Again we see the keen relevance of the bull association with Serapis Bey, for another name for the Sun Center is Mithreaum, outwardly a temple of the old European Mithras mysteries in which the tau-

---

39. The causal body is a designation used in Theosophy to refer to a refined aspect of the mental body. Depending on the classification system, the human has 7 or 9 bodies, all but one of them subtle or energy-based. The causal body has been likened to the true seat or site of the Holy Grail, conceived of here as a pure, empty chalice of gold, an energy "body" equipped to receive the higher Light. The causal body is also called the Spiritual Soul, the basis of the cause, that is, of conditions in the lower bodies, including the material body. Theosophy calls it the vehicle of the universal Spirit. Others call it an abstract force field in a vibratory level one cannot ordinarily comprehend and one that energizes the physical body: its function is to "analyze the lives of the soul-mind as presented to the mental body, find the cause of various happenings, and separate the karmic conditions" so that what has been learned correctly proceeds upwards as wisdom, what is not, heads downwards as a karmic liability to be worked out in subsequent incarnations. June G. Bletzer, *The Donning International Encyclopedic Psychic Dictionary* (Norfolk/Virginia Beach, VA: The Donning Company, 1986): 99.

roctony, the bull-slaying, was performed. Even though the bull-slaying seems to have been performed literally in Mithraic rites of Roman Europe, with vestiges in Spain's bull-fighting today, originally it was symbolic. The Bull of God (Taurus, Apis: the Great Central Sun) let some of its Light flow into the world (the rest of the galaxy and the planets) during the summer solstice. The Bull in effect is the solar oven we bake in during these three days, under the guidance of the Bull-master, Serapis Bey (Osorapis), the Bull of Osiris (God).[41]

Ray Master Serapis Bey notes that at the summer solstice something clicks open and stays open for three days. It is a Blue Door in space. An enigma indeed, but one originally introduced to myself and two English colleagues in the 1980s by the Ofanim. One night in our meditative visits with them, they presented us the Blue Door as an experiential reality: there it was before us and they invited us to open it and pass through. The Ofanim later commented in characteristic laconic fashion: "The Blue Door leads to the other side, the other side of everything." More than 20 years later, Serapis Bey showed me the Blue Door again and quipped, "It comes round again." The mystery.

---

40. Wayland's Smithy, a stone barrow along the Ridgeway in Wiltshire, England, is a Sun Temple, and according to English psychics Grace and Ian Cooke, anciently one went there to receive "'God-shod feet.'" The God-guided initiate was sometimes symbolized by golden shoes, they comment, noting Wayland's Smithy was once a place where great Light was concentrated, a site of initiation that opened consciousness to heaven and other planets. Initiates came here and if their worldly self was "lame" and had lost a "shoe" (that is, their spiritual footing and fluidity), they were "'re-shod' so that they might "travel" onwards. The Smithy was "an ancient centre of power to which traveller's on life's journey came for instruction and initiation into the higher mysteries." Wayland (Weland) is the Anglo-Saxon name for the smith, also called Goibniu, Govannon, Hephaistos, and many others. Grace and Ian Cooke, *The Light in Britain* (New Lands, Hampshire, England: The White Eagle Publishing Trust, 1971): 29-33.

41. In his guise as White Buffalo Maiden, he taught the Lakota the *Hunka Lowanpi*, or Sun Dance.

But perhaps a tiny bit less mysterious, for on the eve of the summer solstice, the Blue Door appeared and clicked open, and I passed through it. Initially, I entered the past life gallery mentioned above with the Nagas, that vast spherical gallery full of all the spirits "I" have been over time. I realized the Blue Door must normally be oblique to our dimension so we only see its edge length, like the great black sleek monolith from *2001: A Space Odyssey* seen only from the side, and easily missed. But now during the solstice as the Sun seems to stop moving for a few days, the Blue Door rotates 45 degrees and faces us front on and we move through it to the other side.

Blue Doors appear and open at sacred sites all over the planet at this moment. Each is an invitation, a beckoning threshold: cross over if you dare. But the dare is worth taking, for the Blue Door seems to be the aperture we pass through to get to the Great Central Sun, the Mithraic oven, and the three-day causal body bake. The summer solstice is the big convocation of souls from around the galaxy (or galaxies) to bake their causal bodies in the Bull's oven, the three-day wake, the solar incubation. The event is a saturation-immersion in the cosmic Bull of Light. You could say: now Mithras, born from out of a stone, goes back into the Stone of Heaven.

Pallas Athena's Magenta Sanctuaries in Greek and Irish Culture

As the Master of the ethereal aspect of the Indigo Ray (a blue violet-magenta, or reddish purple), Ray Master Pallas Athena is also a guide to the Mystery revelation this Ray offers. This is typified in her sponsorship of the itinerant Odysseus whose ten-year journey took him to many Mediterranean Mystery temples (geomantic nodes within Earth's visionary geography for that region). In fact, his name and what he did now is common parlance for expeditions and long trips.

Pallas Athena is well-known for being his steadfast divine intercessor and counselor, higher world friend to that to wily Greek hero and adventure. However, it is closer to the truth of the relationship to construe Odysseus as an adept in Pallas Athena's Ray and his odyssey as a grounding and elaborating of her Ray energies through an initiation arc from Troy to Ithaka. Pallas Athena has a Sanctuary at Troy and at Odysseus' homeland, the Greek island of Ithaka, specifically above its highest peak, Anogi (today's Mount Neriton). So his odyssey through mystical lands was bracketed by Sanctuaries of his Ray mentor.

Odysseus' true home on Ithaka was not his estate but the Ray Master Sanctuary above it. When he touched in at the Ithaka Sanctuary, he could close the "book" on his journey from Troy, for which he had received his imprimatur from Pallas Athena. We might read Odysseus' travels as the sequential, geomantically-based initiation of an apprentice in Pallas Athena's Ray, or, equally, as the expert geomantic adjustment and updating of existing sacred sites in the Mediterranean, again with Hero-Helper Pallas Athena's oversight. The numerous suitors Homer says Odysseus faught off to reclaim his home and wife might be better understood as possibly idle Ray students and apprentices under his charge, awaiting his return to receive their next level of Ray initiation.

The classical Greeks described Pallas Athena as a virgin war goddess who was born—fully grown, completely armed, emitting her war-cry—from the brow of Zeus, chief of the Olympian gods. She personified wisdom and was a manifestation of *metis*, or intelligence, consistent with the qualities of the Ray of Love and Wisdom. We might interpret her birth from the brow of Zeus as telling us she was well-equipped to understand and thus explain the arcane thinking of the highest of gods, her father, *the* Father; she could probe Zeus's brow, his mind (her womb), for wisdom. She could speak on behalf of the Mind of God because that was her place of origin.

As we saw earlier with Ray Master Portia, we can observe the relationship between Ray Master, a people, and a geography in Pallas Athena's association with Athens. Though she was adopted as the divine protectress of many Greek cities, her fundamental role as patron and protector of the citadel was at Athens (virtually named after her: Athena-Town, in effect), ever since she bested the Sea-god Poseidon in a competition to possess the Acropolis. He created a sea-well there but she planted an olive tree, and that was judged the better gift to the Athenians. In legend, she was the ancestor of all Athenians because she birthed their fifth king, Erichthonius.

In the 5th century B.C., the Athenians built the Parthenon (from *parthenos*, "Virgin") in her honor and as a physical place to worship their Pallas Athena. Fittingly, she already had a Ray Master Sanctuary there, so the physical and astral buildings had congruence, the ideal in civic-geomantic planning.

Inside the massive white stone structure was a huge statue of Athena made of gold and ivory; outside the Parthenon once stood an equally formidable bronze statue of her. It was so big that the Greek historian Pausanias wrote that the crest of Athena's golden helmet and her spear tip could be seen miles away from sea. He called her Athene of the City and said "the whole city and the whole country are sacred to Athene." The "holiest of all images" was her statue in the Acropolis (which was once the whole city). "Rumour says it [the statue] fell from heaven."[42] During August, Pausanias added, Athenians staged the Panathenaea, a great civic festival with processions through the city in honor of their patron goddess.

During the time of the Panathenaea, due to the concentrated attention of Athenians on Pallas Athena, in functional and experiential terms it was as if her Sanctuary descended to fit over the Acropolis like a golden helmet. While the Sanctuary per se did not move, the public's focus on Athena made it much easier for her reality to permeate Athens, and for sensitives who walked through the Parthenon at this time it was like being in the other world of her Sanctuary. As Ray Master Portia mentored the Tibetans, so did Pallas Athena her Athenians.

Some of Pallas Athena's Sanctuaries are positioned with respect to a geomantic feature called a landscape zodiac. This is a hologram of a

---

42.   Pausanias, *Guide to Greece, Vol. I, Central Greece*, Translated by Peter Levi (New York: Penguin Putnam, 1979): 75.

selection of the galaxy's stars, the Sun's ecliptic, and the major constellations; it is meant to be an interactive, initiation star wheel templated on a navigable section of landscape of varying size, usually on fairly flat land. There is one at Troy (the Sanctuary is over Hisarlik Hill) in today's Turkey; another on the Plain of Murtheimne (over Ochaine Mountain, *Sliab Tuath*) in Ireland; a third within the city limits of Nürnburg (over the central hill with its castle) in Germany; and a fourth in and around Northampton, Massachusetts (over the Summit House on nearby Mount Holyoke Mountain).

In all four cases, Pallas Athena maintains a Sanctuary of the blue violet flame from which she may oversee, supervise, advise, guide, and mentor the star initiations of her Ray students out in the field of "battle." These battles are really the struggles to birth Einherjar, the self-slain, spiritual heroes who have overcome themselves and the lower personality to become illumined masters. The battle is largely an inner one, based on one's horoscope and waged in its starry landscape. The Trojan War, truly, was about birthing Einherjar out in the zodiacal battlefield; whatever actual physical battle took place there was more of a place-marker for the inner spiritual one.

Over the plains of Troy and Murtheimne and their zodiacs, Pallas Athena observed and sometimes intervened in great, seemingly historical, battles of men, i.e., the Trojan War and the Cattle Raid of Cuailgne, the former involving Odysseus, the latter, Cuchulainn (the Hound of Culann).[43] These battles were spiritual in nature, the strug-

---

43. This highlights an arcane working relationship between Pallas Athena and an Ascended Master called Merlin, famous from the King Arthur mythos. Merlin is a unique planetary worker, a terraformer of geomantic landscapes that will support human illumination; one of his guises was Cuchulainn; another was Padmasambhava, the Indian rishi who tamed the Bön-dominated Tibetan landscape for Buddhism. The exciting link here is that Padmasambhava is directly credited with the periodic release of information (through buried documents) about the location of special mystical landscapes, called *beyuls*, over which Pallas Athena, in her Buddhist guise as Vajravarahi or Dorje Phagmo, presides (see below).

gle by apprentices to master and assimilate conflicting star energies, and the confrontation (again, for understanding and assimilation) of different cadres of Ray Master students within an activated geomantic context, much like the daily mock or training battles the Einherjar engage in at Valhalla.

The Indian and Tibetan Buddhists Pallas Athena's more ontological regality as Vajravarahi (Tibetan: Dorje Phagmo), the Diamond Sow Goddess or the Vajra Sow-Faced Dakini (Tibetan: *Khadroma*, "Sky Walker or Dancer"). She is an exalted manifestation of the Dakinis, female wisdom spirits.[44]

Why is the *vajra* associated with Pallas Athena? The *vajra* (Tibetan: *dorje*) is somewhat like Zeus' thunderbolt or lightning flash, at least in essence, and is known as the splitter, bellowing one, and destroyer. It is depicted as a symmetrical hand-held device, something like two globes with blades passing through them connected by a sphere in the middle. The word *vajra* means diamond or adamantine,

---

44. In Indian lore, the Dakini is usually portrayed as a wrathful, naked, even demonic, female figure who accompanies the gods; but the Tibetan perception is probably closer to the Dakini's reality. There she is the *khadroma*, from *kha* for celestial space or emptiness and *dro*, which means walking, moving, dancing, and *ma* which indicates female gender: Sky Walker. The *khadroma* or Dakini is a female-appearing wisdom deity who moves about at the highest level of reality, representing the inspiring, awakening power of consciousness; her nakedness represents the truth unveiled, direct knowledge of reality, or transcendent wisdom. The Dakini is a "tantric muse who urges adepts beyond logic, reason, and abstract theory and guides them toward the unwalled sanctuaries of the illuminated heart." In the relationship between Pallas Athena and Odysseus we can see traces of the Dakini as mentor to the aspiring adept in his meditations through the hidden-lands. We also see the Dakini in Viviane, the young apprentice-seductress in the Arthurian canon who studies with Merlin then imprisons him in her Crystal Cave when she's finished. But we have to invert the story and read it as Merlin consorting willingly with Dakinis for the intellectual pleasure of their revelation. Ian Baker, *The Heart of the World. A Journey to the Last Secret Place* (New York: The Penguin Press, 2004): 77.

and it refers to absolute truth as a cutting edge and the ontological clarity of vision, which suggests emptiness, true reality, the unvarying, indestructible essence, the spotless purity of all existent things—hence the fittingness of the diamond attribution.[45]

The *vajra*, or *dorje*, belongs to Indra, king of the gods, but ultimately, switching to Greek mythological names, to Zeus, father of the gods. It is an indestructible diamond of immaculate transparency: "The *dorje* is the symbol of the clear immutable essence of reality that is the basis of everything."[46] It symbolizes a path to enlightenment called *upaya*, the quality of skillful means; this is appropriate in that Homer calls Odysseus the wily, cunning, *skillful* one: Odysseus demonstrates *upaya* or continuously applied wisdom in a variety of challenging contexts under the direction of his mentor, Pallas Athena.

More properly, Pallas Athena, in her Vajravarahi guise, could be called the Diamond Goddess *of the Sow*, for the Sow (in myth, the white sow and white cow) was an old, instructive symbol in Celtic and Vedic-Buddhist cultures for a landscape zodiac, a holographic star map templated on a landscape. The Egyptian sky-goddess Nut, for example, was said to contain all the galaxy's stars in her great body arching over the Earth; the Celts saw her as Ceridwen, the Sow-goddess and as the Old White One, or as Phaea, The Shining One. The white sow was an excellent descriptive image for the galaxy of stars, fed, nourished, asnd suckled by the Great Mother and Queen of Heaven in her various cultural guises. Her supply of "milk" (total

---

45.   The *vajra* is the thunderbolt (the Greek *keraunos* of Zeus), representing the urgency of realization. Indra is Vajrapani because he wields the *vajra*. The word and object connote durability, incomparable brilliance, hardness, immutability, the mystery of the mind, the pure awareness of all the Buddhas, eternal strength and constancy, both knowledge and emptiness, that which is enduring, irresistible, indomitable, invincible, indestructible, the absolute *axis mundi*, the impervious, fixed solidity around which all creation turns.

46.   *The Encyclopedia of Eastern Philosophy and Religion*, Edited by Stephan Schuhmacher and Gert Woerner (Boston: Shambhala, 1989): 95, 397-8.

awakened consciousness) for her "piglets" (the stars) was inexhaustible, and she was the white sow because of her effulgence of Light and her numerous "teats" to feed the stars.

With her *vajra*, or diamond consciousness, embodying the wisdom of her father's (Zeus) mind, Pallas Athena guides humans through the interactive star fields. She is the psychopomp of the Sow, the guide through mystical sanctuary of stars within the Great Mother's body.

She is the pre-eminent Hero-Helper, assisting the initiate or apprentice, transiting the holographic stars in the landscape zodiac to overcome ignorance, inertia, unconsciousness, and the abyss of not knowing Zeus' mind. Pallas Athena notes that she interacts with all landscape zodiacs when they are being worked on by humans and the spiritual realms (which takes 180 years), or when they are finally "on" or illuminated (which lasts for 1,080 years).

Each star in the complex galactic hologram is a point of awareness to deepen and expand one's experience of the total mind of Zeus. Pallas Athena takes you from the Sow-goddess full of stars to the Father, the source and reason for the stars, from the sow to the *vajra*. Along the way she reveals the celestial mechanisms. "I help the 'hero' distill this experience into living, embodied wisdom," she comments. "I am thus a mentor in astrology, the practical, interpretive view of this encounter."

Pallas Athena sponsors the Gorgon Medusa Mystery initiation. The Greeks portray Gorgon Medusa (one of three sisters) as fiercely ugly, dangerous, and reclusive, living in a cave at the far end of the universe. One gaze from her eyes and you are turned to stone; instead of hair she has innumerable writhing snakes on her head. Pallas Athena helps the hero Perseus sever Gorgon Medusa's head.

That's the outer husk of the story. The inner aspect entails a human encounter with the cosmic crown chakra, an aspect of the Supreme Being. Isn't it said by mystics that to look on the face of God is to die? Turning to stone is certainly a step in that direction. The writhing snakes are energy currents streaming off the cosmic

crown just as the activated human crown chakra is said by clairvoyants to be like a fire with a thousand flickering flames. Medusa's
snakey, riverine energy currents thread through the "stone" of space
like a golden capillary network.

Why stone? Calling the etheric plane a stone or likening it to a vast
sky of stone is an old esoteric metaphor for the inevitable densifica-
tion of spirit outside the realm of absolute Light. You'll always be
pushed back into the stone of space (where Light is by definition
denser, slower, more stone-like) when you try to see the Gorgon
Medusa's face. You can't *see* it ever in her dimension (the cave)
because there would be no you in there anymore to see something as
outside yourself. You can only see the face by stepping outside the
cave, into the stone. So to see the Gorgon Medusa you turn yourself
back into the stone realm where a distinction between you as per-
ceiver and an object to be perceived is still real. She *does* turn you to
stone.

Ultimately, the human experience with Gorgon Medusa is a portal
to an encounter with the Supreme Being. Qabala talks metaphorically
of God having Three Heads, each more arcane than the previous, one
within the other, and one atop the other. There is the Head of Concealed Wisdom, the Supernal Head (which is the most holy ancient
one), and the Head of all Heads, which is not even a head. Here we
have a more abstract rendition of the three Gorgons in their cave at
the edge of the universe; only one, Gorgon Medusa (the Head of
Concealed Wisdom) is within our reach, if that; the other two are far
too arcane for us.

While Pallas Athena is the psychopomp to human spiritual heroes
transiting the stars and assimilating their energies in the landscape
zodiac (the body of the Sow-goddess, or star map), she is also the presiding presence in a more sublime kind of spiritualized landscape
known in Tibetan geomancy as a *beyul*. This is a mystical sanctuary, a
portion of physical landscape removed from ordinary physical perception and human interaction and set aside as a Light-enriched temple

with chakras (spiritual force and consciousness centers) that are levels of awareness within her expanded "body" as Dorje Phagmo.

Just as the landscape zodiac is inside her body as Sow-goddess, so is the mystical sanctuary and hidden-land with its chakra template inside her apparitional form overlaid on a landscape. We might see this as the outer and inner aspect of the same kind of deified landscape. The *beyul* is a more secret celestial landscape than a zodiac, filled not so much with stars as with the goddess, her "body" and Mind-essence.

Humans granted the opportunity to physically walk through a *beyul* know they are walking through the adamantine, immaculate spiritual body of the tantric Diamond Sow Goddess. Each step is an initiation, a further immersion in her expansive, enlightening field of energy and awareness, itself a reflection of the great mind and reality of her father, Zeus. Walking through a *beyul* opens the human mind to profound, unsuspected levels of awareness and energy.

A *beyul* in a sense is a hologram of a goddess' body overlaid on a secretly veiled landscape, a mystical, Light-enriched landscape thoroughly infused by her presence. A *beyul* is a more secret landscape than a landscape zodiac; the former requires great spiritual merit even to find because though it is a material landscape, it is protected by veils, while the latter is meant for humans to use with relative ease, although it requires a long period of illumination following its initial identification and mapping. The *beyul* is like a numinous glove, in the form of the goddess' tantric body, slipped over a designated landscape; the hand slips inside the glove and becomes invisible.

A *beyul* is like Shangri-la, a paradaisal *hidden* land of perfection; it's beyond the range of normal perception, almost like a parallel dimension, a sanctified place populated by Dakinis and other high spiritual beings, a celestial realm on Earth; it's a paradise for Buddhist practice (and perception) which at one level corresponds "to the flow of intangible energies in the physical body," and at another, it is a "unitary dimension revealed through an auspicious conjunction of person, place, and time." As the mind opens through spiritual practice, so do "new dimensions of the environment [*beyuls*]" get revealed.[47] "This innermost heart of the sublime holy land is identical to a terrestrial pure land of lotus light. In this place, all obscurations of mind and emotion can be released...and the three bodies of the Buddha spontaneously realized."[48] Within each hidden valley, *beyul*, or landscape mandala is one place where the *vajra* is grounded as "an indestructible *vajra*-spot."[49] That is Pallas Athena's power spot.

This adamantine *vajra*-spot is found in landscape zodiacs as well as in the hidden, secret valleys, the classical *beyul*. The two are complementary: the *beyul* is the inner, arcane expression with a chakra sequence but without the star array, while the landscape zodiac is the outer, explicit, more easily interactive form, also with a chakra sequence and *vajra*-spot. But for either, the *vajra*-spot is the absolute first point, the *bindu*, seed of the Dharmakaya, center of the *vajra*, and Ray Master Pallas Athena holds this spot inviolate and energetically intact. It corresponds to Qabala's *Ain Sof*, an extra-monadic point above the Tree of Life.

It is very much like the tiny point of absolute Light and information perceived on a basement stairway that Jorge Luis Borges described in his short story, *The Aleph*.[50] The *vajra*-spot of a landscape zodiac is like a compressed singularity containing, grounding, and reflecting the entire contents of the Light temple. In functional terms, it is the secret, potent center, the mustard seed of the array; it can be no bigger than a few feet across but almost infinitely "heavy" with content; it's similar to the total suction of all light by a black hole. Knowledge of the location of the *vajra*-spot in many respects is

47.   Ian Baker, *The Heart of the World. A Journey to the Last Secret Place* (New York: The Penguin Press, 2004): 9, 11, 15, 24, 26.

48.   Khamtrul Rinpoche, quoted in Ian Baker, *The Heart of the World. A Journey to the Last Secret Place* (New York: The Penguin Press, 2004): 95.

49.   Keith Dowman, *Sky Dancer. The Secret Life and Songs of the Lady Yeshe Tsogyel* (Boston: Routledge & Kegan Paul, 1984): 209.

the key and lock to the mystical sanctuary, and in this Pallas Athena is our guide.

Pallas Athena is a Ray Master full of surprises. Two of her prominent though no doubt unsuspected mythic guises are Morgan le Faye, supposedly "troublesome" sister (and sometimes seducerand even "wife") to King Arthur; and Brunhilde (ON: Brynhildr), mentor and lover to Siegfried (a Germanic Arthur) and leader of the Valkyries, known as Odin's Wish-Girls. The essential equation that helps this identification make sense is that King Arthur (Solar Logos, chief of the Great White Brotherhood) is Indra (owner of Vajravarahi's *vajra*) and Siegfried.

Thus Pallas Athena (Morgan, Brunhilde) is a GWB colleague of King Arthur (Siegfried, Indra), acting independently and in cooperation with him. Appropriately, Morgan is credited by Sir Thomas Malory in his *Le' Morte d'Arthur* with having created the Perilous Valley; this is an allegedly treacherous terrain made as a punishment for unfaithful knights; they become trapped in their own self-created illusions while wandering the valley.

Malory mentions the Perilous Valley, then moves on, not seeming to understand what it is, leaving us this enigmatic reference. It's likely the Perilous Valley is a pure-land *beyul* supervised and infused by Morgan for the enlightenment of her adepts, though they might at times lose their way. The further we get in time from the origin of a myth and the psychic understanding of its contents, the more likely it

---

50. In this *Aleph* on the stairway, no bigger than three centimeters, Borges wrote, you could see all the points in space and all the places of the world from every angle as all co-existing within this tiny point. You could behold infinity, including all the events that ever happened in the world, seen simultaneously, and from all angles of perception. This point contained all universal space, and each individual item could be seen from an infinite number of perspectives. "What a magnificent observatory, eh, Borges!" a character comments in the story. Jorge Luis Borges, "The Aleph," in *Collected Fictions*, Translated by Andrew Hurley (New York: Penguin Books,1999): 281-4.

is to be inverted or demonized: the Pure land *beyul* becomes an evil terrain.

Pallas Athena is also the mentor of the 144,000, a group of humans dispersed amidst the world's populations who have pre-selected themselves to be of service to the Earth's Light grid. *Revelation* calls these the "chosen" who stand with Jesus on Mount Zion, but it is not an elitist group; we can better think of these people as apprentice Einherjar, future GWB members now in training, people who agreed to take responsiblity for awakening something profound within themselves. In the Grail literature, this group was called the Sangreal, the Fellowship of the Holy Grail, or in more vernacular terms, King Arthur's once and future Grail Knights.

Earlier, I described an event at a Valhalla accessed through Ivy Thorn Hill near Glastonbury, England. The beautiful though at the time unidentified (by me) female deity was Ray Master Pallas Athena addressing the Sangreal, the 144,000 assembled in Ursa Major at the original Valhalla. Here the Grail Knights, Einherjar-in-training, were out in the "field" (in human bodies on Earth), not so much in search of the Grail but in quest of wise ways of *using* it to benefit the world. Or we could say King Arthur and *his sister* (i.e., GWB Ray Master colleague) Morgan addressed the group; or Siegfried and his Valkyrie lover-teacher, Brunhilde did; or Indra and Vajravarahi, his Diamond Sow-goddess, mistress of all mystical sanctuaries.

Not only was Pallas Athena addressing the Sangreal, she was administering the Sword in the Stone ritual. This is a test of clairvoyance, the sword being the extension of the sixth chakra into the "stone" of the spiritual worlds as well as into the pure lotus-land of her mystical sanctuaries, both *beyuls* and landscape zodiacs. The ritual also involved a "scabbard," an image with rich nuances: the jewelled array of chakras (spinning vortices with different numbers of bright petals); the triple-chanelled conduit for kundalini along the spine; an aspect of the Tree of Life; the jeweled altar presence of the Great White Brotherhood in support of the sword.

This ritual, as the myths tell us, was the prime test of the young Arthur's fitness to be king of all Britain, but it is a continuing test in the voyage towards clairvoyance and the wise discernment of what one beholds in the stone or spiritual worlds. The Sword in the Stone denotes the ability to penetrate this subtle realm and return to the physical, to penetrate and return, effortlessly and routinely, as a natural extension of your heightened, trained awareness, and to understand what's seen and to speak clearly about it (i.e., using the sword responsibly in the world).[51]

The scabbard equals the Ray Masters' combined blessings on the sword, the jeweled array of colors supporting your active clairvoyance, a kind of miniature Bifrost.

It is fitting that Siegfried first sees Brunhilde lying on a plank in a golden-roofed fortress surrounded by "blazing, wavering" flames, seemingly impassable. "The flames rose to the heavens," yet Siegfried had to pass through them. "No one had dared to do this before." He entered them on horseback, and it was as if he had ridden into pitch-darkness, then the flames subsided and he found Brunhilde inside "a beautiful dwelling;" later, he claimed her for his wife.[52]

This image is wonderfully vivid about how you must pass through the specific color flames or Ray emanations of the Ray Master you wish to encounter. With Pallas Athena, picture the blazing, wavering flames surrounding Brunhilde as a blue violet-magenta; match your

---

51. Pallas Athena makes an uncredited cameo appearance at Camalate where as a "damosel" acting as emissary for "the great lady Lile of Avelion" [probably Avalon was meant] she challenges all the knights of King Arthur's court to draw a particular sword she wears under her cloak out of its scabbard. Nobody could do it. This means at that time none at Camalate had sufficient clairvoyance to accomplish the "penetration;" the next day, a down-and-out knight-manque named Balin succeeds, but with woeful results as he later dies as a consequence of the deed. Sir Thomas Malory, *Le Morte d'Arthur*, Vol. I, Edited by Janet Cowen (New York: Penguin Books, 1969): 60-1

52. *The Saga of the Volsungs*, Translated by Jesse L. Byock (New York: Penguin Books, 1999): 80-1.

crown chakra with that color (it's like painting the top of your head in that hue) until you experience your awareness as surrounded by flames of this color; then, there she is: you have entered this Ray Master's flame-girt Sanctuary and can begin receiving instruction, "marrying" its energy to your aura, chakras, and body.

When Pallas Athena's Sanctuary is situated in proximity to a landscape zodiac, we might think of it as a place for Grail Knights to receive validation, *Hellos!*, counseling, guidance, instruction, and fine-tuning, before and after their voyages.

One of the prime functions of the Valkyries was to select then transport "slain" warriors from the battlefield to Odin's Hall of the Slain, Valhalla. If we think of the battlefield as the landscape zodiac (and its archetype, the horoscope) and "slain" as meaning those who overcome the gravity of body-based consciousness and self-identity—their "death" being a mastery of the ego—then Pallas Athena and her Ray adepts (the other Valkyries) always transport apprentice Einherjar (the Sangreal on Earth) to Valhalla for visits, debriefings, and counseling as part of the Ray initiation.

Master of the Violet Robe—Maha Chohan

In my first experience of this Ray Master I saw him as a Jewish Indian chief—whimsical but true.

This seventh Ray of full purple-violet is, according to Ray Master DK, the Ray of Ceremonial Order, Ritual, and Magic. He uses the following terms, among many others, to connote its qualities: The Unveiled Magician, The Creator of the Form, The Manipulator of the Wand, The Keeper of the Magical Word, The Divine Alchemical Worker, and The Worker in the Magical Art.[53]

The Ray Master associated with the primary Ray color, violet, is known as Maha Chohan, which means Great Teacher.[54] He teaches high, white magic. He is also Lord of the Dharma (the cosmic laws,

---

53. Alice A. Bailey, *Esoteric Psychology. Vol. 1, A Treatise on the Seven Rays* (New York, NY: Lucis Publishing Company, 1962]: 85.

the rightness of *rta* as a principle), which is consistent with maintaining the Ray of Ceremonial Order, Ritual, and Magic.

Here is a summary picture of the nature of this Ray: a Ray Master Sanctuary, filled with books, a massive violet flame burning centermost, all of it set above a landscape dragon. A perfect example of this set-up is at Fajada Butte in Chaco Canyon in northwestern New Mexico. In the same place as the Butte sits coiled one of the Earth's 13 primary dragons; above the Butte in the ethers is one of Maha Chohan's Ray Master Sanctuaries. The juxtaposition of the two gives us original knowledge (Maha Chohan) plus original power (the dragon and its implicit kundalini, the powerful "waters" the dragon is said to contain)—a potent combination indeed.

Applied, energized knowledge is magic, the ability to wield the "magic wand" to manipulate reality. This Ray involves the protean applications of energized knowledge through rituals, protocols, methods, ceremonies, and curricula, and in this Maha Chohan is the master of many arts and diverse magical words and formulae. With this Ray, you have the knowledge (the ritual orders, ceremonies, incantations) and the power (the dragon engaged) to execute it in the world.

In his early Irish guise, he was the Tuatha de Danann god Lugh Lamfada, Lugh ("The Shining One") of the Long-Arm. He was also called *Lugh Samildanach*, "He of Many Skills and Arts" or "Lugh, Skilled in All Arts." Lugh was called "He of Many Skills and Arts" because when he showed up at Tuatha headquarters they asked him what he could do; he said anything and everything, which is why the Tuatha accepted him as a valuable new member. He told them he was competent as a carpenter, smith, champion, harper, poet, Druid sorceror, healer, cup-bearer, bronze-worker—he did them all.

---

54. The word *Chohan* is apparently derived from the Tibetan, from *chös* (law, Dharma) and *Mong khan* (lord); thus "Lord of the Dharma." The term also suggests a spiritual lord, chief, principal, master, preceptor, teacher, or cosmic spirit. Yet the Hebrew term *Cohen* ("priest") has some similarities in connotation: the Cohen was permitted or commissioned to officiate in temple rituals.

The Long-Arm is his spear, for it is a magical spear (the archetype of the "magic wand"), one of four special treasures (or teachings) brought by the Tuatha from the Otherworld, in this case, from the magical city of Gorias presided over by the magus Esras. Hence it was usually known in Irish as the Spear of Lugh, and it was unstoppable and invincible.[55]

The spear was called *Gae Assail* or Lightning Spear; it was also known as the Fiery Spear of Lugh, the Spear of Victory, and the Sun's rays at Midsummer, and it had the same destructive or creative power as Balor of the Evil Eye, whom it killed. It radiated such heat that when not in use, Lugh's spear was kept in a vat of cooling water. Irish lore says the holder of this spear would always be victorious as no battle could be sustained against it. It is likely the *Gae Assail* is the same as the later *Gae Bolg*, the fierce javelin of the Irish hero, Cuchulainn, and possibly the same as the *Gae Dearg* (Red Spear of Diarmait ua Duibne, Angus Og), the *Gae Buide* (Diarmait's Yellow Spear), the *Rhongomynad* (the Welsh Spear of Arthur), and the *Gae Bulga* (Spear of the Goddess Bolg; a forked or twofold spear). This spear was always

---

55. In Norse myth, this spear was called *Gunginir*, Odin's Spear; he was its shaker and user. In Japanese myth, it was a jewelled spear of the gods called *Ama-no-Nuboko*, used by the primal god pair Izanagi and Izanami to stir the primeval brine to bring forth the eight islands of Japan. The Four Treasures, including the Spear, similarly are recognized in esoteric Buddhist and Tibetan lore as being original gifts of the gods. In Irish lore, one Beltaine the Tuatha de Danann manifested out of the mist, coming through the high air down to Ireland, and presented to the Irish the Four Treasures. These had come from four magical cities, each with four wise men (magi) to teach the young men of Ireland skill, knowledge, and perfect wisdom. Among other things, the Four Treasures are archetypes of the four basic elements, and Lugh's Spear is fire. The Western Magical Tradition calls these the "four traditional magical instruments related to the Elemental Quarters," which later became the four suits in Tarot. Gareth Knight, *The Secret Tradition in Arthurian Legend* (Wellingborough, England: The Aquarian Press/Thorsons, 1983): 36.

fatal, always found its mark, and released poisonous barbs when it struck its victim. A terrible yet magical spear, only the gifted and pre-pared warrior could ever wield it, and live.

Lugh was in charge of the Celtic quarterly turning-day and festival event called Lughnasadh observed every year on August 1. Originally, it was celebrated principally at Rodruban *sidhe* at the Hill of Tailtiu in Navan in County Meath, Ireland, in honor of Lugh's mother, Tailtiu, who was buried at that hill. However, that is geomythic code for his "mother" was one of the Earth's 1,053 minor dragons, one of which was centered at the Hill of Tailtiu. Again, this reveals the coupling of Maha Chohan with dragons. During Lughnasadh, Lugh invites peo-ple to travel in vision to the magical city of Gorias to witness the Spear of Victory displayed in a crystal tower.

The surest way to get to Gorias, which is grounded etherically and uniquely for Earth at Tory Island, off Ireland's northwest coast, is by a landscape node that combines a Maha Chohan Ray Master Sanctu-ary and a dragon.

Irish myth remembers this tower and its Spear display case as *Tor Conaind* (Conann's Tower) and also as the glass tower of Balor of the Evil Eye, a Fomorian giant and Lugh's grandfather, based on Tory Island off Ireland's northwestern coast.[56] Again, we are dealing with geomythic code, for Balor of the single, malevolent eye is actually an Elohim (more familiar perhaps by his Greek name, Cyclops, meaning One-Eyed or Round-Eyed). He is a giant like Goliath from whom David secured the magical Sword (see above under Apollo). Goliath,

---

56. *Balor Beimean*, or Balor of the Mighty Blows, had two huge eyes: one in the center of his forehead, another behind his head, covered by his dirty hair. That was the dangerous one, *Suil Bhalair*, Balor's Eye, and every-one hoped he would never "part his hair in the back and release the beams and dyes of venom from his evil eye that could fry men's courage and drop them dead in their tracks." The Eye is normally held down by a heavy iron ring which takes four men to lift; once the Eye fell out of its socket and rolled on the ground, instantly killing 28 warriors upon whom its glance fell. Randy Lee Eickhoff, *The Sorrows* (New York: Forge/Tom Doherty Associates, 2000): 43, 249.

the Cyclops, and Balor were expressions of the Elohim angelic order, once temporarily in the guise of giant humans on Earth to help set up the planet's geomantic terrain and to mentor early advanced humans.

More importantly, the Elohim, whether in human or angelic guise, are the expressions of and the forms for *AL*, the "genes" of magic and high creativity, the secrets of manifestation and of the teachings in their proper usage.[57] Irish myth tells us Lugh killed Balor by blinding that single eye with his spear. More likely, Lugh as Maha Chohan was commissioned by the Elohim (Balor) to transmit the *AL* codes of magic and reality manipulation (symbolized by the Spear, or Fire archetype) under the auspices of this Ray to qualified human individuals. Metaphorically, we might construe Balor's single massive eye as the angelic "gene pool" for these *AL* forms.

The Balor as grandfather and blinding the giant bits seem like myth window-dressing, though these elements are symbolically apt. Arguably, the Elohim as an angelic order is older or more informed than the Ray Masters on certain topics, and thus Balor was Lugh's grandfather in wisdom. The blinding part is descriptive if you reverse the image: say instead that Lugh dipped his Fiery Spear into the deep vat of *AL*-enriched cosmic wisdom that was the "terrible" eye (the unitive vision) of the Elohim.

Other of Ray Master Maha Chohan's guises have included great teachers in different wisdom traditions: Djehuty or Thoth of Egypt; Hermes Trismegistos of Greece; Isaac Luria (1534-1572), the famous Jerusalem-born Qabalist, called the Holy Ari of Safed, the Lion of

---

57. The Elohim are the forms of *AL*, state the Ofanim. "*AL* is the essence of creation, the in-drawn breath, the birthing of something, the point of light, the Star, the essence of Mind, the forgiveness in forgave." The Elohim, as the forms of *AL*, are "the projections or entities or forms which are acceptable to conscious human perception of this essence. *AL* is co-creative power, the seeds of the secret of bringing things into manifestation." *AL* is from the Hebrew: *Aleph* (1), the primal seed or star of Light, and *Lammed* (30), its movement in the world; in Qabala's gematria, this number can be read with equal validity as 13 or 31.

Safed, and the Godly Rabbi Isaac; and the Roman Mercury, with his caduceus or staff of intertwining serpents. The caduceus, the magic wand, Hermes' staff, the Spear of Lugh—these are equivalent expressions and represent the embodiment, activation, and application of this Ray's "magic wand" creative power.

At Hermopolis (the ancient Khmun or Khemnu) in Egypt, you might still perceive Maha Chohan in his Thoth guise as a living, attentive golden head with a massive, vertical rectangular headpiece that rises several feet above his head; behind him is the Spear. You pass through Thoth then enter the Spear, the next dimensional experience of his Ray—the means of executing magic, the magic wand itself. Let's see how the attributes of Hermes-Thoth exemplify what DK said about this Ray.

Hermes was known as the messenger of the gods, the guide for souls in the Underworld, the swift-moving one with wings on his golden sandals and a herald's staff or caduceus in his hand by which he causes humans to wake or sleep as he wills. Hermes "makes safe for the traveller the roads between the Underworld, Earth and Heaven." As such, he embodies the "channels of communication" between Heaven and Earth:" it's a form of intellectual and spiritual commerce he keeps moving at a swift pace.[58]

Hermes is the psychopomp at the temple gates, and he is the hinge that opens the door, the middle point and socket "about which revolves the most decisive issue, namely, the alternation life-death-life." Further, as the inventor of language, he is *hermeneus*, the interpreter, "the begetter and bringer of something light-like, a clarifier, [the] God of exposition and interpretation."[59]

As Thoth, he was the pre-eminent explicator of the Mysteries, the master of hermeneutics, a formidable initiator of humans, and scribe of the gods.[60] He knew the sacred verbal formulae enabling the dead

---

58. Jean Chevalier and Alain Gheerbrant, *A Dictionary of Symbols*, Translated by John Buchanan-Brown (New York: Penguin, 1996): 500.

59. Karl Kerenyi, *Hermes, Guide of Souls*, Translated by Murray Stein, (Woodstock, CT: Spring Publications, 1996): 140, 145-46.

to pass safely through the Underworld; he was in charge of all the "sacred books in the house of life," meaning wisdom documents; and he was "lord of the sacred words," including the hieroglyphs.[61]

Thoth was credited with composing the Smaragdarine Tablet or Emerald Table, the embodiment of ancient occult knowledge, part of which is remembered today as the seven Hermetic axioms (one of which, abbreviated, says: *As above, so below*); these are the foundation of the Western Mystery tradition and Hermetic philosophy. "He embodies the revelation to mankind of wisdom and the way of eternal life." His spoken word "penetrates to the very depths of people's consciousness."[62]

Thoth was the Great Teacher, the Maha Chohan, the Violet Ray Master. He presided over almost all aspects of cult and ritual activity, their texts and formulae, as well as magical proceedings and the occult powers of the gods. He was viewed as having "a leading role in the drama of creation itself, as a demiurge who called things into being merely by the sound of his voice."[63] (Congruently, Qabalistic mysti-

---

60. The hermeneutics aspect, in the sense of scholarly, intellectual analysis and interpretation of spiritual matters finds application in Judaic mysticsm through Qabala and Maha Chohan's guise as Isaac Luria. But hermeneutics here is more on the order of a high spiritual interpretation not the dry analytical approach common today. "Interpretation is not a futile game but a fundamental attitude...Through interpretation, man becomes an 'infinitive man,' stretched in a transcendental movement towards the infinite." A text, says Qabala, is "always open to new interpretations," and a text, ultimately, is the entire universe and everything in creation for they were created by permutations and combinations of the basic 22 Hebrew letters, Qabala teaches. Thus to interpret reality is to read a text, and here mysticism and metaphysics are hermeneutical. Marc-Alain Ouaknin, *Mysteries of the Kabbalah* (New York: Abbeville Press, 2002): 67.

61. George Hart, *A Dictionary of Egyptian Gods and Goddesses* (New York: Routledge, Chapman and Hall, 1986): 214-218.

62. Jean Chevalier and Alain Gheerbrant, *A Dictionary of Symbols*, Translated by John Buchanan-Brown (New York: Penguin, 1996): 500-501.

cism emphasizes the creative potency of the Hebrew words when spoken on their own and in different combinations and permutations.)

The Jewish Indian chief? The Jewish part of this was as the Qabalist Luria, with Maha Chohan's Ray Master Sanctuaries situated at several key locales for Qabalist exploration including Gerona in Spain and Safed in Israel. The Native American part comes from a lifetime he spent as a chief among the Cree of Canada (I have not yet secured the name of that Cree chief). The feeling of the Ray is deep, still, rich, revelatory, midnight-hued, with a *soupçon* of amusement, and perhaps that captures the essence of the Jewish and Native American strains.

Saint Germain's Lilac Ray of Transmutation

As mentioned earlier, the Ray Masters work with the Earth's dragons and dragon network, but at least one of the 14 has a reputation, though disguised, as a "dragon-slayer," or as he prefers, "dragon plumber." You can observe a little of this dragon plumbing function of Saint Germain (his name is from *Sanctus Germanus*, "Holy Brother") in a few of the world's myths, if you look through the façade to the geomantic reality. Saint Germain was the famous St. George, patron saint of England but earlier, the dragon slayer of Sylene, Libya, where, legend says, he dispatched a fearsome dragon in the 4th century A.D.

He was also the mythic Greek figure Bellerophon, who rode Pegasus, the white, winged celestial horse to defeat the Chimaera somewhere in Lycia, Turkey. The Chimaera had three heads—lion, goat, and serpent—and was a terrible creature, swift and strong, exhaling invincible blazing fire. A dragon, in other words. Greek myth says Bellerophon killed this dragon, but geomantically what happened was Saint Germain adjusted its release valves. Over Sylene in Libya and somewhere in Lycia, Turkey, sits one of his Sanctuaries of the Lilac Ray.

---

63. Garth Fowden, *The Egyptian Hermes. A Historical Approach to the Late Pagan Mind* (Princeton, NJ: Princeton University Press, 1986): 22-23.

It is more accurate to think of St. George's dragon-slaying as a per-petual engagement of the dragon energy (per the analogy of plumbing valves), making suitable adjustments according to the overall energy flow from it through the Earth's plumbing network (its visionary geography) at given time periods. We might adjust the Greek image slightly: Saint Germain astride the mighty Pegasus wielding his flam-ing lilac sword upon various dragons means Saint Germain as a Ray Master is making various expedient applications of the Lilac Ray—as flames, tubes, containment columns, or other forms—to keep the dragon system in trim and to periodically let some of its life force or kundalini dribble out to refresh and energize the world.

Many of Saint Germain's Ray functions with respect to the Earth and humanity have been either mentioned or alluded to throughout this book. In our time, Ray Masters Portia and Saint Germain are the two primarily assigned to work with the Archangel Michael and the Ofanim in the refreshment of the Earth's Light grid and to midwife its tumultuous morphing into a new shape. As the anecdotes of my visits to the GWB headquarters and glimpses of their current projects indicate, Saint Germain is at the forefront here as well, both as expli-cator to humans of GWB responsibilities and projects (some of them) and as a leader in their fulfillment. The Lilac Ray of transmutation and the Orange Ray of discernment in the transmutation process are foremost among Rays in operation on the Earth today.

Saint Germain is also commissioned to help the United States, as a country and landmass, pass through its current dark, materialist phase and achieve the seemingly unbelievable destiny of being a Cup of Light, a veritable Grail chalice, to the world, as he foresaw in the 1930s. I say "seemingly unbelievable" because in recent years the U.S., with respect to the Earth, its environment, and its Light body, has acted more like the Antichrist in toxic fulmination than the Christ on the world stage.

Ray Masters of course take the long view, master plan in hand, and perhaps Saint Germain's forecast of America as the world's Cup of Light is congruent with the Native American vision of the Ghost

Dance from the 1890s. The day was soon coming, Paiute visionary Wovoda proclaimed from near Pyramid Lake in Nevada, when all the Indian ancestors (the "ghosts") will return to the Earth, alive and vibrant, in response to ritualized dancing; the buffalo will return in vast numbers and the invading white Europeans will be removed from the land as it is regenerated and restored to its archaic purity, health, and abundance.

Wovoda and all those he influenced expected the apocalypse to happen in the 1890s. Instead, Wounded Knee happened, in which over 300 Ghost Dancers were murdered by U.S. government forces in South Dakota, shutting off the Ghost Dance vision. But a regeneration of the land and its restoration to an original purity is congruent with Saint Germain's Cup of Light vision for America, and possibly the way this will be achieved in our future is through a re-engagement of humanity with the Earth's Light body and and a reinvestment of our spirituality with the geomantic terrain. Leading and inspiring this long-term effort is Ray Master Saint Germain.

The inimical White Man ways of non-perception of Earth's visionary geography and its abuse of Gaia and the planet will be ended, like wiping away a taint from the soul, and a new spirit of cooperation among white-European Americans with Indians, both living and functioning as spirit ancestors and land guardians, may be initiated. In other words, we can have the Ghost Dance fulfilled without anyone leaving the country; what will leave are the ignorant, abusive, derelict attitudes of this country's residents.

This is what I mean: the Spanish then English colonialists and then the rest of the European nations took over North America and expunged its natives without ever learning the protocols of landscape maintenance, that is, how to interact with the implicit visionary geography and its spirits to maintain the health of land, wildlife, all of Nature, and humanity. The planet gained a powerful country whose residents had no concept of the spiritual mechanisms of its own context, the land, and who began a period of settlement characterized by complete unawareness of the true price of land habitation. The Native

Americans did know the protocols, and though the vast majority of them are no longer physically embodied, they still work from the spirit world to look after the land. The Ghost Dance may be fulfilled when we start calling on them for guidance in how to finally take up our responsibility as American residents to mainain the land.

An earlier expression of this perhaps may be found in Saint German's life as Francis Bacon (Baron Verulam, Viscount St. Alban: 1561-1626), the English founder of modern Freemasonry and Supreme Master and President of the Brotherhood of the Golden Rose-Croix. He wrote copiously about a regeneration of culture and consciousness through the "Great Instauration," the restoration of the world through a renovation of the arts and sciences. His life was dedicated to creating "the Baconian temple of light, built as a landmark or starting point for a worldwide temple of enlightened humanity," and for this he was the "herald or harbinger of a new age…a renovator or reviver of the ancient and original wisdom teachings taught via the Mysteries and based on love…." The Great Instauration was to involve the rebuilding of the Temple of Solomon, understood to be an initiate's brotherhood and the systematic regeneration of paradaisal conditions on Earth and in humanity.[64]

Some of Saint Germain's planetary functions involve an overlap with the work of other Ray Masters concerning the operation of complex geomantic nodes. One function pertains to creating massive lilac flame containment fields for particular geomantic features. One such complex node is Sicily's Mount Etna. Saint Germain has a Sanctuary high above fiery Mount Etna (the Greek *Aitne* from *aitho*, which means "I burn;" elevation: 10,902 feet), the still active volcano that dominates the island of Sicily off the southwestern coast of Italy. Geologists estimate it has been active for about 2.5 million years, and the Greeks tell a marvellous tale about it.

64.   Peter Dawkins, *Building Paradise. The Freemasonic and Rosicrucian Six Days' Work* (Warwickshire, England: The Francis Bacon Research Trust, 2001): 2, 4, 62.

Long ago, Zeus threw Mount Etna like a giant boulder at a monster called Typhon to pin him down forever, and there he remains today, and when Etna bellows, shakes, or erupts, it is Typhon groaning in his imprisonment. Typhon was so tall his head grazed the stars; he had one hundred serpent's heads; his lower torso consisted of two intertwining serpents; he yelled and hissed constantly; his body was covered with wings; his eyes were made of fire; flames shot forth from them and his nostrils and one hundred mouths; and he frequently uttered horrible imprecations or threw stones or barked hideously at the gods.[65]

This is more than a prolix, antique description of a volcano's power. Typhon was the Greek perception of a formidable angelic being imprisoned on Earth. Biblical lore has it that Lucifer, after rebelling, was flung out of Heaven and plummeted towards Earth like a falling star; Dante's *Inferno* has him imprisoned headfirst in the icy bowels of the Earth in the 9th level of Hell. However, as we saw with the centaurs, to understand the story we have to strip away the bad press and demonization surrounding Lucifer and approach it geomantically.

It's a huge story, too big to explicate in full here, but the concise version is that humanity has been generated twice on Earth. First-generation humanity had great freedoms and psychic largesse, which it eventually abused prodigiously. Using mythic imagery to explain this, let's say they grossly abused the Sword of Nuadu and the other Trea-

---

65. Virtually the same story is told of Iran's sacred peak, Mount Demavend, in which long ago the demon Azi-Dahaka (also called Bevarasp; Zohak; Dahak; the Evil One) was bound and imprisoned after a reign of 1,000 years. Here again we see the motif of a huge mountain being placed over the "demon" to effect a seemingly permanent imprisonment. Azi-Dahaka was said to have three heads, three mouths, six eyes, and was of enormous size; or he was a winged dragon-snake with three heads yet a humanoid torso and head. His wings were so vast that when outstretched, they obliterated all view of the Heavens from Earth. The occasional rumblings of the mountain are his groans, and the sulfurous vapors and venting steam are his exhalations.

sures of the Tuatha de Danann, precipitating the Dolorous Stroke that created the Wasteland. The gift of their awesome ontological freedom came from Lucifer who was commissioned by the Supreme Being to sponsor and look after this first Adam. In modern terms, he had to co-sign the bank loan, act as surety in case the borrowers defaulted. They did, and Lucifer was stuck with the "bill." His payment was to be bound into the Earth, his spiritual essence reduced and constrained. Our payment was to arrive in the world in which the Wasteland was a dominant characteristic.[66]

For Lucifer to mentor first-generation humanity, embodied humans living on an organic planet, he had to incarnate some of his essence into the planet. He spread his energy and "parts" out across the Earth, investing himself literally in the bold project of materialized humans and a fairly densified planet, both of which had the potential to fully evolve into their Light body or celestial form. As Light Bringer and Light Bearer, Lucifer was implicit in all projects involving humanity and that sought to incorporate the Light (and the freedom to wield it) into organic, mortal bodies living on an organic Earth.

As humanity "fell," that is, fell short of the agreed-upon goals, so Lucifer "fell." But the Light he embodied and brought to Earth is still here, distributed in over 3,400 different locations, awaiting its eventual re-release into humanity.

In his guise as the Mayan Quetzalcoatl (or Kukulcan), he buried his "heart" at a site near Oaxaca, Mexico; in his guise as Typhon, he buried his "spleen" at Mount Etna. The Mayan perception paints Quetzalcoatl's glories, while the Greek view emphasizes Typhon's fiercesomeness, yet both suggest his great puissance, for they are the

---

66.   I use the term Wasteland in a broader sense than usual to denote a condition of reduced freedom and psychic mobility, and increasingly, a condition of spiritual amnesia in which humanity forgets its origins and lives ever more so under conditions of darkness, materialism, atheism, fundamentalism, and pain.

same being, two guises among many for this monumental and singular spiritual being.

Mount Etna is one of the planet's 3,496 Lucifer Binding Sites. At each, a portion of Lucifer's planetary expression has been bound, that is, limited. Sometimes, a little is let out into the world; sometimes, some of it is bound tighter. Mount Etna has an additional geomantic factor that supports the seemingly exaggerated nature of Typhon; certainly the reduction and fragmentation of a high angelic being in the realm of matter and its etheric overlay is worthy of groans, but Mount Etna also contains a reservoir of Lucifer's life force or *prana* in the form of his spleen chakra.

Technically, the "spleen" belongs to the Earth, and as the spleen chakra, this site is a vital energy well. This is one of the 72 minor chakras (on a human and planetary level), "an invisible individual power-plant of concentrated energy" that "absorbs vitality from the sun and disperses it throughout the body" as well as spirit from the air to distribute to the etheric body and nervous system.[67] When Lucifer touched down onto the Earth, at this and other sites, his presence electrified all matter in the vicinity, and some of his energy merged with the spleen's inherent geomantic energy at this location.

Within or below Mount Etna, this planetary spleen chakra looks like a roiling sea of yellow-white, and Typhon actually is protecting this reservoir of *prana*. His fierceness and all-seeing quality are perfectly suited to the task of guardianship.

The geomantic structure of Mount Etna is complex and straddles several dimensions or reality layers. Typhon sits upon the roiling yellow-white cauldron of life force; around and through him sits a Sun Center (one of the eight Celestial Cities, as mentioned earlier); and superimposed on this Sun Center is a Ray Master Sanctuary of Jesus in his guise as Hephaistos, the Olympian smith-god, working his forge and solar fires, fueled in part by the spleen chakra.

---

67.   June G. Bletzer, *The Donning International Encyclopedic Psychic Dictionary* (Norfolk/Virginia Beach, VA: The Donning Company, 1986): 586.

Helping him are three Cyclops (which means Elohim), and numerous Cyclop caves with an estimated one hundred Cyclops (according to Virgil in the *Aeneid*) punctuate the slopes.[68] Also on the outer flanks of the volcano graze Helios' 360 Cattle of the Sun, a subsidiary geomantic feature to do with parcelling out the Sun Center fires. Above and around Mount Etna spans an etheric dome many miles wide and high, transmitting the energies of a star in the constellation Corona Borealis.

Above the dome is the Sanctuary for Saint Germain, and surrounding all of these features and a portion of Sicily itself is a towering lilac flame containment field, miles high and miles deep into the Earth. This containment field protects the Earth and humanity from premature exposure to the pure ontological puissance of Lucifer as Light Bringer until such time as we and the planet can assimilate some of this potent energy. The lilac field also protects the entire geomantic complex and its treasure hoard—the vast *prana* reservoir—from outside disturbance, interference, manipulation, or inimical incursions from other powerful energies.

The lilac flame around Mount Etna is shaped as a hollow column that encases the mountain and rises straight upward for many miles; it transmutes unwholesome or entropic energies potentially focussed upon the *prana* reservoir. In this sense, it is like a defensive shield, but

---

68.   Virgil called this the Brotherhood of Etna and said the Cyclops lived in the bays and mountainsides of the island, but especially in the vicinity of Mount Etna. This conclave of Cyclops is a geomantic feature maintained by the Elohim, an angelic order involved in much of the building, both physical and etheric, of the Earth and its Light grid. For a time, they took physical form as giants, about 18 feet tall; the single-eyed aspect of the Cyclops refers to their unitive vision, their constant awareness of the Supreme Being and His plans for a given area; and in a more humanized sense, it represents the unity of the psychic 6th and 7th chakras. The Brotherhood of Etna had their own geomantic feature there which I call an Elohim Citadel, a kind of massive, very tall, cathedralic-like, dark blue temple space in which the 100 or so Elohim assembled.

it deflects unsavory energies by entirely changing their nature; the lilac flame disassembles the intent and content of the energy. As for the inward-facing function of the flame, it transduces (or steps down) the powerful frequencies of the *prana* reservoir and Typhon's presence there so as not to destabilize all of Sicily or larger regions, and even the Earth itself.

Saint Germain explains that he administers a similar lilac flame containment field at about 20 other Lucifer Binding Sites on the Earth, including Mount Demavand in Iran and Mount Kilimanjaro in Kenya. These sites preserve Lucifer's celestial Light-filled presence in a pure form, almost as demonstration sets, with the understanding that eventually, as humanity ripens for this, that awesome Light (of consciousness, freedom, and reality manifestation) can be let back into the world. That will be coincident, no doubt, with America becoming the world's Cup of Light and with the Ghost Dance vision coming to fruition and the planet's dark grid and Antichrist (see below) being transmuted and removed from Earth reality.

How to Interact with the Ray Masters in Their Sanctuaries

It is my impression that the Ray Masters generally will respond to sincere, respectful requests for an audience put forth by people in a concentrated meditative state of mind. If you know you have contractual spiritual agreements with individual Ray Masters, then you may be sure you will get a fairly swift response; if you do not, you may still get their attention for a short while. As each Ray Master is capable of 1,746,000 manifestations, that means their attention can be in that many places at the same time—including having a dialogue or visionary encounter with you.

The preferred or most efficient way is to use your crown chakra as a beacon, though this may not be the easiest method at first go. Everyone has a crown chakra but like muscles and skills, this center needs to be developed and used regularly to work optimally. Create a *golden* bubble (do not use white) around you that is perhaps 10-20 feet in diameter; visualize a cord of golden light that goes straight up from the top of the bubble to the Supreme Being; from the underside of the bubble, visualize a hollow tube that goes straight to the center of the Earth. Ask the Supreme Being to assure the purity and integrity of your psychic contact through keeping the *golden* bubble around you intact.

Bring your awareness to the top of your head, as if you were standing on the roof. Surround yourself with the specific Ray color as a series of flickering flames. If you are seeking contact with Saint Germain, picture yourself (inside the golden bubble) surrounded by brilliant, flickering lilac flames (which are also inside the bubble); immerse yourself in them until they fill the field of your awareness within your crown chakra. Matching yourself with the desired color (lilac) is like knowing the Ray Masters' correct telephone numbers; it is also sending them a psychic *Hello!*

Then you wait; depending on circumstances, timing, and your own karma and intent, the Ray Master may visit you, indicating his presence in some manner appropriate to you, possibly in terms of knowledge, symbols, or signs personal to you. Using telepathy (your mental voice), tell the Ray Master what your intent is: for example, you want to experience his energy and color; ask some questions, visit some Sanctuaries; receive guidance on a spiritual matter.[69] When you are finished, thank the Ray Master for her time and information, return your attention to its normal distribution pattern throughout your physical body, and take down the golden bubble and its top and bottom cords, and psychically throw them out.

---

69. Keep in mind the Ray Masters are many steps in evolution above spirit guides, the deceased among humanity, or other conventional sources of spiritual guidance. I recommend against asking questions of a personal or mundane nature; this is not the brief of the Ray Masters and may cost you their audience. Try to come up with questions that have some gravitas, that, for example, pertain to energy, consciousness, Rays, karmic destiny of nations, or cosmic structure.

An alternative, easier approach is to create the towering Ray flames around your body and then follow the same steps as above. If you can occupy your sixth chakra as a kind of viewing space while doing this, all the better. Remember, you are contacting a Ray Master in the spirit of "I'll meet you half way"; realistically, the Ray Master comes far closer than just one-half the way, but since their level of vibration and awareness is vastly enlarged compared to our normal cognitive range, to interact with them in a dependable, certain way, you need to make the "phone call" from at least your sixth, and better, your seventh chakra. Otherwise, the vibrational differential may be too great for your body and your awareness.[70]

As a preparatory mnemonic, a few days before you plan to "make the call," wear some clothing of the Ray Master's color or surround yourself in various ways with the color. That way the color becomes more actively familiar to you.

The "15ᵗʰ" Ray Master, the Cosmic Joker Called Merlin

Merlin, the famous magus of King Arthur's Camalate, is not officially a Ray Master, but is a free-ranging, free-lance, independent member of the Great White Brotherhood. He is like Mercurius or Quicksilver, the Holy Fool or Joker, wiser and older than most. He says he is a

---

70. Successful, reliable contact with the Ray Masters presupposes some degree of systematic psychic training. Obviously, the use of one's sixth and seventh chakras is not something easily acquired in a weekend, although many people have "raw" talent. For the contact to be dependable and clean, you need confidence in the use of these higher energy centers, and that confidence comes from responsible training. Good psychic training also reduces the likelihood of your connection becoming a "party line," the way home telephones used to be set up in the early 1950s in America. You don't want other voices speaking in your phone when you thought you were having a dedicated contact with just one source, the Ray Master.

member of the GWB "when it suits me." There is no 15th Ray as such that emanates from Ursa Major, yet Merlin manages a color frequency: silver, the Ray of the Great Mother.

Merlin manifests or is reached through silver, the Ray of the Great Mother, a connection encoded in his name: Merlin means Mer-Line, the line of connection to the Great Sea of Consciousness or Cosmic Mother, *Mer.* In one of his many cultural guises, as the Greek hero Herakles, this implicit connection to the Great Mother is unambiguously encoded in the name for *Hera*kles means the "Glory of Hera." Herakles-Merlin is the effulgent agent for the Great Hera. Merlin is or holds the line of connection for all sentient beings to the Mother and her Love from Above that seeks always to flow down the Mer-Line to humans. Merlin is the umbilicus between humans and the Great Mother, and he keeps it always open for us.

In this capacity, Merlin is associated with a geomantic feature called a Heraeum. This is a sanctuary dedicated to the Great Mother using her Greek name of Hera, though of course it could equally be called a Danu temple or any other name given to the Great Mother. The Heraeum, or Hera Room, is a vast silver temple in the astral plane, though with Earth landscape grounding points (notably, Hera's sanctuary at Euboia, five miles from Argos in the Pelopponese in Greece); its ultimate origin might be in the Canopus star system somewhere, as this is the source of the primary silver line that encircles the Earth.

Once a year, the Great Mother is particularly honored in an event I call Silver Line Adjustment Day, November 22; the essence of this observance is to realign humanity with the Great Mother through the Mer-Line implicit in each human's auric field. All the star-gods and the Tuatha de Danann (the GWB) gather in the Heraeum to honor her. You have a good chance of meeting up with Merlin at a Heraeum.

Merlin's other chief spiritual affiliation is with the Ofanim, called in various medieval texts "Blaise:" Merlin is said to be in retreat in his invisible Glass House (or *eplumoir*) with his master, Blaise. Blaise is also described (in Thomas Malory's 15th century compilation of legends, *Le Morte d'Arthur*) as Merlin's priest-confessor, companion on a journey to the Grail Castle, and historian, writing down the events of Camalate and the Grail Quest. The correct way of understanding this relationship is that Master Blaise, who is the Ofanim condensed by the storyteller into seemingly one person, conveys the celestial plans to Merlin who then executes them.

The Irish maintain a vivid mythic memory of the *Mer* at the end of the Mer-Line. The Great Mother was known as Brigit (different than the Ray Master Nada as Bridget), and she was the possessor of Brigit's Mantle, a rolling carpet of silver flame-mist that she and the Tuatha de Danann unrolled across Ireland in the earliest days of its land formation (i.e., its terraforming) to create and settle its various features. Merlin is the agent of the Silver Ray as Brigit's Mantle for all terraforming activity.

Terraforming and energizing new landscapes in many respects is central to Merlin's commission for the Earth, and it has figured, along with geomantic maintenance and landscape blessing, in his many guises which include the Polynesian Maui, the Indian Padmasambhava, the Irish Cuchulainn, the Navajo Monster Slayer, the Persian Zal, the Gaelic Saint Columcille of Iona, the Christian St. John of Patmos, and others. So pivotal was Merlin's role in the original energizing of the British Isles that in the Welsh mythic memory that land was known as Myrddin's Precinct, the first of its three original, ancient names.[71]

Merlin is credited with pulling up entire islands from the sea (Hawaii), with ridding landscapes of inimical, autochthonous beings (Tibet, New Mexico), christening prepared geomantic locales (Iona, Patmos), defending sacred lands (as Cuchulainn, the Hound of Culainn, at the Plain of Murtheimne, Ireland), and initiating new geomantic terrains and their features (as Herakles at Mycenae in Greece).

Merlin says: "I prepare planets for habitation. I do the heavy-lifting, i.e., raising up land masses. I prepare the land for the birth of the

Solar Logos, the Arthur Light [culturally, these rare places become Camalates, or centers for Arthurian activities, of which there have been 26 so far in Earth's life]. I don't have sanctuaries as such. I perch where I please."

His "perches," as recognized by humans, tend to be Shambhala portals, such as his legendary but enigmatic Glass House on the Welsh Island of Bardsey or Merlin's Mound in Marlborough, Wiltshire, in England. Mount Oeta in Greece, site of his dramatic immolation in the pyre as the wearied Herakles and his elevation in glory to Mount Olympus (see Sophocles' *The Women of Trachis*), retains today his silver flame imprint and is de facto a Merlin Sanctuary.

The Ofanim characterize Merlin as "an adept, a Grand Square Master" and say they have worked collegially with him on many occasions during the course of the Earth's existence (notably, transporting the stones of Stonehenge from Africa to Ireland then Salisbury Plain in England). They noted that Merlin was trained in the cultural milieus of Mu and Atlantis in the synthesis of the unitive and individuative approaches to consciousness development, and that part of his

---

71.　It is as if Merlin left a little signature of his formative presence in Tibetan history for the Tibetan word (in transliteration) for the vital principle of the element of Fire is *me-rlun*. Merlin as primordial energizer of landscapes is the one who uses spiritual Fire to do so. In fact, Merlin (in shortened form as *rlun*) is implicit in the four elements: as the pranic essence (prana, in Tibetan: *rlun*) of the earth element; of water (*chu-rlun*); and air (*rlun-gi-rlun*). This seems to further account for his role as primal landscape energizer because he masters the foundational elements that comprise all physical matter. All this also implies that the Love from Above of the Great Mother gets embodied (through the Mer-Line) in the four foundational elements and in the land masses that Merlin energizes. As Padmasambhava, the Indian Buddhist missionary, Merlin prepared the Tibetan landscape and its wealth of protector beings and spirits, to receive the new Buddhist impulse. This blend would become Tibetan Buddhism. Lama Anagarika Govinda, *Foundations of Tibetan Mysticism* (London: Rider & Company, 1960): 182.

brief involved initiating King Arthur's Grail Knights (both men and women) during the 15 epochs in which this archetypal and cosmically based myth found grounding in human expression.

The Ofanim put the relationship among Merlin, humans, and the Ofanim on a more exalted perspective when they say that through the Mer-Line, or Mother's Line, the Father (the male aspect of the Supreme Being) shines through them (the Ofanim) as angelic intermediaries, to reach human awareness. The Ofanim's work with people moves through the Mer-Line connection and through Merlin who embodies it. "It is Love from Above through the Mer-Line," the Ofanim say.

Merlin recently facilitated one step in the progressive illumination of an important geomantic node in New Mexico called Frijoles Canyon, part of Bandelier National Monument near Los Alamos, about 50 miles from Santa Fe. Every geomantic node, in addition to its particular features, sits upon a generic template that consists of a sequence of the 9 major and 72 minor chakras. As part of any progressive site stimulation, these 81 chakras need a Light infusion. In July 2005, Merlin brought Brigit's Mantle to Bandelier to infuse the 72 minor charkas in its landscape.

He rolled out Brigit's Mantle like a flaming silver sea which flowed through the long thin canyon, and numerous angelic faces arose out of it like bobbing buoys. These faces belonged to space-holders for the 72 minor chakras within the canyon geomantic template. The 72 minor chakras at any level of expression express a cymatic pattern, a living, organic spiritual shape compounded of the various vibrations of the individual energy centers, known in Qabala as the 72 Names of God (*Shemhamforesh*, "The Name of Four Parts"). This is a mystical reality in which the angels at the chakra temples are known in Judaic mysticism as the Angels of the *Shemhamforesh*, each of them named. As I looked out over the silver sea of angelic faces and temples in Frijoles Canyon, it was as if the angels of the Names of God were registering one by one in my awareness: *Haqem, Menad, Aunem, Vamet,*

Yebem, Haiai, until the full Name of God was sounded and the 72 chakras that transmit that vibration were activated in silver.

The array of minor chakras occupied an area of about 4-5 square miles. Infusing it with Brigit's Mantle, Merlin explained, "restores the conformity" of implicit Light grid to actual landmass quality and current status. The minor chakras became more apparent and easier to see within this silver sea, and they looked like silver button mushrooms each with a white bulbous top. Each "mushroom" in fact was a Light temple for that Name of God and minor chakra. Each could be visited and interacted with (they had an open rotunda shape). The reality and nature of each is maintained by the specific vibratory pattern of that chakra and Name and is superintended by a presiding *Shemhamforesh* angel. Merlin's Silver Ray inundation awakened them and brought them more into present-day planetary life.

Ray Master Dedicated Outposts, and How to Interact with Them

At numerous locations throughout the Earth you may encounter (on a visionary level) solitary flames burning in an urn but without a Ray Master or Sanctuary structure as such. These flames usually are a single color and may rise 100-500 feet above the ground and span perhaps 30-100 feet across, and in some instances much more; they burn in a concave urn seemingly set inside a hill, mountain, or even a church, or on top of (but not above) a hill.

For example, a massive lilac flame burns in the Japanese city of Hiroshima to purify the terrible effects of the nuclear explosion and the mass deaths there in 1945; at Chimayo, a New Mexico sacred site and small country Catholic church near Santa Fe, a scarlet and lilac flame burn in an urn inside the church, though they are much larger than the physical church. Here Ray Masters Jesus (scarlet) and Saint Germain (lilac) have established a joint Dedicated Outpost.

Within Santa Fe, a yellow flame of Ray Master Lao Tzu burns at the top of the Hill of the Martyrs, a small hill a few blocks from the

Plaza; a dark blue flame dedicated to Ray Master Paul the Venetian burns within a breadloaf-shaped small mountain—in the next dimension but in the same location—outside the country town of Lamy, 20 miles from Santa Fe. At Taaiyalone mesa, the Zuni sacred peak in northwestern New Mexico, the pale yellow flame of Ray Master Kuan-Yin burns within and beyond the entire extent of the mesa, flaming upwards many hundreds of feet; it is set in a large, shallow crystalline urn, itself more than a thousand feet wide, filling the mesa's interior.

The purpose of a Dedicated Outpost is to produce a continuous purification and permeation by the specific Ray flame of a given area. Analogically, it is like placing a fat stick of lit incense in a burner in a room to freshen and focus its atmosphere then going somewhere else, coming back now and then to check on things. In the judgement of the Ray Masters, a given locale (say a church or hilltop) will benefit from a specific and single Ray flame permeation for a period of time, so they light the flame. The total planetary count of these Dedicated Outposts is at present unknown, and most likely it is not a fixed number but dependent on changing circumstances.

A Ray Master is not usually "at home" at a Dedicated Outpost. Rather, the Ray Master has left an energetic simulacrum of his essence and vibration in the form of a massive living flame. Interacting with a Dedicated Outpost will serve you well in getting a basic experiential introduction to how the Ray color feels and how it effects you.

Let's say you have located a Dedicated Outpost for the rich yellow Ray, that of Ray Master Lao Tzu. If you can physically sit in proximity to the flame (sometimes you can't, or can't easily, as the Outposts can be on mountain tops), then surround yourself with a visualized towering yellow flame (as explained above in terms of interacting with Ray Master Sanctuaries); do it as if you sit within the center of a yellow candle-flame. This will align you with the actual, though much larger, Ray flame burning before you at the Outpost. Do not expect an encounter with Lao Tzu here (though it's possible), but rather an introductory or deepened experience of the Yellow Ray.

8

THE GREAT WHITE BROTHERHOOD IN CURRENT TIME

You may wonder: what is the GWB doing today and why should I make the effort to interact with such sublime or arcane spiritual beings as these? Here are five reasons why the Great White Brotherhood is very active on Earth at this time and how you can help the Earth and humanity progress by participating in the GWB's plans and programs.

Reasons to Interact with the Ray Masters

I offer five reasons to consider: 1) The Ray Masters and their Rays are constituent parts of the Earth's spiritual anatomy and thus reality factors in our environment. 2) They represent and embody the primordial structure of Light and consciousness and are fundamental to Creation. 3) They are implicit in our spiritual constitution and energetic anatomy. 4) They oversee the soul's development by means of initiation and progressive awakening in individual lifetimes. 5) Through them, you may start to align yourself with the spiritual energies and higher reality of the galaxy in whose life our Earth is embedded.

See Table 8 for a summary of the essential qualities of each major Ray.

Table 8
Essential Qualities of the 7 Major Rays

RED, Rays 1, 2	Christ smith, Logos carrier; surrender, softening; fullness of the Love of God the Father-Mother; Eros; sound, vibration, mantras
ORANGE, Rays 3, 4	Justice, mercy, discrimination and discernment; truth alignment; transcendental insight, knowledge; revelation of God's Mind
YELLOW, Rays 5, 6,	Harmonizing contrary energies; secret landscapes of the Spirit; taking the high view; penetrating the opposites
GREEN, Rays 7, 8	Cosmic law teachings; universal analyzer-systems-maker; quickener of growth and activity; mentoring; Christ-advent preparation
BLUE, Rays 9, 10	God's force-will applied for healing, inspiration, prophecy, divination, self-divestment; death initiations
INDIGO, Rays 11, 12	Guided voyages to truth, knowledge, wisdom; Mystery initiations in mystical sanctuaries; explaining the Mind of God
VIOLET, Rays 13, 14	Applied esoteric knowledge (magic); transmuting negativity; alchemical change; creation, activation, awakening, purification, freedom

Current Activities of the Great White Brotherhood on Earth

Probably the broadest statement to make about this topic is that the GWB's thrust is twofold: the dissolution of the Antichrist or dark grid from the Earth and the activation, enlightening, and upgrading of the planet's original Light grid. Neither will happen quickly; both will take most of the 21st century to accomplish in full.

By way of definition, the Light grid is the Earth's total array of visionary geographic features, the 105+ different types of energy-receiving and conducting nodes that constitute the planet's esoteric anatomy and physiology. These features, the entire Light grid, were implicit with the creation of the planet and remain its primary receptor and distribution system for Light and higher consciousness—the benign input from the celestial spheres and angelic realms. The Earth's Light grid represents the receipt (through many forms) of the absolute Light at a lower level. These forms must continually be purified, upgraded, and realigned with the source.

See Table 9 for a selected list of geomantic locales Ray Masters work with.

Table 9
Selected Associations of Ray Masters with Geomantic Features

Jesus, Ray 1, Scarlet	Sun Temples-Centers (Mithraea)
Nada, Ray 2, Pink	Ixion's Wheels
Portia, Ray 3, Orange-Gold	Labyrinths; energy funnels-star temples; national egregors and omphalos points; the 72 Crowns of the Ancient of Days
Lao Tzu, Ray 5, Yellow	Og-Min Cave Heavens; *Sipapuni*-Hollow Earth; Naga Cities
Paul the Venetian, Ray 9, Cobalt Blue	Underworld Entrances; labyrinths
Apollo, Ray 10, Pale Blue	Arcs of Developing Consciousness
Serapis Bey, Ray 11, Indigo	Mystery Pyramids; Naga Cities
Pallas Athena, Ray 12, Violet-Magenta	*Beyuls* (mystical sanctuaries); landscape zodiacs; *vajra* spots
Saint Germain, Ray 14, Lilac	Dragons; Lucifer Binding Sites
Merlin, "Ray 15," Silver	Heraea (Heraeum); Shambhala portals

The dark grid is an artificial, human-made, partial overlay upon the Light grid. It has no fixed geometric pattern, no inherent cosmos or beauty to its structure, no celestial imprimatur other than this is a planet of free will and thus aberrations such as this must be tolerated. It is more like an opportunistic, lawless, cancerous growth consisting of thousands of dark tendrils that insert into cities and locales to secure the distribution of dark grid consciousness, more popularly, if warily, called the Antichrist—the antagonist of the Christ Light.

Seen from afar, the dark grid appears as a black cancer, a pathogenic organism that is asymmetrical, ugly, and chaotic with a firm sucker-like hold with many rope-like tendrils binding up areas in a kind of demented open-mesh black sack. A massive splotch of it, for example overlays the U.S. East Coast like a black storm cloud glued to the land or like an octopus hideously flattened and stuck to the face of the land.

How did the dark grid get anchored into the Earth? It's home grown.

The dark grid largely is the residue of an after-death possessive state of the former civilization of Atlantis. The height of Atlantean culture manifested a highly sophisticated spiritual-consciousness technology whereby scientists and engineers were able to interact with the energies of the galaxy through a materially augmented spiritual technology. It was a combination of radar, deep space telemetry, and something like the phased-array of the Very Large Array of astronomy telescopes at Socorro, New Mexico. Not only did this system enable the Atlantean researchers to interact with the stars and their intelligences, but to subtly influence and eventually manipulate the galaxy from the Earth. Eventually, the feedback from this continual DSL connection with the galaxy destabilized Atlantis at its geological and geomantic roots and the island imploded then sank cataclysmically.

From our perspective today, we might say it was a classic case of scientists over-reaching their mandate, going way beyond the boundaries of safety and responsibility, and carrying on in a foolhardy, reckless manner oblivious of possible consequences. After the complete demise of the Atlantean landmass and all its people, many engineers in their after-death state expressed themselves as a psychotic collective, a kind of possessive, life-desiring, vampiric organism—a giant thoughtform reaching out of the sunken continent like a malign black hand trying to claw its way back into planetary life and its former presumption of control.

This "black hand" had innumerable, unlimited fingers, and each finger sought an anchor point, a place from which to sink into a portion of Earth physical reality. Each finger was like a dark tendril seeking a grounding point so that the Atlantean engineering collective could continue to influence and manipulate Earth reality. The problem was in its after-death state, this Atlantean collective had become dark, troubled, unbalanced, and acted radically inappropriately, like angry ghosts, Earthbound, restless, even demented, spirits. They sought footholds in human reality, and they did this largely through Atlanteans who began reincarnating on Earth while maintaining their allegiance to the disincarnate group.

Eventually, many thousands of "fingers" or dark tendrils got established in the human world, in cities of power, government, commerce, and worldly or religious influence. The planet got enmeshed in the spidery dark webs emanating from the after-death state of the destroyed Atlantis; after a while, this network of tendrils or "grounded fingers" grew so large it had a shape, a planetary mass, although it was (and remains) a deformed, non-beautiful, toxic growth like a metastasized tumor. The placenta for the Earth's dark grid and its thousands of umbilical cords is Atlantis, physically vanished but still psychically very active.

Now it is the planetary Shadow, humanity's unexpiated Atlantean dark side, and the matrix for the emergence and extrapolation of the Antichrist.

Say Goodbye to the Antichrist

The dark grid cannot be removed by some marvellous *deus ex machina*, such as the way Greek tragedians got their characters out of hopeless messes. Allegiance to the dark grid or Antichrist must be repudiated one person at a time because every person, in terms of their soul history, has made agreements over time with the dark grid as well as the Light grid to fit the contingencies of given lifetimes. These agreements remain in place across the many lifetimes a soul undertakes unless they are consciously revoked. The refurbishment of the Earth's Light body requires we start doing this today.

Worldwide at this time each human must, if one chooses so, end these agreements. It can't be done for us for that would make a mockery of free will. We must do it on our own of our own free choice, then the change is binding.

It is important to not think of the Antichrist in terms of a single if monolithic individuality opposed to everything the Christ stands for. It is more useful to conceive of the Antichrist as a decentralized pervasive influence with many points or "faces" of manifestation. The Antichrist has been on the planet for a long time, at least since Atlantis whose demise the Ofanim place at more than 150,000 years ago.

It is true that the Antichrist's influence and presence has intensified since the start of the 20th century, and this could be interpreted as the imminence of its coming to Earth. But this intensification can also be seen as a product of our growing salutary awareness of our vast collective Shadow with its Atlantean dark grid allegiances and the imminence of its tumultuous bringing to light and expiation.

The Antichrist is the opponent of the Christ, but that alone is too simplistic. This is not a matter of Christianity but of the cosmic Christ. The Antichrist fosters qualities opposed to the celestially ecumenical spirit of the Christ as a cosmic being, as the Logos and the Light. They include: atheism, materialism, literalism, the apotheosis of the personality as a celebrity, patriarchalism, scientific imperialism, rationalism, genetic and blood line identities, mechanization, militarism, intolerance, ideological fanaticism, hatred of matter (of body and Earth), hatred of the feminine and the soul, a disavowal, even demonization, of clairvoyance, true metaphysical knowledge, and independently attained (and wielded) higher consciousness.

The Antichrist is opposed to human freedom, the full, unhindered, *wakeful* use of free will, and the ability of every person to achieve the highest state of independent knowing possible (without priests or dogma authorities). It wants to cram the spiritual world down into matter and have us focus exclusively on this level. It abhors truth and thus continuously encourages lies and righteous or thuggish behavior to enforce the cloak of false reality and deception. It uses fear or artificially induced piety (based on dogma, not experience) to create an adversarial, confrontational, elitist, punishment-based, paranoid, and perpetually millennialist world view in which only the submissive, well-behaved "elect" will be favored to survive.

The dark grid fosters these attitudes, providing them a kind of plant food, while the Light grid, embodying the original intentions for Earth, provides a climate of higher consciousness enabling humans to individually make *free* and wakeful choices as to their allegiance. The Light grid cannot compel choices; it creates conditions in which one can comprehend each choice and its likely outcome and then freely choose knowing this. We must be wary of judgemental and punishment-based fundamentalist attitudes in religion, and be cautioned by C. S. Lewis' prescient portrayal in *The Screwtape Letters* of the Antichrist tarted up to fool us in Christ's clothing, the real "Devil" hiding in plain sight as a priest.

The Antichrist, through the dark grid, currently is pounding Lucifer, the spirit of beauty and freedom and the celestial Light-Bearer, into the Earth, hammering stakes into his heart as if he were a foetid vampire. We cannot re-establish our fluidic link-up with the planet's Light body and its galactic life until this stops, for Lucifer is the expression of the freedom and form of the Light given to both Adams that the Earth's Light grid literally embodies. The Antichrist pounds Lucifer into demonized matter because should we catch on to the truth of the situation and start liberating the Light-Bearer, the act of redemption itself would repudiate the Antichrist completely. The tricky part is that the Antichrist keeps us thinking Lucifer is the Antichrist, so that we are disinclined even to approach this celestial being to start his redemption.

One part of the Great White Brotherhood's plan for the Earth is to help us dissolve the dark grid so that it is entirely removed from the planet. They expect this will take all of the 21st century to complete and that, for America, the best place to start is the West Coast and the states west of the Rocky Mountains. These areas present a sufficient number of people in support of the repudiation of the dark grid and Antichrist and the flowering of the Light grid so the GWB's work, dependent on human cooperation, will enjoy some early traction there. In fact, it's already begun.

We might picture this as a wave of vibrant pale yellow light rolling across the U.S. from the West Coast, dissolving the dark grid tendrils as they're met and feeding the land and ethers with new life. For a time, the western half of the U.S. will be under this yellow wave, the rest of the country still living in the spiritual darkness cast by the dark grid and, shockingly, for the most part, not even knowing it, presuming they live in the salvific Christian Nation founded at last in the United States.[1]

East of the Rockies is more deeply entrenched with dark grid influence, and the seat of power in Washington, D.C., as well as London and Rome, likely will be among the last places to be freed of the dark

---

1.   Remarkably, in 1932, the British novelist Aldous Huxley wrote in *Brave New World* that the only enclave (more like a concentration camp) for the misfits who refused to conform with the societal protocols regarding suppressing emotions and using test-tube birthing (as well as the remaining Native American population) was just outside Santa Fe, New Mexico. Even then, sensitive writers like Huxley intuited that the areas west of the Rocky Mountains, including certain cultural oases (representing true, not mass, culture) like Santa Fe, would be the refuge of the nonconformists (i.e., the free).

grid encasement. In at least a psychic sense, the U.S. will undergo a kind of ontological civil war: there will be two divergent realities present in the U.S. and the Rockies will be the divider. In one reality, the Light grid is being rejuvenated and enriched; in the other, the dark grid will continue to churn out its grim and brutal Antichrist scenarios, killing the soul even more thoroughly.

We could say the Ghost Dance vision is finally born on American soil west of the Rockies while everything east of it is immured in a perpetual Wounded Knee massacre of the psyche, truth, and higher consciousness.

One of the ways the GWB will accomplish this vast project of removing the dark grid is to plant massive lilac flames in selected communities west of the Rockies. Again, there has to be sufficient human agreement for this to happen. A *deux ex machina* or some miraculous single-stroke Earth change coincident with the end of the Mayan calendar in 2012 or any other easy apocalyptic schedule is a myth with no reality. This Earth change, in the Light grid and the human psyche, will happen one person at a time, grassroots, door-to-door, as agreements with the Antichrist are recognized and cancelled. Even worse, it is a distraction to expect a miraculous world-changing rescue, a deflection of our attention to outside ourselves so that we fail to do the unavoidable inner spiritual work.

The GWB has dispatched numerous adepts, under Ray Master Saint Germain's direction, to monitor these towering lilac flames in the U.S. West. The flames, embodying and transmitting Saint Germain's Ray of freedom and transmutation, will create a favorable environment for those people wishing to repudiate the dark grid in their locale and from their own auric field, chakras, body, and the entire soul lineage of their past lifetimes. The flames will gradually burn off the black tendrils anchored into the lands of the western states and that bind up reality in dark rope sacks. The Ascended Masters monitoring the lilac flames will create local Light sanctuaries for those willing to enter them freely; think of these as zones of freer, lighter, *truer* reality, all of it with a lovely lilac tinge.

The placement of these flames to an extent is free of pre-existing geomantic features; for example, they are not part of the Dedicated Outposts system. But in many cases their placement is coincident with geomantic features that can support, protect, and amplify the flames, such as the Plaza at the heart of Santa Fe, New Mexico, where a huge lilac flame burns amidst a Sun Temple and other features.

Throughout most of the 21st century, it is likely the U.S. will experience a bifurcation in identity and even in the quality of reality people live in. The long-term goal is surprising and from today's perspective, nearly unbelievable, given the dubious political behavior of the United States in the last 100 years.

As mentioned earlier under the discussion of Saint Germain's Ray, during his 1930's communications with Godfre Ray King, Saint Germain made this remarkable statement about America's destiny.[2] It is to be the "Cup of Light" for the entire world, he declared. America, he said, is the "Heart-center of the Spiritual Progress" on the Earth; through America, the Cosmic Christ will find a firm anchor and foundation "in the Hearts of mankind;" America is the Grail or Cup that carries the "Light of the Cosmic Christ" for the whole Earth; and America will be the Heart center of the coming Golden Age.[3]

---

2. It is important to distinguish these pronouncements from the seemingly similar statements from militant, evangelical Christian fundamentalism about the triumph of the Christ in America. Those types of statements actually derive in large measure from dark grid, Antichrist influences and are not of the Cosmic Christ nor what Saint Germain was indicating. Nor should the Golden Age and time of the Cup of Light in America be confused with the chaise-longue chiliasm mode of "New Age" expectations.

3. Godfre Ray King, *The Magic Presence* (Schaumburg, IL: Saint Germain Press: 1935): 137-8; Godfre Ray King, *Unveiled Mysteries* (Chicago, IL: Saint Germain Press, 1939): 97.

Reassuring the Nation's Egregor, the Eagle

Every nation has an angelic watcher and protector known as an egregor. It assumes characteristics, over time, appropriate to the landmass and the soul type of the people living there. In America, the egregor has the form of an Eagle of Light, and it has a material grounding point in western Pennsylvania where we might say its astral body casts a large shadow over the land so that you could interact with the Eagle through specific landscape nodes. The U.S. Eagle predates the formal founding of the U.S. in the late 18th century; in earlier days, the Native Americans took responsibility for the interaction and probably helped create its eagle guise over time.[4]

The Eagle is "a national figure representing the Logos of the nation," explain the Ofanim. "Its role is as the Logos of a nation which is the Word in the landscape. It is the character of a country. It is the teacher and the predator. It is the eye that sees far and the heart that embraces all. It is prone to deception. It needs harmony and truth. The biggest form of deception is self-deception. What is needed is self-perception and then the eye that sees far functions from the heart." To a large extent, America's Eagle has been deceived or at least interfered with by the dark grid influences operating within its own landmass and people.

Although the Eagle represents the negotiated fusion of landmass and people over time (including its essential soul qualities and destiny or intended evolutionary goal), in recent decades, as the dark grid influence has dug in deeper into America, this has affected the Eagle and its ability to accurately reflect the spirit of America (using this term in the true and neutral sense) as it was originally set down. In November 2004, Saint Germain and selected GWB adepts visited the

---

4.   National egregors start as empty angelic containers; over time, they assume an agreed-upon form in interaction with the people of its landmass; that form is usually congruent with and symbolic of essential qualities of the land and the soul composition of its people (its ethnos: French, Italian, Greek, etc.).

American Eagle, and they offered myself and a colleague a few glimpses of the state of things.

The Eagle appeared glum, forlorn, beat-up, and neglected. The GWB group surrounded the Eagle with towering lilac flames, many miles high and wide, to start the process of transmuting the astral pollution, lies, deception, and dark grid energy that had accumulated in its being. On a visionary level, these flames about the Eagle lit up the northern East Coast in a massive purification and restoration, an *auto-da-fé* of the Antichrist—or at least the opening flames of the operatic cleansing. Thousands of angels with upraised swords stood as sentinels during this process.

Meanwhile, representatives of the dark grid swarmed the outskirts of the event but were barred from coming close to the Eagle and certainly from touching it. The GWB had put the Eagle inside an impenetrable glass mountain, a kind of spiritual alchemical retort in which it could begin its rejuvenation and rebooting to its original programming and parameters. At least at this exalted level, the dark grid agenda is now incongruent with the national egregor whose spiritual vision is being recalibrated by the GWB to match the original intention for how its energy and consciousness should be set for this landmass and its people.

A few weeks later, the GWB field unit returned to the Eagle for more healing. The Supreme Being sent down a tube of golden light into the Eagle's crown chakra. We were asked to stand in spirit form within the golden tube because some human representatives had to be part of this process and more crucially, as a minimum, a few Americans, since *being an American* is a conditioning on the soul (as being any other nationality is too) that puts us as embodied humans in congruence with the conditioning of the American egregor. Saint Germain explained that at least a few Americans had to be in resonance with this resetting of the national "god" or it would have no reality (or grounding) in the American psyche.

For our part, we were asked to repudiate all our hidden or karmic dark grid allegiances so we could be congruent with the incoming pure spiritual energy. Just because we wish to act as a so-called Light Worker in one lifetime, does not mean we don't have a full resume of dark grid-affiliated past lifetimes. As soldiers say, Watch your back! In this case, we should say, Watch your Shadow!

The gold light flowed down the tube in a swift spiral and contained symbolic information or encodings in a language of Light. Saint Germain said this was a "column of Truth" from God, a "blood transfusion" of the Supreme Being's essence, a profound reminder to the Eagle (and the land) of its true nature and of the continuous benevolent regard from Above.

Such a resetting will probably take some time to percolate down into the material side of America, Saint Germain suggested. The Eagle will not be healed overnight. In fact, symptoms of the healing initially might take a negative aspect, so that for a time it may seem that the dark grid influence is actually strengthened; this will be the Light causing a radical purge of the darkness and for the discerning, only a seeming, transient heightening of Antichrist activity. For a time, the worst and most virulent aspects of the dark grid will be purged out of the Eagle (and American culture) as the profound purification continues. It may look and feel bad only because the toxic soul substances are now finally coming to light as they leave the foetid shadows to be disgorged into daytime consciousness for transmutation.[5]

---

5.   This principle is understood in natural medicine in the context of liver and colon detoxification where it is called the Herxheimer Effect. As the liver collects and neutralizes toxic substances for removal from the body, for a while the patient feels shockingly sicker than before the cleansing started; he is experiencing the transient, toxic effect full-bore of the substances being mobilized. This passes in a few days or less, and its effects can be ameliorated somewhat by high dose vitamin C ingestion. The lilac flame purification of the U.S. egregor tracks this biological process quite clearly: the seeming intensification of dark grid activities in the U.S. would be the same as the mobilized toxic substances in the liver being neutralized, and we might think of the lilac flame as both the purgative herb and the palliative vitamin C.

During the night of December 20, 2005, on the eve of the winter solstice and part of a GWB global event known in folklore as the Wild Hunt (see below), Saint Germain and his colleagues revisited the Eagle and reaffirmed the lilac lame around it. Saint Germain revealed to me at this time that the Ray Masters maintain a Light City on the crown of the U.S. Eagle as well as a phase-shifted, cave-situated Physical Retreat underground at the same site. "This is a very important place, the Eagle and its environs," he said. Saint Germain explained that he is responsible for the well-being of the national egregors of Canada, the U.S., and Mexico, and that he oversees activities of the continental egregor of all North America (one of the planet's nine at this level). This egregor's territory spans north to the North Pole and south to the tip of South America, and includes the activities of the three national agregors just cited.

All three national egregors and the continental egregor were wrapped in brilliant lilac flames during this pre-solstice evening. In fact, the lilac flame for the continental egregor was a gigantic lilac lotus as large as all of North America; the lilac flames of the three national egregors burned within this much larger lilac flame. Saint Germain indicated the other 13 Ray Masters look after the other national egregors.

The point of this lilac flame infusion was to help "de-obscure" the Eagle's eyes. "This infusion will help the Eagle inspire some Americans to come to terms with their country's dark side," said Saint Germain. "America must confront its dark father, and see beyond its borders to witness the effects of this dark father on the world, effects which have been kept from them by the government." The revelation of the American Shadow starts with the Eagle; when his eyes are cleared, then so can ours be. The "dark father" refers to the particularly American blindspot of not being able to see the negative aspects of its national behavior, to the ingrained tendency to see the President (what Native Americans used to call the "Great White Father") as in some circumstances a dark, demonic, destructive figure and not a benevolent one.

The continental egregor is being engaged in this lilac infusion and the project of confronting the dark father Shadow side of American life and culture, Saint Germain said. In many respects, this larger egregor is less susceptible to the deceptions and Antichrist machinations underfoot in America, which tend to overwhelm or certainly interfere with the clear seeing of the American Eagle. Saint Germain said the lilac flames would be maintained at this heightened intensity during that pre-solstice the night as a "steady, insistent pressure of the truth and as a way of burning off some of the resistance among Americans and the Antichrist influence."

On this Wild Hunt, Saint Germain and his fellow GWB "riders" were "collecting souls to work with us in this great, urgent project of clearing the Eagle's eyes so it can help Americans do the same." The intent was to get this "de-obscuring" going voluntarily at this point so that a more violent "shake-up" or cataclysmic event would not be needed later to push people into confronting their national Shadow.

The Plan Calls for Geometry

One of the prime reasons for the global purification process is that the geometrical structure of the Earth's Light grid is changing. It is slowly morphing from its original form to a more complex one.

Technically, the Light grid is transforming from a combination of the five Platonic Solids (regular polyhedra with unique properties), but principally (and outwardly) the dodecahedron (with 12 facets) and icosahedron (20 facets), to a more complex form known as an Archimedean Solid. This classification includes 13 possible shapes: the one chosen for Earth is an icosidodecahedron (with 32 facets). Although the new form seems but a combination of the previous two, it is a completely different geometric shape, with different angles and facet shapes, and a new effect on planetary and psychological reality.

The significance of this transformation is radical: for one, the Earth Light grid has never changed shape since it was installed, which was partly coincident with the creation of the Earth itself; for another, it will take 50-100 years for the morphing to be complete; third, it will generate a host of new and newly defined sacred sites; fourth, it will deeply change the nature of our material, planetary reality as its defining mathematical and geometrical parameters are expanded. Its installation is, at least analogically, akin to changing one of the "constants" of Nature.

As the new Archimedean Solid for the planet's Light grid comes into shape, the dark grid overlay on the Earth's original, classic Light grid will be dissolved. The new Light grid, to be successfully anchored into Earth reality, requires the eradication of the toxicity accrued by the old grid, and the process of imposing the new grid will force that dissolution. The original Earth Light grid will remain in place, but it will have a "second story," so to speak, with the icosidodecahedron emerging and expanding out from it to create a new multidimensional shape.

That's one way to picture it, but when it's completed you could see it also as the new grid being superimposed over the old form, so that both are present. Experientially, in terms of how we experience and *feel* our reality, on psychological, bodily, and planetary levels, it will be as if the old grid facets have erupted into many new angles, vertices, and planes. Many talk about Earth changes, how we will soon be living in the fourth dimension or in Light bodies; ancient mythologies speak of Ragnarok, Judgement Day, the End of the Mayan Calendar, and End-Times. These are ways, mostly fear-based and in need of an upgrade into present time, of describing the expected experienced effect of this change in the geometry of planetary Light.

Fortunately—in fact, one might almost say, amusingly—the dark grid will be incongruent with this new Light grid geometry and lose all its traction. The Antichrist will have nowhere to stand on the Earth because "his" footing was dependent on manipulating the original Earth Light grid and the psychological and material reality it supported. All that will be different soon. The Antichrist will have no foothold on the new grid; it will be for the Antichrist like the Glass

Mountain was to the valiant but ineffectual knights of myth who could not scale it and slid off.

The Global Geomantic Liturgical Calendar

During the course of the year, the GWB, in cooperation with certain angelic orders, facilitate numerous infusions of the Earth's visionary geography with celestial Light. Often, these infusions correspond with well-known festivals, holidays, and days highlighted in folklore such as May Day (Beltaine) and Halloween (Samhain).

Beltaine on May 1, for example, involves Ray Master Apollo (in his guise as the Celtic god Bel); Lughnasadh (Lammas Day) on August 1 sees Ray Master Maha Chohan as the Celtic deity, Lugh Lamfada directing events. In the spring equinox (March 21), Ray Master Jesus (as Rama) is central to events, while for the summer solstice (June 21), it is Ray Master Serapis Bey at the forefront.

See Table 10 for a selected list of correlations between Ray Masters and geomantic festivals.

Table 10
Selected Correlations of Ray Masters with Geomantic Festivals

January 6	Epiphany	Jesus, Scarlet Ray
February 2	Candlemass	Nada, Pink Ray
March 21	Spring equinox	Jesus as Rama, Scarlet Ray
Variable, May Full Moon	Wesak	Djwhal Khul, Green Ray
May 1	Beltaine	Apollo, Pale Blue Ray
June 21	Summer solstice	Serapis Bey, Indigo Ray
August 1	Lughnasadh	Maha Chohan, Purple Ray
September 22	Fall equinox	Jesus as Balder, Scarlet Ray
November 1	Samhain, Hallowmass	Lao Tzu, Yellow Ray
November 22	Silver Line Adjustment Day	Merlin, Silver Ray
December 20	Winter solstice, Wild Hunt, Yuletide	Saint Germain, Lilac Ray
December 21	Heaven on Earth Day	Portia, Orange-Gold Ray

I call this annual sequence of planetary infusions the global geomantic liturgical calendar. The events are global as they affect the entire planet; the Light infusions work through sacred sites or geomantic nodes; the activities follow a kind of script or procedural, much like a liturgy; and it's a full year's schedule consisting of perhaps five dozen regular events plus special energizations that arise during the course of a year and which may not be repeated in following years.

The relevance here is that humanity is invited to participate in all of these. Once we did, as the folkloric record amply illustrates, but increasingly since the 19th century, public participation or even understanding of the geomantic nature of these festival days has been greatly diminished until today, certainly in the U.S., many of these days are barely acknowledged and appreciated even less often. Ideally, humanity is asked to take part in this calendar because humans are needed to ground and transduce the incoming energies for the Earth through the geomantic nodes.

The set-up is like this: the angelic and hierarchical realms channel down pure energies appropriate to each calendar date, but these need to be received by organic sentient beings for maximum benefit to the Earth, Nature, and people. That so few people today participate in most of the events (the summer solstice is still popular, especially in the British Isles) means the Earth is deprived of some of its cosmic nutrient feed. Metaphorically, if Gaia needs 1,000,000 "straws" (human receivers) to sip the divine nectar settling like dew on her flowers (geomantic nodes) to get an ample intake, these days she gets "juice" from only 1,000 straws, or maybe far less.

Think of the calendar as the planet's regular maintenance schedule and each of its many dates as our collective responsibility to show up as its mechanics. Ours is a designer planet tailored for human conscious evolution, but its vitality is predicated on regular human maintenance in accordance with this calendar.[6]

Overall Purpose of the Great White Brotherhood Geomantic Locales

Despite appearances, Earth is pre-eminently a free-will planet where freedom of choice is paramount. At the same time, we are not left here on our own, to fumble in the cognitive dark, making what may prove to be ill-informed or entirely uninformed choices. Through their variety of geomantic nodes, the GWB maintains a mentoring presence on Earth, always offering life guidance to people, if they wish it.

Probably the biggest picture we might form of the GWB's purpose is to keep open for us a portal for information, energy, and consciousness from Ursa Major to flow into the Earth and human culture through its visionary geographic nodes. We might think of it in terms of plumbing: Ursa Major connects to the Earth through a big pipe through which flows higher consciousness and spiritual life; this celestial flow empties into the Earth's Light grid through seven different spigots. Each of these spigots is one of the GWB geomantic locales we've considered.

In many respects, Ursa Major's role with Earth is similar to what a landscape angel or national egregor does. A landscape angel ensouls a given landmass, be it a valley, mountain, state, country, or continent. It cycles higher, angelic energy down into the landscape, into both its etheric and physical aspects, so as to enrich and support all life in its purview. The landscape angel is also aware of the "plan" for its region of responsibility, having been briefed by "larger" landscape angels who oversee and ensoul greater areas of land and population.

So the landscape angel's assignment is to keep the energy, consciousness, and frequency range within the parameters set down by the plan for that region; to maintain the energy pure and intact. In

---

6. See: Richard Leviton, "Taking the Earth in for Maintenance," at Articles on Visionary Geography; see also on-going issues of *Welcome to Your Designer Planet! Newsletter* for information about calendar events; both at: www.blueroomconsortium.com

clairvoyant language we call this "setting the energy" and "holding the space" for that energy to flourish and support life.

The Ray Masters have done that on a larger scale for the entire planet. A certain frequency range for human evolution was set at the beginning of the planet and fine-tuned at humanity's advent. That's why we regard the Earth as a *designer planet*: it was planned and designed for humanity's benefit. The Ray Masters, along with the angelic hierarchy, know that plan and administer it for us.

The Ray Masters, working through Ursa Major and its various geomantic outposts on the Earth, maintain these parameters for conscious evolution in bodies on this designer planet and in accordance with the plan for Earth. Just as a landscape angel ensouls a topographical region, so do the Ray Masters ensoul the Earth with galactic life, continuously bringing in and grounding Ursa Major consciousness even if, from our worldly perspective, we are never aware of it.

Ursa Major's energy or galactic reality is too big to be grounded at just one point on the Earth. In a sense, to do so would make it explosive. Far better to install numerous outflow valves (i.e., the GWB geomantic locales, all in multiple copies) to allow the energy to percolate, like drip-feed irrigation used in the desert, into the planet's visionary geography and eventually into its physical reality and our lives.

It is more than a quantitative allocation of Ursa Major energy through numerous geomantic nodes. It is too big an energy for the Earth to receive it at 100% strength even if at a thousand intake points. So the spectrum of Ursa Major's galactic reality is divided up into at least seven different filters, and these exist each in multiple copies around the Earth to ease the assimilation which comes in at differing amounts, but never at 100%. For example, you get the assembly of the GWB through the Valhallas; the residences of the 14 Ray Masters of the GWB at the Amaravatis; the individual Ray Masters at their Sanctuaries; and their Ray flames at the Dedicated Outposts.

So the Earth and humans get a steady infiltration of Ursa Major energy through these numerous outlets, but the efficiency of the "drip-feed irrigation" depends on regular human interaction with these geomantic nodes. If we think of these as celestial houses built on the Earth, they all have front doors, and these doors need to be opened and kept opened by us. That's our responsibility to the Earth.

Often in the life of humanity on Earth episodes of high culture coincided with keeping these doors open. I call such cultures Lands of Light (notably, Sumer; ancient Ireland and Egypt [around Heliopolis or An]; classical Greece [around Mycenae]) because they flourished based on an understanding of and regular informed interaction with the Light grid. They were cultures that grounded, embodied, and transmitted this Light across the young planet through their local, highly-charged geomantic nodes through regular ceremonial interactions.

Enlil, the high god of Sumer (equivalent to the Greek Zeus or Norse Odin), had his seat called *E-Kur* at Nippur from which he administered his *ellilu'tu*, or royal, spiritual authority and proclaimed his choices for human kings. Nippur was the site of a Celestial City of Amaravati, which means the seat of temporal authority for Sumer geomantically coincided with the seat of spiritual authority, itself a grounded conduit for the galactic government in Ursa Major. Appropriately, *E-Kur* translates to mean "The House is a Mountain," which matches the Glass Mountain or crystal pyramid found over this Celestial City. In this Land of Light, for a time, Heaven and Earth were congruent, their goals and activities largely coinciding harmoniously.

The placement of Nippur at the overlap of the hologram of Amaravati points to another purpose of the GWB locales. They are always open for humans seeking guidance for themselves, communities, cultures, or nations. While the GWB is not likely to reveal the entirety of the Plan for Earth, or even too much detail on the specifics for a given time period, their members are willing to offer enough "higher view" information—what you get when you can see around a few corners in probable human cultural and consciousness evolution—to enable human leaders to guide their societies in accordance with these spiritual trends. Should they wish to.

On a personal, individual level, there is great benefit to ourselves when we make our own authentic contact with the energies of the Great Bear. It starts to answer the fundamental question many people ask: *Why am I here?* And the perhaps deeper ones: *Why is there reality? Why is the world here?* By learning your soul's Ray color and making preliminary contacts with the Ray Master of your Ray, you start to provide your own experiential answers to these questions. You realize it is possible to get answers, and you may be surprised, even encouraged and inspired, by the direction suggested by the specifics of your answers. This may lead you to find deeper, more satisfying, ways to engage yourself spiritually with the Earth through regular interaction with its geomantic nodes.

All of Earth Lives in the Womb of Amaravati

Much of what I've described here is by way of an anatomical view of a stationary, seemingly inert system. It's important to remember the Earth's Light grid is not static, but a living, dynamic organism, with a vibrant physiology operating in real-time. So what does the Light grid of Earth look like while operating in real-time?

Ray Master Portia helped me gain a view of the living Earth with the "motor running," at least with respect to the presence and activity of its GWB geomantic locales. The Great Bear uses the seven stars of the Big Dipper to focus the GWB energy and consciousness onto Earth. Ursa Major holds all of Earth inside a womb of Light made of the 14 Rays and the Celestial City of Amaravati with its numerous differentiated parts we've visited in this book.

A primary component of this Ursa Major womb about the Earth is the geometrical network formed by the 12 Oroboros Lines that come from it. These form a regular array of lines and intersections around the Earth, the overall impression of which is like a fishnet sack of many colored threads.[7] Each Oroboros Line, transmitting the essential energy of a zodiacal sign (e.g., Taurus, Cancer, Scorpio), also conveys the Ray associated with it (e.g., Djwhal Khul's Green Ray, Portia's Orange-Gold, Paul the Venetian's Blue, respectively).

In real-time, with every changing of astrological month (i.e., the start of Scorpio on October 23, for example), the corresponding Ray pulsates with that Oroboros Line, transmitting a combined astrological and Ray influence to Earth. In a sense, this combination of Scorpio (as constellation) and Blue Ray emission flavors all of the GWB locales around the Earth's visionary geography during that month. We might picture the Ray for the zodiacal influence as an extra layer of insulation around the "wire" that carries the "current" from Ursa Major.

Seen from above, all of Earth resides within the womb of Indra's heavenly Amaravati. Everything that exists within that pure realm is part of our celestial-terrestrial Earth environment. Although the seven different GWB locales have multiple copies around the planet (more than 2,000 in all), all of them are subsumed in the single presence of this one Celestial City. The total presence of the GWB of Ursa Major is the *one Amaravati* which encases the planet and its Light grid like a womb; it effects a total planetary infusion and permeation. And it also like a placenta for it continuously feeds the Earth. We live inside our great Bear Mother, Ursa Major.

All of the GWB activities pertinent to Earth happen in Ursa Major, but we participate in them (should we wish to be aware of them clairvoyantly) holographically. All the GWB geomantic locales are holograms or virtual reality presentations of the original in Ursa Major. When we interact with a Light City or Valhalla, for example, these locales seem grounded and present within Earth reality, but truly we are interacting in a hologram of Ursa Major projected onto this planet.[8]

---

7.   There are a total of 15 Oroboros Lines encircling the Earth;12 are zodiacal, while the three that are not zodiacal pertain to solar, lunar, and neutral currents (from Sirius, Canopus, and Polaris, respectively). The 15 Lines form an oscillating network around the Earth consisting of 62 points of intersection and 120 equilateral triangles.

It gets better, for the same is true of the other seven Celestial Cities: each of these offers a total presence and placenta-womb environment around the Earth. Our planetary reality is enveloped by, for example, the Celestial City of the Nagas (through 144 copies and their singular, total presence) and its galactic reality as well as its host star or constellation (Orion). Each of the eight Celestial Cities is grounded through a specific star or constellation just as the GWB's locales work through the constellation Ursa Major. This means at one level of perception, Earth is embedded in the galactic reality of the Naga City and its great cosmic life and level of wisdom and insight; similarly, it is embedded in the Celestial City of the Sun (called Tejovati, with 144 copies); of the Moon; and the rest of them. That alone is an eight-dimensional view of our planet, possibly as culturally shocking as the first NASA pictures of Earth.

This gives our Earth's Light body eight primary aspects or levels, if you like. Each is a total, supportive, and interactive environment comprising dozens of holographic copies of the same original location in the spiritual world. Each is grounded through a primary host star, and were we to abstract our planetary spiritual experience to focus on but one Celestial City, we could accurately say we live on the planet of Soma (Moon temple), of the Grail, the Underworld, Shambhala,

---

8. The hologram model is a helpful metaphor for describing how the Earth's Light body works. As scientists explain it, a hologram is a two-dimensional object, but when you view it correctly (focus coherent light on it), it generates a three-dimensional image, a convincing simulation or simulacra of the original object that was encoded into the 2D hologram. "All the information describing the three-dimensional image is in essence encoded in the two-dimensional hologram." Some astrophysicists are now querying whether "the entire universe could be a kind of hologram." Juan Maldacena, "The Illusion of Gravity," *Scientific American*, Vol. 293, No. 5, November 2005: 57-58. In the case of the Earth's visionary geography, we might say all the information describing its fourth dimensional image (i.e., the bulk of the Earth's visionary geographic features) is encoded in the planet's three-dimensional reality as a hologram.

or the sublime pleasure-world of Avalon, for each of these Cities is a complete *celestial environment* (i.e., a heavenly, beatific realm) for us right here on the physical Earth.

When we work with the GWB and the angelic hierarchy to start the long process of energizing and illuminating a GWB geomantic node, it starts to expand and ground into our three-dimensional Earth reality. A GWB locale in the Light grid of Earth, as far as human consciousness goes, is like a compressed computer disk, full of information and "gigabytes." Our interactions with it helps it to start uncompressing its gigabytes, so that the site can unfold and express its true and full shape.

As for the dark grid, to the Ray Masters this is of little concern, Ray Master Portia explains. From our vantage point as embodied humans living mostly in three-dimensional, consensus reality and within the propaganda trance of materialism and atheism, the dark grid (once we realize it's there) can seem a formidable, invincible, and unquestionable reality. Yet, ultimately, it is just a toxic, dark cloud layer of the planetary atmosphere trying to make everyone think it is an absolute, immutable reality. The dark grid and its personification, the Antichrist, is but an "emperor-manque" whom the GWB, out of great tolerance and compassion for human free will to create and experience this darkness, allow to run things, for a little while.

Basically, the dark grid is a thin toxic layer sandwiched in between the Earth and its Light body of eight Celestial Cities. You have Gaia, the magnificent, angelic spirit of the Earth, whose benevolent face is the size of the planet; and you have the benevolent, higher Light womb of the eight Celestial Cities. In between is the dark grid, a stormy, angry-god atmosphere, threatening thunder and lightning (more bravado and bluster than anything else; to the celestials, the Antichrist is a poseur), packed between two more puissant layers of enlightenment or Buddha-Mind.

Every time we interact out of wholesome intention with a GWB locale and its galactic reality starts to ground into our physical reality, this "penetrates the false but obscuring layer of the dark grid materialism atmosphere so that the celestial reality and *truth* of our presence starts to become unassailable to all those who can see it and have it as their true planetary reality," says Ray Master Portia. Something pure starts to be discernible through the "black obscuring muck" of the dark grid. Portia says her job is to help people get the *view* of this big process underway on Earth, to see the pattern and rationality of the great transmutation Saint Germain is leading.

"The dark grid is an infernal dream world spun by those in resonance with it, but it is truly an illusory reality, all smoke and mirrors, a permitted aberration," Portia continues. The dark grid is a toxic delusional state, seemingly very persuasive but ultimately a delusory state, like a *bardo* apparition. "It would be useful to read the *Tibetan Book of the Dead* to the planet at this time [like the radio broadcast of *War of the Worlds* in 1938] to give people a perspective.[9] They are in the after-death state between the original world created by the primary Light grid and the new world and reality being born through the morphing of this grid into its next phase. All the 'demons' of the dark grid are *bardo* manifestations of humanity's own undigested, unconfronted mental states."

Bifrost Planet—The Earth Is on the Rainbow Bridge

Ray Master Portia offers another picture to describe the Earth's participation in Amaravati. Recall from our earlier discussion that Bifrost is the Rainbow Bridge of 14 Ray flames that leads to Asgard, the Norse name for this Celestial City of the GWB and the Ray Masters. Our planet is enwebbed in the 14 Rays so we could say the Earth is on Bifrost, like a pilgrim on the way to the city of the gods, striding along on the quivering bridge of flames.

Everywhere you stand on Earth, you are on the Bridge; you are always heading towards the Celestial City of Asgard, to the galactic revelation of Amaravati. Bifrost symbolizes the all-encompassing presence of the GWB on the Earth. Our Ray-enwrapped planet leads us into Asgard, which is both the perception of the Celestial City as a total planetary environment *here*, as well as its galactic original in Ursa Major, seemingly *there*—both are in the same place. Spending a wakeful day on Bifrost could be a life mission, or one of many lifetimes.

Gaia, our planetary spirit, perpetually has her "face" in Bifrost as well as in Asgard, as she enjoys the refreshing vista which reminds her of the ultimate salutary outcome of her long commission as the soul of Earth. Portia emphasizes that Amaravati is more of a process or a dynamic of consciousness than an actual place as we conceive of such things. "It is a reference point in a cosmic process, a step in a metabolic chain. This Celestial City is one of eight overlapping states [with

---

9.   The *Tibetan Book of the Dead*, or *Bardo Thodol*, attributed to Padmasambhava, was found in the 14th century A.D. as a buried treasure text; it is used as a liturgical text to help the recently deceased pass through the after-death state (the *bardo*) without being ensnared in fear, delusion, or ignorance so as to pass into the Clear Light and supreme reality and escape rebirth. *Bardo* means "in-between state," as in being between bodily form and enlightenment; the full name of the *Bardo Thodol* is "The Book of Liberation through Hearing in the In-Between State." The experiences one has in the *bardo* are explained as manifestations of either the delusory state of mind (as darkness) or of the mind's true nature (as Light). The goal is to recognize while you're in the *bardo* for 49 days after death (the true length of the "wake") that what one sees are projections or symbolic visions of the nature and state of one's own mind, and thus ultimately unreal. These are "hallucinations created by the *karmic* reflexes of actions done by him in the earth-plane body...thought-forms, having been consciously visualized and allowed to take root and grow and blossom and produce, now pass in a solemn and mighty panorama, as the consciousness-content of his personality." One is subjected to tests of the "hallucinatory visions directly resultant from the mental-content of the percipient." W.Y. Evans-Wentz, "Introduction," in *The Tibetan Book of the Dead*, Compiled and Edited by W.Y. Evans-Wentz (New York: Oxford University Press, 1960): 29, 66-67.

the other seven Celestial Cities] of the inner heart [the eight-petalled *Ananda-kanda*], the place of bliss."

"Our job, originally, was to place the Earth on the Bridge," Portia says. "Now, we do maintenance, adjustments, updates, and cleansings of this placement." The overall, summary purpose of the GWB locales and of Amaravati as a whole, she says, is to "protect, nurture, midwife, and shepherd the unfolding of the Light on Earth, that is, as higher consciousness in embodied humans. Our job is to look after the great life of these 14 Rays of Light and higher life and awareness and their elaboration in the human context through our many sites which act as release or containment 'valves.'"

Ray Master Portia suggests we picture the Earth and ourselves as perpetually on Bifrost wherever we stand on the Earth, to see ourselves as always walking along this bridge of 14 lights on the way to the Celestial City. This is a solid preparation for the assimilation of the full reality of Amaravati in 3,000 A.D. The opulence accorded to this City by the Vedic psychic poets symbolizes the richness and delight of this level of consciousness as seen from outside it, Portia explains. In a sense, the almost dizzying opulence of the place is meant to be an inducement to us to come visit it, to sample its offerings of "flesh" and "drink," to get rich with the Light.

The perpetual feasting on the boar and the constant drinking of the mead as reported by the Norse and Irish seers represent the state of total permeation by the Christ Consciousness. It speaks of the saturated awareness one has there of the Christ Light comprising one's body of Light, that the ascended state is an environment of Light, promising us that a Philosopher's Stone is reserved for every soul, that everyone one day will enjoy the Messianic Banquet. The Ray Masters and GWB residents of this place in consciousness always have this, always are there, because the Christ Light is now their ascended "flesh" which they bear in glory for us to emulate.

The Blue Room Consortium

The Blue Room Consortium, based in Santa Fe, New Mexico, and founded/directed by Richard Leviton, is a cosmic mysteries think tank for Earth energies, mapping and interaction. It's the authoritative information source for the Earth's visionary geography, the experiential guide to interacting with sacred sites and their Light temples, and to understanding the Earth's geomantic plan and function.

Offering: Research, workshops, classes, field trips, tours, designer pilgrimages, geomantic maps, trainings, consultations, initiations, publications, articles, newsletters.

Subscribe to our *Welcome to Your Designer Planet!* a monthly newsletter on participating in Earth maintenance through interacting with sacred sites.

Keep current with innovative and original visionary geography research through our continuing *Primers on Earth's Geomantic Reality* series.

Website: www.blueroomconsortium.com
Email: blaise@blueroomconsortium.com

About the Author

Richard Leviton is the author of 14 books, including many on myths and the global landscape, notably *The Galaxy on Earth*, *The Emerald Modem*, *Signs on the Earth*, and *Encyclopedia of Earth Myths*. He is the director/founder of the Blue Room Consortium, a cosmic mysteries think tank based in Santa Fe, New Mexico. He has been studying Earth mysteries and sacred sites for 22 years and regularly conducts workshops ad field trips on the subject in the U.S. and Europe.

978-0-595-38339-9
0-595-38339-4

CPSIA information can be obtained
at www.ICGtesting.com
Printed in the USA
FSHW011949211020
75111FS